Illustrated Guide to
WILD
FLOWERS

Illustrated Guide to
WILD
FLOWERS

Stephen Blackmore

Galley Press

Page 5 : Wild flowers, such as the Corn Marigold (Chrysanthemum segetum), *are a beautiful part of our heritage, and we must ensure that there are always suitable places for all of them to grow.*

Previous page : Alpine meadows are amongst the richest European wild-flower habitats, especially above the tree line, where there is plenty of light and space.

Right : A field full of Meadow Buttercups (Ranunculus acris). *All are flowering together in response to seasonal conditions, and their great profusion attracts many insects.*

Contents

Foreword

The number of varieties of cultivated flowers must now far exceed the world's three hundred thousand wild species. It's a matter of routine horticultural practice to produce bigger, earlier, more bountiful blooms. Yet there is still something perennially engaging about a truly wild flower. Perhaps it is an economy and subtlety that is lost in the extravagances of cultivated varieties. Perhaps it is wildness itself, that indomitable ability to survive – when we give them the chance – in patterns which are unfailingly suited to place and season.

The sadness, of course, is that our resurgence of interest and affection for wild flowers has come about because such chances are fading away. At every point, the natural habitats of flowers are being eroded by development and the increasingly intensive techniques of modern agriculture and forestry. Species that men have lived close to for thousands of years and taken into their cultures are vanishing before our eyes. Indeed in some parts of the world the pressure is so great that species which might have been the source of a new drug or crop, or a garden plant, may be becoming extinct even before we have seen them.

Stephen Blackmore's book is principally concerned to give a clear account of the lives and habitats of wild flowers. But it never loses sight of the manifold ways in which they can enrich human life. It is a welcome contribution to the fight to save the Earth's wild plants before it is too late.

Richard Mabey

Left : Giant Hogweed (Heracleum mantegazzianum) *has become widely naturalized along stream banks in northern Europe. Contact with the plant can cause allergic reactions.*

Part One

The Life of Wild Flowers

Left: Musk Mallow (Malva moschata) was formerly used in the preparation of herbal cough medicines. It takes its name from the musk-like smell of the leaves when crushed.

What Is a Wild Flower?

Human beings have always had a vital interest in plants of all kinds. In ancient times a knowledge of which plants were useful, generally as food, and which were harmful was essential to their survival. Later, as civilizations became more sophisticated, plants came to be used for a wider variety of purposes, including medicines, fibres, dyes and as superstitious or religious objects. Most people could recognize the more important plants, and each region or culture developed its own names for each kind of plant. In modern times the need for every individual to be able to recognize plants has diminished. Many medicines are still derived from plants and many plants are still used as culinary herbs or spices, but now they are usually obtained in a processed form, ready for use.

Fortunately this does not mean that interest in plants, their names and traditional uses has been lost. The more attractive wild flowers have long been prized for their beauty and planted in the gardens around mankind's dwelling places. Added to their aesthetic appeal has been the growing awareness of the fact that there are fewer and fewer places where plants can be seen in their former profusion.

Defining the Term 'Wild Flower'

Whilst all kinds of plants have their own attraction, it is to the wild flowers that most people are drawn at first. The term wild flower is in daily use and is familiar to everyone. Despite this, it is difficult to give a precise definition of a wild flower and opinions vary widely as to exactly what may be considered a wild flower and what may not. One characteristic feature of wild flowers is precisely that they produce flowers, which at once excludes such plants as Mosses, Liverworts and Ferns, which reproduce by spores and have no flowers. The possession of flowers places wild flowers in the group known to botanists as the *Angiosperms*, one of the two groups of seed-producing plants. The second group of seed plants comprises the *Gymnosperms*, which have cones instead of flowers and which include such plants as the Conifers, Cycads and the Maidenhair tree (*Ginkgo biloba*).

It is also clear from their name that wild flowers are essentially wild plants – that is, they grow naturally where they do, without mankind's influence, and indeed often despite it. Plants which people have crossed and bred selectively for decorative, or other, purposes are not wild flowers although they all have their wild relatives. Neither are plants which have been imported to a region from elsewhere strictly wild flowers, and it is here that the difficulty begins. It is often difficult to be certain whether a plant is truly native to a particular place or was introduced, perhaps unintentionally, by people in the past. In some cases such introduced plants rapidly flourish and become so widespread that they are said to have become *naturalized*. The Pineappleweed (*Chamomilla suaveolens*) is now common in Europe, and yet it only arrived as recently as the late 19th century from North America, where it is also a weed. Where plants have become so well established, they are usually

Right: Pineappleweed (Chamomilla suaveolens) *is an introduced weed which has become widespread, especially on trampled ground and pathways where few other wild flowers can survive. Each head, or* capitulum, *contains hundreds of tiny flowers called* florets.

Above: Chicory (Cichorium intybus) is a plant which has many uses, and its distribution reflects this fact. The leaves can be eaten as a salad vegetable and the roots roasted and added to coffee.

Below: Bird's Nest Orchid (Neottia nidus-avis) photographed by flash light in the deep shade of a Beech wood. The plants entirely lack chlorophyll, the substance which makes most plants green.

numbered amongst the wild flowers. In other cases, that of the Chicory (*Cichorium intybus*) for example, it is not known for certain whether the plant was an early introduction by mankind into the British Isles or occurs there naturally.

So far the question of defining wild flowers has been quite straightforward, apart from the problem posed by introduced plants. Another difficulty arises over exactly which of the indigenous Angiosperms are wild flowers. Many are clearly trees, some with attractive or showy flowers, some without. Some are shrubs, distinctly woody-trunked plants which are usually quite large. Usually it is the smaller shrubs, especially those with large or colourful flowers, and the soft-stemmed or herbaceous plants which are considered to be wild flowers. Thus the Dog Rose (*Rosa canina*) and the Elderflower (*Sambucus nigra*) are considered wild flowers, whereas the smaller Willows (*Salix* species) are not. Then there are those flowering plants, such as the Grasses or Sedges, which have very small and inconspicuous flowers. They are often not thought of as wild flowers, which, strictly speaking, they are.

Variety in the Earth's Wild Flowers

Amongst the wild flowers, however one defines them, there is an enormous variety of shapes, colours, sizes and structures of every part. The smallest wild flowers are the Duckweeds (*Lemna* species), which consist only of minute floating leaves with very reduced roots and tiny flowers which are rarely seen. Other water plants have partly submerged leaves and carry their flowers above the water, as do the Lesser Spearwort (*Ranunculus flammula*) or the Bladderwort (*Utricularia vulgaris*), which has minute traps for catching and digesting small water animals (see page 35). There are also carnivorous plants on land, such as the Sundew (*Drosera rotundifolia*), a plant of peat bogs which traps insects on sticky-haired leaves (page 35). There are flowers of very simple construction, like the Wallflower (*Cheiranthus cheiri*), with its four petals arranged in a cross, and others, like the Orchids, with flowers of amazingly elaborate construction.

This vast array of different wild flowers has not arisen randomly. Much of their fascination come from the fact that the form and colour of each feature are closely related to the way the particular plant functions and lives. Wild flowers are very demanding of the right conditions for their growth, and as a result many are found only where the soil acidity, rainfall, wind and other environmental factors are just right. With some experience it becomes possible to recognize places where certain plants are likely to grow. The Bird's Nest Orchid (*Neottia nidus-avis*), for example, is a saprophytic plant which grows in very deep shade and is most likely to be found in thick Beech woods. Armed with such knowledge about plants, it may be possible to track down the places where they occur.

It is precisely because many wild flowers have such precise requirements, and are not able to grow just anywhere, that they are so vulnerable and may be endangered by mankind. The greatest threat to most of our rarer wild flowers is the destruction of suitable places for them to grow as towns, roads and cultivated farmland expand into the countryside.

The Structure of Wild Flowers

On a short walk along a hedgerow or through a field in spring or summer it is possible to see wild flowers in an almost infinite variety of shapes, sizes, forms and colours. But despite their obvious differences, thay all have the same four main parts: roots, stems, leaves and flowers. Sometimes one or more of these parts may not be apparent; the stems or leaves, for example, may be very reduced in size or even completely lacking. Each of these four parts, or *organ systems*, functions in certain ways in the life of the plant, and the variations which occur are closely matched to the way of life of the plant.

Plants live in very different ways. The Coltsfoot (*Tussilago farfara*) and the Wood Anemone (*Anemone nemorosa*) are both plants which put on a sudden burst of growth in order to flower in the early spring. In this way, they are amongst the first flowers to appear after winter and so are eagerly sought by insects, which pollinate them. They also have the opportunity to take advantage of the sunlight before the buds of trees and later wild flowers open and shade them. To achieve this early start most of the spring flowers rely on a source of energy stored from the previous year. Often this energy store takes the form of an underground *bulb*, as in the Lily family (Liliaceae), which includes the Snowdrop (*Galanthus nivalis*) and the Wild Tulip (*Tulipa sylvestris*) as well as many other familiar early garden flowers. Other wild flowers survive the winter in the form of *seeds* and begin their growth afresh each year at the start of more favourable conditions. Since the seed contains a more limited store of energy, such plants generally flower later in the year after a period of growth. During this growth the plant builds up a supply of energy-giving sugars by a process known as *photosynthesis*, which is mainly carried out in the leaves (see page 28). The plant also needs certain nutrients from the soil for healthy growth, and these are obtained by the roots. Thus each organ system has a part to play in the life of the plant, and their various forms are described in the following chapters. The flowers show the greatest diversity of all, although this is not always realized because the floral parts are often rather small. Consequently, when looking for features or characters to distinguish one wild flower from another in order to identify it, it is the flower which is most important. Most of the *families* of wild flowers are recognizable by their particular type of flower. However, when identifying exactly which individual member, or *species*, of a plant family one has found, the stem, leaf and root characters can also be important.

There is always some variation between the individual species of plants, just as there is between human individuals. This variation is due partly to hereditary factors and partly to the influence of the *environment*. The environment is the place and prevailing conditions in which the plant grows. Differences between individual plants which show the influence of the environment include such things as

Above: The Spring Squill (Scilla verna) *is a Monocotyledon and has parallel-veined leaves and a fibrous root system. Like many Monocotyledons it has a fleshy bulb which stores food reserves over winter.*

Below: A diagram of the Meadow Buttercup (Ranunculus acris) *showing the main parts of a Dicotyledon. The tap root and net-veined leaves are characteristic of Dicotyledons.*

the variations in size of plants receiving different amounts of water, growing in different kinds of soil or living at different altitudes. The lushest growth occurs when plenty of water, nutrients and light are available, although the exact balance required by particular plant species varies.

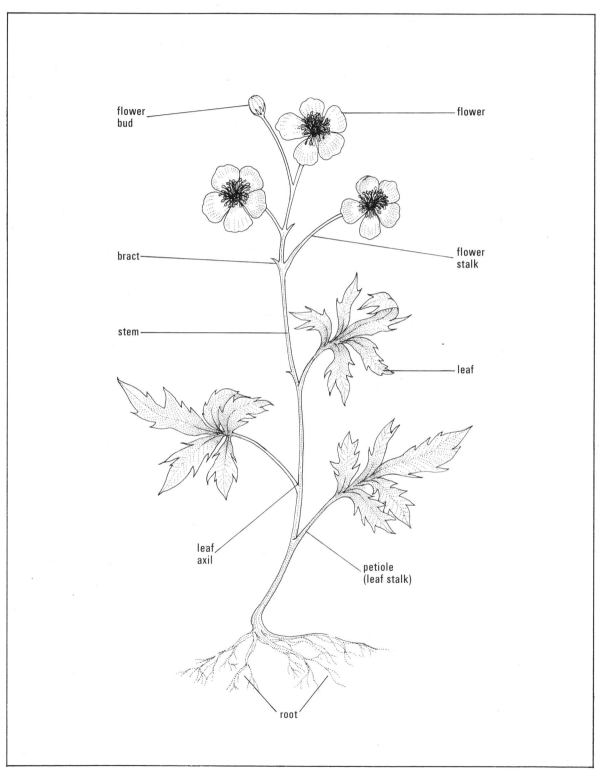

flower bud

flower

bract

flower stalk

stem

leaf

leaf axil

petiole (leaf stalk)

root

Roots

The roots of wild flowers are their least commonly seen parts, although most people have encountered the tough, deeply buried roots of some of the persistent garden weeds such as the Ground Elder (*Aegopodium podagraria*) a member of the Carrot family (Umbelliferae).

Roots perform two important functions in the life of the plant. First, they anchor it firmly to the ground so as to provide firm support for the rest of the plant. For wild flowers which grow in deep soil this presents no great problem, and the roots can easily penetrate the ground. Plants such as the Ivy (*Hedera helix*), which grow on walls or attached to the bark of trees, often have extra roots, known as *adventitious roots*, along the length of their stems to provide

Below : Ivy (Hedera helix) has woody, bark-covered climbing stems, which are attached to the rocks and tree trunks the plant grows on by the adventitious roots which arise at intervals along the stems.

them with sufficient anchorage to maintain their hold. In this way, such plants are able to grow in places where other plants cannot, because there is insufficient soil or too much shade. Plants with adventitious roots are thus able to grow more successfully than those without in certain circumstances. Some wild flowers can grow on the faces of rocks or boulders in the shallowest pockets of soil. The Saxifrages (*Saxifraga* species) have perfected this way of life and take their botanical name, which literally means 'rock-breaking' from this fact. The name is derived from an ancient belief that the plants themselves caused the cracks in the rocks in which they grew.

The second, and most important, function of roots is the extraction of water and dissolved nutrients from the soil. Water is vital to plants; without it their cells eventually collapse and die. The first signs of water shortage are seen in wilting plants, which can often recover if given water, provided a certain critical point has not been passed. As the wild flower grows new stems and leaves, its demand for water increases and, to keep pace with this, the roots grow in proportion below the ground. Plants of well-drained habitats, such as sand dunes, have very deep root systems and features which enable them to retain and hoard their water. When the ground freezes and water is only present as ice, even those plants which normally have a plentiful supply of water may be deprived of it because it cannot be absorbed in this form.

How the Roots Work

The water is taken into the root by specialized cells called *root hairs*, which absorb water by a process known as *osmosis*. In this process, the water flows through the cell membranes into the more concentrated cell sap. If seedlings are grown in water instead of soil then the root hairs can easily be seen as a thicker part of the root just behind its growing tip. There are many thousands of these root hairs, each of which resembles a minute thread-like extension into the soil. As the root grows and advances through the soil, the older root hairs wither and die and are replaced by newly grown ones nearer to the root tip. In this way, the part of the root with the water-absorbing root hairs effectively advances through the soil as the root grows. Once inside the tissues of the root, the water is transferred from cell to cell until it reaches a central core of conducting or transporting cells known as the *xylem*. Xylem cells have no living contents and consist simply of microscopic, capillary-like tubes running alongside one another through the root and up into the aerial parts of the plant. Each xylem cell is reinforced along its length by rings or spirals of strengthening material.

The Nutrients in the Soil

Various dissolved substances are taken into the root along with the water. These include nitrates, phosphates and traces of other minerals which are essential for plant growth. Many of these substances are needed in only the most minute amounts, but without them a healthy plant cannot grow. It is to supply such substances that fertilizers are added to the soil by farmers and gardeners in order to encourage better growth of crops. In nature there are no such artificial fertilizers to maintain the quality of the soil. Wild

Above: The first root produced by a germinating seed soon develops the root hairs needed to obtain water for further growth.

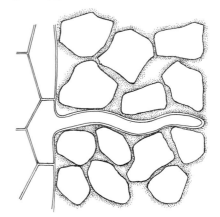

Above: A root hair cell penetrating the water film between soil particles.

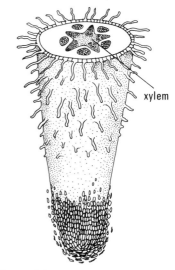

xylem

Above: The growing tip of a root sliced off to show the arrangement of the various tissues inside.

flowers rely on obtaining most of their nutrients from mineral sources in the soil and from those released when dead plant remains are decomposed, although some even feed through their leaves.

There exists a delicately balanced cycle in which nutrients are absorbed into plants from the soil and then returned to the soil after the death of the plant by a variety of decomposing organisms, including invertebrate animals, fungi and bacteria. As in the formation of garden *compost*, these plant remains break down at first to a rich brown material known as *humus*. Any interference in this natural re-cycling of materials can have disastrous results. For example, when woodlands or forests are cleared, the nutrients in the soil may be lost by the rain falling directly on to the ground and washing them away. On steeper ground, the top soil itself may even be washed away. Soils develop over very long periods of time and, once left impoverished in this way, cannot easily regain their former condition.

Not all soils are equally rich in nutrients. They also differ in being either acidic or alkaline. Plants are very sensitive to differences in the nutrient content and acidity of the soil, and for this reason the distribution of many wild flowers reflects the occurrence of certain types of soil. Surprisingly little is known about exactly how and why plants differ so markedly in their ability to grow in different soils. Some wild flowers seem to be able to grow on any kind of soil without any distinct preference for acidic or alkaline conditions. Others are only to be found where the soil is exactly right, and this means that certain soil types have their own characteristic flora associated with them. The soils which develop on chalk, for example, often have a characteristic chalk grassland flora, with plants such as the Common Rock-rose (*Helianthemum chamaecistus*) and the Pyramidal Orchid (*Anacamptis pyramidalis*). It may seem strange that such an obviously important question of how plants and soils interact should be unanswered. To find the answers needs careful observation and experimentation and for some plants, if not all, this has been done.

Types of Root System

There are two main types of root system in wild flowers and the one which any particular plant possesses gives a good indication of which of the two main groups of flowering plants it belongs to. In one group, the *Monocotyledons*, the root system is fibrous, consisting of many equal-sized roots arising from the base of the stem, which is often a swollen bulb. In the second group, the *Dicotyledons*, there is a taproot with a large central part from which arise smaller secondary roots. In addition to anchoring the plant and taking up water and nutrients, the roots often have the extra function of storing a starchy food reserve. The Wild Beetroot (*Beta vulgaris*, page 98), a plant of sandy coastal areas and of salt marshes, has a swollen taproot. It was this important underground part of the plant which caused it to be brought into cultivation as a crop plant. Plants with such underground food reserves can better survive through periods of adverse conditions caused by the weather or by heavy grazing by animals. Most gardeners know just how well the Dandelion (*Taraxacum officinale*) can continue to sprout fresh

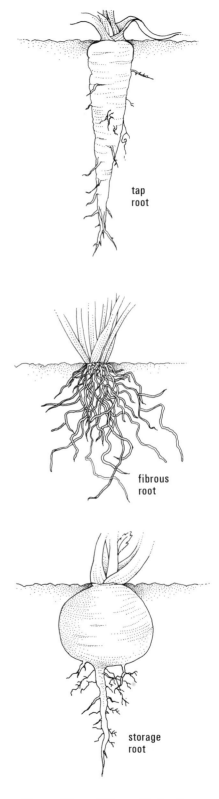

tap root

fibrous root

storage root

Above: Three different kinds of root system. In each the shape of the root is suited to the functions which it performs.

21

shoots from its taproots no matter how often the leaves are cut back.

A few plants have specialized roots which actually penetrate the tissues of other plants and take some of their supplies of water, nutrients and food products. Some of these *parasites*, the Common Dodder (*Cuscuta epithymum*) for example, are totally dependent on their host plant and are incapable of leading a separate life. The Dodder plants have no leaves and consist of a tangled mass of reddish stems entwined around their host and swollen roots entering it. Other parasites, like the Lousewort (*Pedicularis palustris*), are semi-parasitic and only partly dependent on their hosts. They have normal-looking leaves and, without digging up their roots, cannot be seen to be parasitic.

The roots of some wild flowers form another kind of close relationship, not as parasites on other plants but as a form of mutual benefit with fungi or algae in the soil. Many members of the Pea family (Leguminosae) have small rounded lumps known as *root nodules*, which contain certain kinds of algae, the presence of which greatly benefits the plant. The algae are capable of using nitrogen directly from the atmosphere and converting it into the nitrates which the plant needs. The algae benefit from the host plant in obtaining nutrition directly from its cells. This important property of certain members of the Pea family makes them important crop plants as they actually improve the soil in which they grow rather than depleting it.

A similar situation occurs in the Orchid family (Orchidaceae), where the association is with microscopic soil fungi. Orchid seeds will not grow unless these fungi are present with them in the soil. The fungi are able to extract nutrients from the soil which the developing Orchid seedling cannot extract itself. As the Orchid grows – a slow process taking place over a number of years – so the fungal cells become distributed in fine strands through the cells of the root. It is the necessity for this relationship with fungi which makes Orchids so difficult to raise from seeds. It is possible to by-pass the need for the fungus if the seeds are grown on a special medium containing supplies of certain nutrients, as they are in the commercial Orchid-growing industry. Even so, it takes many years for such efforts to be rewarded, for many Orchids do not flower for the first five to ten years of their lives

Above: The roots from the tangled mass of red-coloured Dodder (Cuscuta epithymum) *stems penetrate the living stems of the Broom* (Sarothamnus scoparius).

Right: Although the Red Rattle (Pedicularis palustris) *has normal-looking leaves which carry out photosynthesis, it also obtains some nutrients by having roots which parasitize those of other plants.*

Below: The roots of the Clover (Trifolium *species*) *and related plants have root nodules containing bacteria. Those of the Crocus contract to keep the corm underground.*

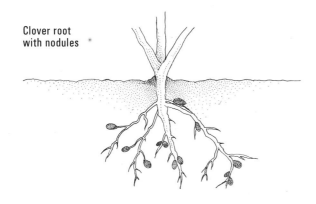

Clover root
with nodules

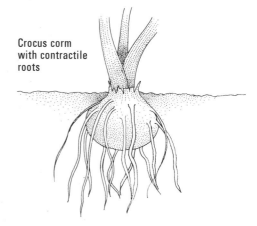

Crocus corm
with contractile
roots

Stems

The stem is the simplest of the above-ground parts of a wild-flower plant in structure and function. Like the leaves, the stem is often green and contributes to a certain extent to the production of food for the plant. But its main functions are to provide both support for the leaves and flowers and a transport system for the distribution of substances within the plant. To provide support for the leaves the stem needs to be both strong and have a degree of flexibility, and it achieves these things by its internal structure, which is quite different from that of the root.

The Structure of the Stem

In the root the water-conducting cells of the xylem, the cells which give the root its toughness and wiryness, are in the centre. This permits the root to be very flexible and bend in and out between stones and soil and yet gives it sufficient strength to withstand strain and anchor the plant. A more rigid structure is needed to support the leaves and flowers in the air, and so in the stem the strengthening cells of the xylem are arranged in an open cylinder around the outside. Often the centre of the stem is a hollow space or consists only of large, soft-walled cells making up the *pith*. This open framework of strengthening cells consists of *vascular bundles* made up of groups of xylem cells together with cells of other types, including fibres the only function of which is to add to the strength of the stem. The arrangement of vascular bundles is often likened to the iron rods used to reinforce concrete in buildings. Some stems have extra reinforcement on their outsides. The characteristic square stems of the Mint family (Labiatae) owe their shape to four rows of strengthening cells running along their length.

As well as supporting the other aerial parts of the plant the stem acts as a transport system conveying water and nutrients to parts of the plant where they are needed. Water enters the xylem cells in the root and is carried up through a continuous series of xylem cells through the stem. In some stems the number of xylem cells is large and the stem is rather woody as a result; indeed, the wood of trees is mostly made up of xylem cells in the vast numbers needed to supply a tree with water.

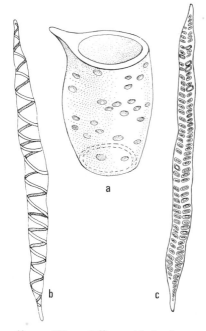

Above: Three different kinds of xylem cells. The one marked a *is a short cylindrical cell the ends of which join on to other cells of the same kind. Those marked* b *and* c *have tapering ends which overlap with other cells and transmit water through thin areas.*

Right: Traveller's Joy (Clematis vitalba) with its feathery, plumed fruits and reddish stems climbs over a Dogwood (Cornus sanguinea).

Dicotyledon   Monocotyledon

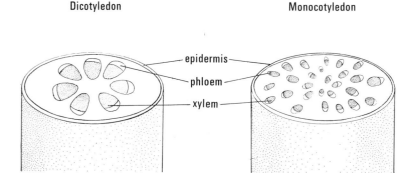

epidermis
phloem
xylem

Left: A cross section of the stems of a Dicotyledon (left) and a Monocotyledon (right) showing the different arrangements of conducting cells in each.

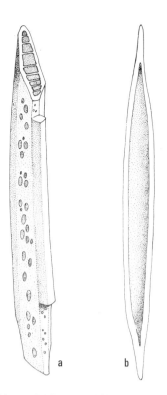

Above: Phloem and fibre cells. (a) a long phloem cell and associated companion cell, *whose precise function is unknown. (b) a fibre cell; some are many times as long as the cell shown.*

A second system of cells, known as the *phloem*, transports a sugary solution of the food produced in the leaves of the plant. Exactly how the transport within the phloem takes place is not known. Unlike the xylem, the phloem cells are living cells, not simply hollow tubes. The sugary sap they contain has to pass through the walls between the cells to move from one place to another. There are several theories which attempt to explain how this happens, but none satisfactorily fits all the facts. The main problem with the theoretical explanations is that they do not account for the very fast speed of phloem transport as it occurs in plants. Another complication is that it is well known that transport in the phloem can be in two directions, both up and down the stem and sometimes both at once in a single stem. Upward transport of food is important when the plant is growing flower buds at the end of its stems.

Types of Stems

The stem supports the leaves in such a way that they can best absorb sunlight, since light is the source of energy the plant uses in its food-synthesizing processes. To this end some stems climb over other plants to reach above their shade and take advantage of the best position for absorbing light. Amongst European wild flowers the Traveller's Joy (*Clematis vitalba*) is the master of this art. It is an unusually woody member of the Buttercup family (Ranunculaceae) which smothers shrubs and low trees, particularly along sunny lanes and in woodland glades. Its thick woody stems are the only temperate counterpart of the climbing lianas so characteristic of tropical forests and jungles. Other plants climb on a less ambitious scale, and many are quick to take advantage of man-made structures.

Left: The Spear Thistle (Cirsium vulgare) takes its name from the formidable, spine-tipped bracts which help protect the flowers from being eaten. The other parts of the plant are also spiny.

Wild Strawberry runners

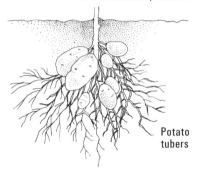

Potato tubers

Above and right: Stems of different kinds serve different purposes; Wild Strawberry (Fragaria vesca) runners produce new plants; Potato (Solanum tuberosum) has underground storage stems or tubers; Lilies (Liliaceae family) have bulbs made up of a short stem surrounded by swollen leaf bases; Gladiolus corms are underground storage stems; and Iris rhizomes are for storage and propagation.

Right: Buckshorn Plantain (Plantago coronopus), a plant common on dunes, walls or footpaths in coastal places, is virtually stemless and has its leaves in a rosette against the ground.

The Bindweed (*Calystegia sepium*) is a familiar and attractive sight threading its stems between wire fences even in the middle of built-up areas in towns.

Many stems have prickles or spines and often these also play a part in helping the plant to climb. The young branches of the Bramble, or Blackberry, (*Rubus fruticosus*) grow vertically into the air at first, but when their weight becomes too great to be supported they arch over the surrounding vegetation and become held in place by their prickles. Spines can have the added function of making the plant difficult for grazing animals to eat, as in the Thistles.

Some plants have entirely given up the struggle towards the light and have almost no stem at all. In certain situations such a form or habit is necessary for the plant's survival. Familiar wild flowers such as the Daisy (*Bellis perennis*) and the Plantains (*Plantago* species) are well suited for life amongst other short plants in places where there is continuous exposure to strong winds or to trampling and grazing

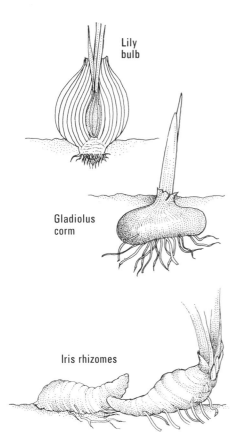

Lily
bulb

Gladiolus
corm

Iris rhizomes

by animals. In these situations height is a disadvantage, making the plant an easy target for the teeth of herbivores or the blades of lawn mowers. The stemless plants protect their leaves by keeping them pressed firmly against the ground, and in order to make the most of the sunlight available at this level, their leaves are usually spread in a rosette pattern. This arrangement gives the least overlap of leaves and the most exposure to light.

Other plants stay close to the ground by having horizontal stems, called *stolons*, which creep along the ground. Usually there are adventitious roots at intervals to anchor them. As the stolons grow longer and begin to branch, large colonies of plants develop. Eventually the older parts of the stolons die, leaving a number of separate plants all derived from one original individual. This is a process known as *vegetative reproduction*, which differs from *sexual reproduction* in that it does not involve flowering and fertilization. Vegetative reproduction is important in many wild flowers and allows them to cover extensive areas. The Ground Ivy (*Glechoma hederaceae*), which is not a true Ivy but belongs to the Mint family (Labiatae), often forms quite large colonies in woods in this way.

The stems of wild flowers which grow in water are often unusual. At first glance the underwater stems of the Milfoils (*Myriophyllum* species), for example, may not seem much different from those of land plants, although their finely divided leaves do. When a handful of the plant is lifted out of the water, it hangs completely limp, because the stem has lost its supporting function. It also has only a small number of xylem cells, since it does not need an extensive water-transporting system because it grows surrounded by water.

Leaves

The leaves are the most variable green part of a plant. They range from the filamentous, finely divided leaves of some aquatic plants to very large simple leaves, with almost every conceivable intermediate shape between. But whatever the shape of the leaves, their function is almost always the same: the production of energy.

The Energy-producing Process

The cells of the leaf contain special coloured substances called *pigments*, which can absorb the energy of the sun's rays and convert it into a form of energy which can be stored within the plant as its food supply. The energy is used to power a series of reactions in which sugars are built up, or *synthesized*, from their basic building blocks – atoms of carbon, hydrogen and oxygen. The whole process is known as *photosynthesis*, because it depends on light. Photosynthesis is the most important process on earth. Animals do not have the ability to carry out photosynthesis or manufacture their own food, so they are obliged to obtain their energy by eating plants, or by eating other animals which themselves have fed on plants. Without photosynthesis the human race itself could not survive, as there would be nothing to eat.

Not only is photosynthesis the ultimate source of food for all organisms, it is also vitally important in maintaining the composition of the air. During photosynthesis plants take in carbon dioxide, a gas abundantly available in the atmosphere, and produce oxygen as a by-product. In this way they re-cycle the gases in the air, since oxygen is used up by fires and the respiration of animals and carbon dioxide is produced. Without the continuous balancing process of photosynthesis, the oxygen in the atmosphere would eventually be depleted. On a global scale, the trees and forests that cover many vast areas are crucially important in maintaining the balance of gases in the atmosphere, although the smaller wild flowers also play a significant part. Photosynthesis is thus at the core of the most important interactions between plants and animals and is central to the whole balance of nature.

Right: Woodruff (Galium odoratum) *has groups of 7–9 leaves in whorls around the stem, a common arrangement in the Bedstraw family* (Rubiaceae).

Below: A diagram showing the process of photosynthesis in a leaf with a simplified representation of the chemistry of the process (right).

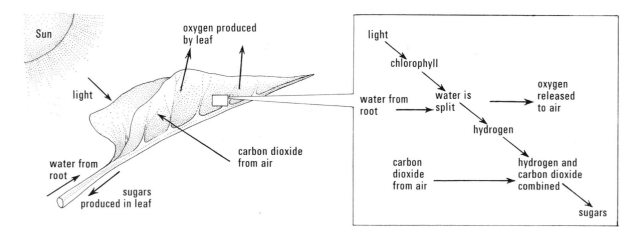

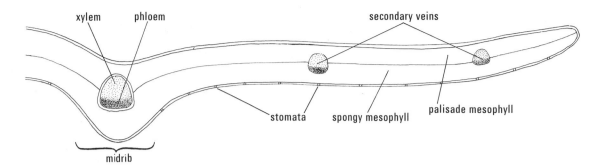

xylem   phloem   secondary veins

stomata   spongy mesophyll   palisade mesophyll

midrib

The Structure of the Leaf

The internal structure of a wild-flower leaf is like a perfectly planned factory for photosynthesis. There are facilities for the arrival of the raw ingredients, the process itself, the distribution of the manufactured product and the disposal of waste by-products. The raw ingredients are simply water and carbon dioxide, both of which are readily available to the plant. The water is carried from the roots, up through the stem into the network of veins in the leaf. These veins end in finer and finer capillaries of only one or two xylem cells. So fine are these branches of the veins that no cell in the leaf is more than a few cells away from a supply of water. Carbon dioxide is obtained directly from the air, which enters the leaf through minute pores in its surface called *stomata*. Far from being solid, the interior of the leaf contains minute spaces between the cells through which air can pass. The central layer of the leaf is known as the *spongy mesophyll*, because of its large air spaces.

On the upper side of the leaf, is the *palisade mesophyll*, the layer of cells in which most of the photosynthesis takes place. The cells take their name from the way they are arranged in rows like a palisade. The overall shape of the leaf – a very thin, flattened structure – is ideal for the maximum absorption of light, and the palisade mesophyll cells are best positioned to receive the light before it has to pass through any other cells, apart from a thin, transparent, skin-like *epidermis*. The light is trapped inside tiny, green bodies called *chloroplasts*, which occur in large numbers in the palisade cells and in smaller numbers elsewhere in the plants. The chloroplasts contain several light-absorbing pigments, the most important of which is *chlorophyll*, which gives the plant its green colour. Chlorophyll absorbs light of various wavelengths or colours, but not green light, which is reflected back and makes the leaf appear green. The leaves of wild flowers which appear red, such as the Sorrel (*Rumex acetosa*) or Herb Robert (*Geranium robertianum*), do so because they have much less chlorophyll in their red parts, and so red light which would normally be absorbed by the chlorophyll is reflected.

The leaves are rather like solar energy panels, evolved millions of years before mankind started to look for ways of harnessing the energy of the sun. Recently some of the most efficient photosynthesizing plants, such as the Sugar Cane or Cassava, which produce large amounts of sugar, have been fermented to make alcohol as a fuel for mankind. The possibility for tapping the sun's energy in this way offers great potential.

Above: A cross section through part of a leaf to show the arrangement of tissues in the midrib and leaf blade.

Below: The structure of stomata seen in (a) a surface view of the underside of a leaf, and (b) part of a thin section through a leaf. Both views are greatly magnified.

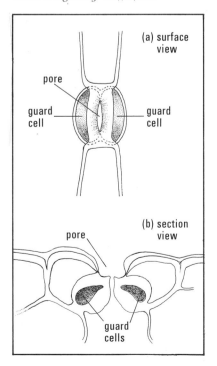

(a) surface view

pore

guard cell   guard cell

(b) section view

pore

guard cells

Methods of Controlling Water Loss

Some of the oxygen produced during photosynthesis is used immediately in the plant and some is released into the air. This diffusing of gases in and out of the leaf presents the plant with a dilemma. Not enough air can diffuse into the leaf without the presence of the minute stomata pores in its surface, but at the same time these offer an easy way for water to escape from the leaf by evaporation, a process known as *transpiration*. If the plant has a plentiful supply of water this water loss presents little problem, but for plants in drier places it can mean the difference between life and death. Fortunately the stomata can open and close and so the plant has some means of regulating its water loss. In most plants the stomata close at night, when there is no light for photosynthesis, and open again in the morning. If a plant becomes short of water and begins to wilt, the stomata will close, even during the day, to protect the plant against further drying out.

For some wild flowers even this control is not enough, and other ways of conserving water must be found. One of the commonest methods which plants use is a reduction of the size, or surface area, of the leaves. This of course means a loss of area for photosynthesis but can permit plants to be suitable for life where they would otherwise not be able to grow. The Cacti are the ultimate examples of reduced leaf area; their leaves have evolved into spines, and photosynthesis is carried out in their swollen, water-storing stems. We need not look so far afield for examples of wild flowers with very reduced leaves. Biting Stonecrop (*Sedum acre*), which grows on stone walls, and many coastal or salt marsh plants, such as the Glasswort (*Salicornia perennis*), are good examples. Even the familiar compound leaves, which are divided into a number of leaflets, are that shape as a result of their surface area having been reduced from that of a large, simple leaf.

Above: Pennywort (Umbilicus rupestris) *has fleshy peltate leaves.*

Below: Biting Stonecrop (Sedum acre) *has small, succulent leaves which are often tinged with red. The plant grows in dry places such as rocks and walls.*

Identifying Plants by the Leaves

The shape of the leaves and the form of their edges are of great importance in identifying wild plants. Indeed, when they are not in flower there is often little else by which they can be recognized, and those with distinctive foliage can be identified all year round. Leaves may be *simple* – that is, with a single leaf blade and a stalk, or *petiole* – or *compound*, consisting of a number of leaflets arranged on a petiole. Compound leaves are either *palmate*, with their leaflets radiating like the fingers of a hand, or *pinnate*, with the leaflets along the two sides of a longer petiole. The number of leaflets varies considerably and can be an important aid to plant identification. The Clovers take their botanical name, *Trifolium*, from their characteristic leaves, which are divided into three leaflets, or very rarely into four. Other members of the same family, such as the Vetches (*Vicia* species), have more leaflets and often have the end ones modified as tendrils. These tendrils consist mainly of the mid-vein of the last leaflet without a leaf blade. They are an important means of climbing over neighbouring plants and are found in a number of quite unrelated plant families.

The *venation*, or pattern of veins, of a leaf is another important diagnostic feature and is one of the best ways of distinguishing the Monocotyledons from the Dicotyledons. Monocotyledons almost always have leaves with parallel veins which do not form a network. The leaves of Grasses, Lilies or Irises are good examples of this type of venation. Dicotyledons, on the other hand, always have a network

Above: White Bryony (Bryonia dioica) *often grows in hedgerows, where it climbs over other plants by means of the tendrils which arise at the base of the leaf stalks. The palmate leaves usually have five lobes.*

Right: A diagram showing some of the commonest varieties of leaves, their shapes, margins, tips and arrangements. These features are important in identifying wild flowers.

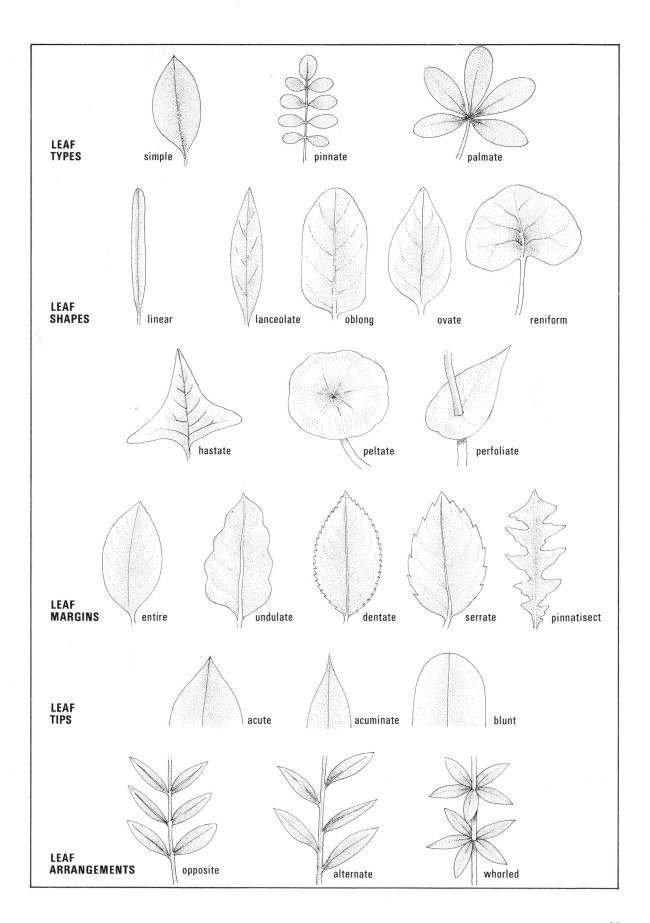

LEAF TYPES — simple, pinnate, palmate

LEAF SHAPES — linear, lanceolate, oblong, ovate, reniform, hastate, peltate, perfoliate

LEAF MARGINS — entire, undulate, dentate, serrate, pinnatisect

LEAF TIPS — acute, acuminate, blunt

LEAF ARRANGEMENTS — opposite, alternate, whorled

Left: Yellow Flag (Iris pseudacorus) *is a member of the Iris family (Iridaceae) which, like most other Monocotyledons, has long narrow leaves with parallel veins.*

Below: Yellow-wort (Blackstonia perfoliata) *belongs to the Gentian family (Gentianaceae) and has perfoliate leaves; the stems grow between pairs of fused leaves.*

of veins even though it is not always obvious. The Plantains (*Plantago* species) are Dicotyledons, although at first glance their leaves seem to have parallel veins. However, when examined closely, the cross connections of the network can be seen. One common Monocotyledon with unusual leaf venation is the Lords-and-Ladies (*Arum maculatum*), which has leaves with a clear network of veins. Monocotyledons with this unusual type of venation always have a single outer vein running around the edge of the leaf, but even so they are not always easily recognizable.

The arrangement of leaves on the stems is also of interest. In certain families, such as the Mint family (Labiatae), the leaves are arranged *opposite* to one another. In the Bedstraw family (Rubiaceae) they are either opposite or in *whorls*, as in the Sweet Woodruff (*Galium odoratum*). In the Daisy family (Compositae) they are usually *alternate* along the stems, not opposite, but often this is not obvious if the leaves are crowded in a circular, flattened *rosette*.

The hairiness of leaves is another important feature. Hairy plants are often given the botanical name *hirsutus* or *hispidus*, as in the Hairy Vetchling (*Lathyrus hirsutus*) or the Hairy Bird's-foot Trefoil (*Lotus hispidus*). In a few cases the type of hair present is important in identifying wild flowers. The Cat's Ears (*Hypochoeris* species) have simple hairs on their leaves, whereas most Hawkbits (*Leontodon* species) have forked hairs. The plants are otherwise very similar in appearance, but to distinguish them by their hairs needs acute eyesight or a hand lens, the invaluable tool of the botanist.

Special Leaf Adaptations

In some wild flowers the leaves have taken on the unusual function of trapping small animals and digesting them. Such plants are said to be *carnivorous* and are of three main kinds in Europe. All grow in areas where the soil is lacking in certain nutrients, and it is to compensate for this that animals, mostly insects, are trapped. The

Right: Sundew (Drosera anglica) *growing in a peat bog. The red hairs on the leaves secrete drops of a sticky substance which traps and then digests small insects.*

Below: One of the minute traps of the Bladderwort (Utricularia vulgaris) *seen with a microscope. The fine white hairs (left) are the trigger which, when touched, cause the trap to work.*

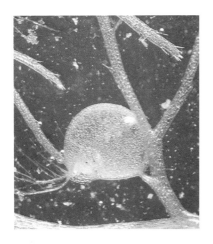

Sundews (*Drosera* species) are probably the best-known examples. They are small plants of wet, acidic bogs whose leaves have special hairs that secrete drops of sticky liquid. Insects are attracted to this and become caught in it. The movement of the trapped insect stimulates the hairs to curl around it firmly. In the liquid there are enzymes which gradually break down the insect, releasing nutrients which are absorbed into the leaf. In similar habitats the Butterworts (*Pinguicula* species) also grow. These have a simpler trap consisting of a rolled leaf with a sticky surface off which insects cannot crawl.

The third type of carnivorous wild flower in Europe is the Bladderwort (*Utricularia* species). This is an aquatic plant with minute bladder-like structures on its underwater leaves. The mouth of each bladder is surrounded by sensitive hairs which act as a trigger. If a small water animal brushes against them, the lid of the trap swings inwards carrying the animal inside in a rush of water. It is prevented from leaving by backward-pointing hairs in the trap and then slowly digested. The more spectacular tropical carnivorous plants include the famous Venus Fly Trap and the Pitcher plants, but European examples, though less dramatic, are equally intriguing.

Flowers

Flowers are, without doubt, the most interesting parts of a plant. Their purpose is the reproduction of new individuals and is essential for the survival of the species.

Flowers may grow singly, or in groups known as *inflorescences*. An individual flower has four main components, although they are not always all present. The component structures are generally arranged in whorls or in spirals around a central flower stalk and are attached to the part known as the *receptacle*.

Parts of the Flower

The outermost parts of the flower are the *sepals*. These are usually green and often look like tiny leaves. In some plants the sepals are more colourful and look like the petals, as in many flowers of the Lily family (Liliaceae). The sepals are known collectively as the *calyx*. Sometimes the sepals are fused together for part of all of their length, giving the calyx a tube or cup-like form. The main function of the sepals, unless they are brightly coloured, is to protect the young flower from insects and from drying out whilst it is still in bud.

Right: The Pasque Flower (Anemone pulsatilla) *is one of the most beautiful members of the Buttercup family (Ranunculaceae). The structure of the flower, with its hairy sepals, purple petals, many anthers and central stigmas, is clearly seen.*

Below: A diagram of a Buttercup (Ranunculus) *flower, cut vertically in half to show the four different kinds of organs it is made up of.*

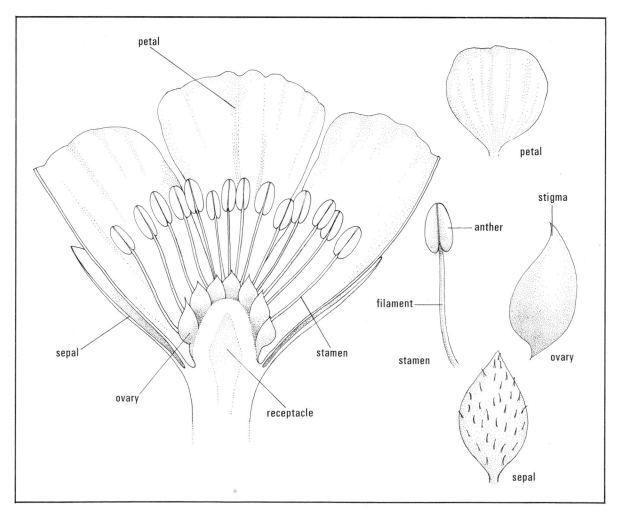

Just inside the sepals the *petals* are found. They are usually larger than the sepals and are often brightly coloured. In certain flowers, such as that of the Yellow Water-lily (*Nuphar lutea*), the petals and sepals are not so distinct; the sepals are gradually transformed into petals from the outside towards the centre. The petals of most flowers are brightly coloured in order to attract insects. Insects are very important in the life cycle of the plant because they carry out the process of pollination, an important part of the reproductive methods of plants which will be discussed in the following chapter. In flowers which are not visited by insects in this way, the petals are often small and inconspicuous.

At the centre of the flower are the reproductive parts themselves. The male parts are known as *stamens* and consist of slender stalks called *filaments* which end in sac-like structures called *anthers*. Inside the anthers are produced thousands of minute *pollen grains*. When the anther is fully developed it splits open and releases the pollen, which looks like yellow dust. Seen through a microscope each pollen grain is found to consist of a hard outer protective case containing only two or three cells. One of these cells is a male sex cell, or *gamete*, which can fertilize a female egg cell.

Above: The Fritillary (Fritillaria meleagris) *usually has chequered white and purple flowers but most groups include some plants with pure white flowers. Drainage of the wet meadows the plant grows in have made it rarer.*

The female part of the flower is known as the *pistil* and varies in form from one plant family to another. At its simplest it consists of a protective structure called the *ovary*, or *carpel*, which contains one or more ovules. The *ovules* contain the female egg cells, one in each ovule. At the top of the ovary is a slender projection called the *style*, which ends in a specialized pollen-receiving region known as the *stigma*. More complex structures made up of several ovaries fused together, with the styles separate or fused, are often found. When the flower of a particular plant is very small, it is often difficult to see exactly which arrangement of pistil is present, even with a magnifying lens.

For the female egg cells to be fertilized by a male sex cell, a pollen grain must first become attached to the stigma, where it then germinates to produce a *pollen tube* which grows through the style to the ovule. When the pollen tube reaches the ovule the male and female sex cells fuse and an *embryo* is formed. This embryo will develop into a *seed*, which may grow into a new plant and so complete the life cycle.

Not all flowers contain both male and female reproductive parts together. Where both do occur together, the plant is said to be *monoecious* (meaning living in one place), whereas *dioecious* plants have unisexual male or female flowers on different individual plants. The familiar woodland Dog's Mercury (*Mercurialis perennis*) is dioecious; the male flowering plants are found along the edges of woods whilst the female flowering ones grow deeper in the wood.

The numbers of parts present in flowers provide one of the best ways of distinguishing Monocotyledons from Dicotyledons. Monocotyledon flowers have their parts in threes or multiples of three. The flowers of the Lily family (Liliaceae) have six petals (three of which are really sepals but are coloured like the petals), six stamens and three ovaries fused together. In the Dicotyledons the floral parts are groups of two, four or five or more.

Above: Moschatel (Adoxa moschatellina) *is a tiny woodland wild flower with unusual cube-shaped inflorescences which give it another of its common names – Clock Tower.*

Below: A diagram showing the stages in the life cycle of a member of the Pea family (Leguminosae). All other flowering plants have the same life cycle.

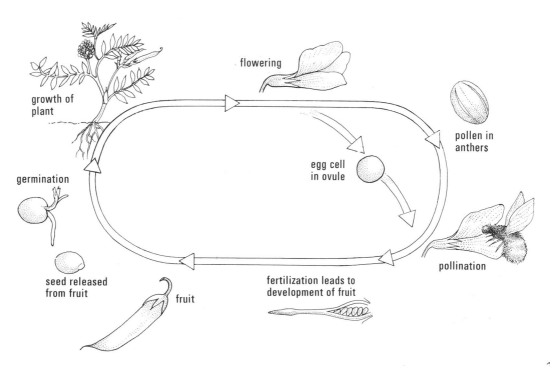

growth of plant

flowering

pollen in anthers

egg cell in ovule

germination

pollination

seed released from fruit

fruit

fertilization leads to development of fruit

Right: The flowers of Cuckoo Flower (Cardamine pratensis), which grows in damp grassy places, may be lilac or white. Each flower has four sepals, four petals in a cross shape, six stamens and a central stigma.

Below: The Creeping Bellflower (Campanula rapunculoides), like other members of the Bellflower family (Campanulaceae), has petals which are fused along most of their length to form a bell-shaped flower.

Flower Shapes

The sepals, petals, stamens and pistils are the basic units of flowers, but there is great diversity in the ways in which they are grouped together. The Buttercup (*Ranunculus* species) is often taken as an example of a typical flower, but it really represents only one of a number of main types of flower. The Buttercup flower has each part represented in relatively large numbers and there is considerable variation in the exact number of each part from one flower to another. Similar parts, such as the petals, are not fused together. This construction of flower is thought of by most botanists as being a primitive type from which a variety of other kinds of flower have evolved. This is not to say that the Buttercup is the actual plant from which other flower types have evolved, but simply that it combines a number of features thought to occur in the ancestors of many other kinds of flower.

In more advanced types of flower there are usually fewer of each floral part and much less variation in the numbers of parts between individual flowers. In the Cabbage family (Cruciferae), for example, there are four sepals, four petals, four or six stamens and a pistil of two fused ovaries. These low numbers of parts are fairly constant, with the exception of the number of stamens, throughout the family and are a good way of recognizing its members. The four petals arranged in a cross are characteristic of flowers of the Cruciferae, but members of other families sometimes look very similar. The Greater Celandine (*Chelidonium majus*) also has four petals in a cross but differs in having many stamens and belongs to the Poppy family (Papaveraceae).

More advanced families often have the parts of the flower fused together. Thus the sepals may be connected, as they are in the Potato family (Solanaceae), and the petals may be joined together to make a tubular flower as in the Harebell family (Campanulaceae), the Mint family (Labiatae) or Foxglove family (Scrophulariaceae). The individual flowers of the Daisy family (Compositae) also have fused petals although this is not always obvious because so many flowers are crowded together in a head.

The Symmetry of Flowers

Despite the great range in the shapes of flowers, they are all remarkably symmetrical in structure. Some flowers are said to be *radially* symmetrical, others *bilaterally* symmetrical. In a radially symmetrical flower there are a number of planes of symmetry, or possible mirror images, when seen from above. The flowers of Buttercups (*Ranunculus* species), Wallflower (*Cheiranthus cheiri*) and Dog Rose (*Rosa canina*) are all examples of radially symmetrical flowers.

Some of the flowers with smaller numbers of parts are bilaterally symmetrical rather than radially symmetrical. Bilaterally symmetrical flowers have only one plane of symmetry running through the middle of the flower when seen from above. If a bilaterally symmetrical flower is cut in two through the middle, both halves will be identical. Such flowers are characteristic of certain families, including the Pea family (Leguminosae), the Foxglove family (Scrophulariaceae) and the Orchid family (Orchidaceae). Those of the Pea family are very characteristic and enable the members of the family to be recognized easily. Each flower in the family has a large petal called the *standard* at the back of the flower, two outer *wing* petals and two inner *keel* petals. The stamens and pistil are enclosed within the wings and keel. Some members of the Daisy family (Compositae) have a mixture of flowers with both types of symmetry;

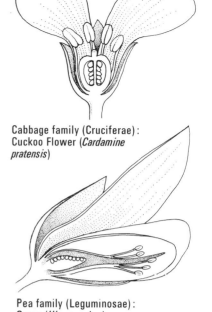

Cabbage family (Cruciferae): Cuckoo Flower (*Cardamine pratensis*)

Pea family (Leguminosae): Gorse (*Ulex* species)

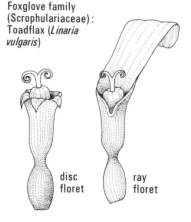

Foxglove family (Scrophulariaceae): Toadflax (*Linaria vulgaris*)

disc floret   ray floret

Daisy family (Compositae): Common Ragwort (*Senecio jacobaea*)

Above: The construction of several kinds of flower. The top three are shown as flowers which have been cut vertically in half.

Left: The Dog Rose (Rosa canina) is a common hedgerow plant. The flowers have many stamens and large pink or white flowers. The plant is closely related to garden roses, which have been bred from such wild species.

41

Left: A flower head of Corn Marigold (Chrysanthemum segetum) *showing the large outer ray florets and the smaller, more numerous, central disc florets. The plant is a common weed of cereal crops.*

Below: An inflorescence of the Fragrant Orchid (Gymnadenia conopsea) *displays the typical shape of Orchid flowers: a three-lobed lower petal with a long nectar-containing spur, and upper petals which form a hood over the pollen masses.*

the outer *ray florets* are bilaterally symmetrical and the inner *disc florets* are radial.

The petals of some wild flowers have narrow sac-like projections known as *spurs*, containing nectar, which may make the flower bilaterally symmetrical, as in the Orchids and members of the Foxglove family, where there is only one spur on each flower. Some flowers, such as the Columbine (*Aquilegia vulgaris*), have spurs on each petal and remain radially symmetrical.

Types of Inflorescence

The ways in which flowers can be grouped together in arrangements called *inflorescences* can also be important in identifying wild flowers. The simplest arrangement occurs in plants with a single flower at the end of a flower stalk, as in the Violet (*Viola* species) or the Primrose (*Primula vulgaris*). Where there is more than one flower there are several ways in which they may be grouped together on the flower stalk. One of the simplest inflorescences is the *spike*, in which a number of flowers grow directly along an upright stalk. The Pondweeds (*Potamogeton* species) and the Amphibious Bistort (*Polygonum persicaria*) are two examples of wild flowers with inflorescences in the form of spikes. Where the flowers are borne on short side shoots called *pedicels*, the inflorescence is known as a *raceme*. Racemes are found in many wild flowers, including the Bladderwort (*Utricularia vulgaris*) and the Common Toadflax (*Linaria vulgaris*).

In the other types of inflorescence the main flower stalks are branched, giving a more complicated appearance. A *panicle* is a raceme in which the pedicels branch. The Figworts (*Scrophularia* species), common plants of damp places and woodland margins, and many Grasses (Graminae) have flowers in panicles. The second type of branching inflorescence is the *cyme*, in which the main stalk ends with a flower, and younger flowers grow on side branches. Cymes are often repeatedly branched and have a broad, flattened outline, as in the Elder (*Sambucus nigra*) or the Valerian (*Valeriana officinalis*).

There are a few other types of inflorescence which are, in fact, variations of the cyme or the panicle. The Carrot family (Umbelliferae) has a characteristic inflorescence called an *umbel*, from which the botanical name for the family is derived. An umbel is a panicle in which the branches all arise at the same point and end in flowers held at the same level. It may be a *simple umbel*, in which this pattern occurs only once, or a *compound umbel*, with each main branch of the inflorescence ending in its own umbel. From a distance an umbel may appear to be a single large, white flower, although when seen closely it is obvious that it is made up of many very small flowers held next to one another.

The Daisy family (Compositae) has an inflorescence known as a *head*, or *capitulum*, in which many small flowers are grouped together on a flattened receptacle and surrounded by small green bracts. *Bracts* are small, scale-like leaves associated with an inflorescence and, in the case of the capitulum, look rather like sepals.

Below: Diagrams showing the arrangement of flowers in some of the commoner kinds of inflorescence.

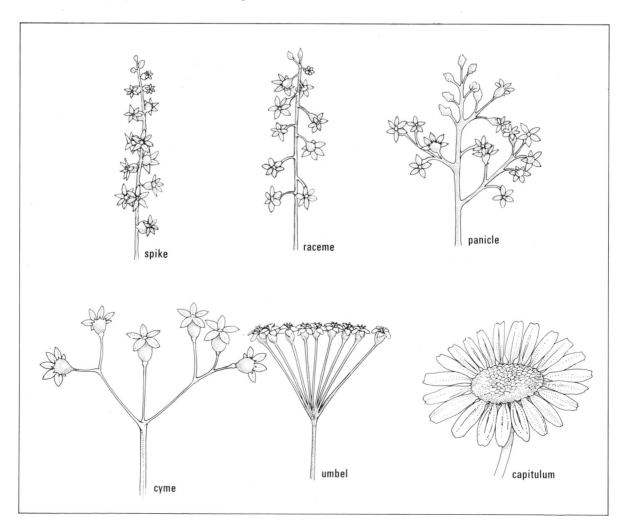

spike

raceme

panicle

cyme

umbel

capitulum

The Pollination of Wild Flowers

Pollination is one of the most remarkable processes in the life of a wild flower. It is so essential to the reproduction of the plant that many interesting adaptations have developed to make certain that it takes place. Pollination is the transfer of pollen grains from the anthers of a flower to the receptive surface of the stigma of a flower of the same kind. After pollination has taken place, fertilization of the female egg cell can occur and a seed eventually develop. The pollen grain is a self-contained microscopic unit of great complexity and contains a male *gamete*, or sex cell. This sex cell has a set of *chromosomes* carrying all the genetic characteristics of the parent plant within it.

Self-pollination and Cross-pollination

In *self-pollinated* plants pollen grains are transported from the anthers to stigmas on the same individual plant, whereas in *cross-pollinated* plants pollen is transferred to the stigmas of different individuals of the same species. There is a great difference between these two systems when fertilization takes place. In self-pollination the chromosomes from the male gamete fuse with a set of chromosomes in the female egg cell which have the same parent, and there is no possibility for a completely new mixture of characteristics resulting. However, there is a limited possibility for some reshuffling of chromosomes, which may result in small differences between parents and progeny. But when cross-pollination takes place, a completely new genetic mixture is formed. This has various advantages to the plant; for example, it often results in the production of a greater proportion of vigorous seeds, and the plants which grow from them are often healthier.

The chromosomes control the outward appearance of every aspect of the growing plant. In nature much of the variation between members of the same species is due to the different combinations of chromosomes present in their cells. The dwarf varieties of many garden flowers are plants which have been selected because of particular genetic characteristics. The mixing of chromosomes that follows cross-pollination provides an opportunity for new varieties to develop, some of which may be better suited than their parents to life in a particular environment.

Because cross-pollination has these advantages many plants have ways of encouraging cross-pollination and preventing self-pollination. Often this is achieved simply by having the male and female parts of each flower mature at different times, so that when the pollen is being released it is at the wrong time for fertilization of that same flower to occur, either because the ovules are immature or because they have already been fertilized. Alternatively, the construction of the flower may be such that pollen cannot easily be transferred to the stigma of the same flower. A few plants, including many members of the Daisy family (Compositae), such as the

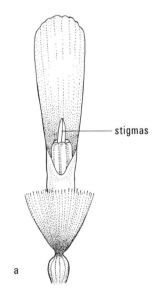

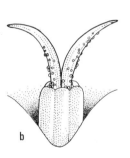

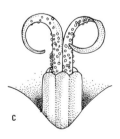

Above: Different stages in the flowering of the Dandelion (Taraxacum officinale); (a) pollen is forced out by growth of the stigmas; (b) the cross-pollination stage, in close-up; (c) the self-pollination stage. Self-pollination will not occur if the flowers have already been cross-pollinated.

Goat's-beard (*Tragopogon pratensis*), have an arrangement which allows self-pollination to succeed if cross-pollination has not occurred within a certain time. In this way the plants have the best of both worlds.

Two different means of transport are used by pollen grains to travel from the anthers to the stigma: the wind and animals of various kinds.

Above: A bee collecting nectar and pollen from a Purple Loosestrife (Lythrum salicaria) flower. The pollen is gathered into sacs on the bees hind legs but also becomes caught in the hairs on its body, from where it may be transferred to a stigma when the bee visits another flower.

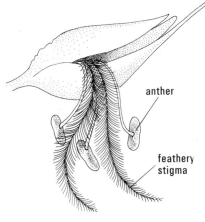

anther

feathery
stigma

*Above: Wind-pollinated flowers.
Top: a diagram of a single Grass
flower, much magnified. Centre:
Salad Burnet (Sanguisorba minor),
a wind-pollinated member of the Rose
family (Rosaceae). Bottom: Hoary
Plantain (Plantago media) with its
numerous white anthers.*

Wind Pollination

Wind pollination simply involves the wind blowing pollen grains, which are small and very light, through the air. This is a hit-or-miss process, since the chances of a pollen grain landing on a stigma of the right species are very small. For wind pollination to succeed pollen grains must be liberated into the air in enormous quantities. sufferers from hay fever, an allergic reaction to certain pollen grains, know this only too well. Most of the plants whose pollen grains cause hay fever are wind pollinated.

Despite the seemingly random nature of wind pollination it obviously works very well in practice. As well as many trees and shrubs, a number of wild flowers are pollinated by wind, including two very large families of plants, the Grasses (Graminae) and the Sedges (Cyperaceae). Such plants often grow together in large numbers, forming continuous areas of fairly uniform vegetation. The close proximity of the plants increases the chances of success in wind pollination. The flower of a Grass is a very reduced structure without petals or sepals and consisting mainly of anthers and stigmas. Both of the latter parts hang outside the flower so that the anthers can release the pollen directly into the air and the feathery stigmas can catch it readily.

Wind pollination also occurs in other families. The Salad Burnet (*Sanguisorba minor*) is an unusual wind-pollinated member of the Rose family (Rosaceae) which lacks the usual showy petals of the family. It is in fact a general characteristic of the flowers of wind-pollinated plants to be inconspicuous and lack colour, since they do not need to attract insects. Even the pollen grains themselves differ from those of animal-pollinated plants in being smooth-surfaced and not sticky.

Pollination by Animals

Plants which are pollinated by animals differ from wind-pollinated ones in having more brightly-coloured flowers, scent and nectar. The flowers are also more varied in shape and their pollen grains are larger. These often have spines or surface projections and are sticky so that they cling to the bodies of animals. The most important animal pollinating agents are insects, but other animals such as birds, bats and even snails are sometimes important pollinators, especially in tropical regions. Almost all the animals visit the flowers in search of food, such as nectar, and in so doing accidentally pick up pollen on their bodies which can be brushed off on to a stigma when the animal moves to another flower.

Animal pollination relies on the fact that animals behave in certain ways, regularly feeding on the same type of plant and often visiting one flower after another of their preferred kind. Because it can take advantage of the behaviour of animals, the plant does not need to produce such vast amounts of pollen, since the chances of any particular pollen grain reaching a suitable stigma are much higher than in wind pollination. Animal pollination can also work well between relatively scattered plants, and there is no need for such close spacing of the individuals.

At its simplest, insect pollination takes place because insects such as beetles visit flowers to eat them. In doing so, they may damage the flower to the extent that it cannot set seed, but if they do not cause so much damage they may very well effect pollination. This was probably the first relationship between plants and insects to evolve hundreds of millions of years ago in the Cretaceous period, when flowering plants first appeared.

Since that time the close dependence of insects on plants for food has led to the gradual evolution of more sophisticated systems of pollination in which the plant is not damaged. This has been accomplished mainly by providing an alternative source of food instead of the flowers themselves. Often this food is provided by a surplus of pollen grains, themselves highly nutritious. Some plants produce a sugary secretion called *nectar* as an alternative food.

Some insects are specially adapted for collecting pollen or nectar. Bees, for example, have baskets on their hind legs into which they load pollen grains to transport back to their hives. Bees make ideal pollinating agents because they are highly efficient foragers. They will select a particular kind of plant which is at the peak of its pollen production and concentrate on visiting it, working systematically from one flower to the next. The bee has a hairy body which is ideal for pollen grains to become stuck to. This foraging behaviour of bees greatly increases the likelihood of successful pollination with less wastage of pollen, even though much is removed by the insects. Those flowers which produce nectar are mostly visited by insects with fairly long sucking mouth parts through which they can drink the sugary solution. Bees are well suited to sucking up nectar as well as collecting pollen, but insects such as butterflies and moths, which have even longer mouthparts, are best suited to nectar feeding.

If a flower is able to restrict itself to insect visitors of only one kind, it may gain the advantage of becoming the main source of food for the insect and so increase the number of visits it makes. This will increase the possibilities of pollen being transferred directly from one individual plant to another as if by a special messenger service. On the other hand, those flowers which attract a great variety of kinds of insect may have a larger number of visitors in all. One of the commonest ways in which flowers restrict the kinds of insect which visit them is to have the petals fused together so that the mouth of the tube will only allow insects of a certain size to reach the pollen or nectar. Flowers of this construction are found in the Foxglove (Scrophulariaceae) and Mint (Labiatae) families; in both of these, the fused petals have a lower lobe which acts as a 'landing stage' for incoming insects. Often this lower lobe is distinctively coloured or patterned to attract the insect to land. Some flowers have brightly coloured lines leading into the entrance of the flower which are called 'honey guides' or 'nectar guides' because they help the insect to locate the nectar.

The flowers of the Meadow Clary (*Salvia pratensis*) are visited by small bees, which crawl into the tube-like flower. As they push into the base of the flower to reach the nectar, they cause the anthers to pivot and deposit pollen on to the back of the insect, where it is perfectly placed to come in contact with the stigma of the next flower visited. The pivoting action is caused when the bee pushes against two sterile anthers which do not produce pollen and which are connected to the functional anthers and cause them to move.

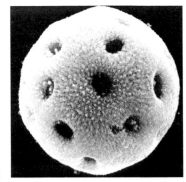

a

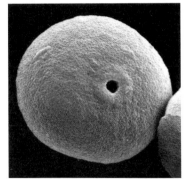

b

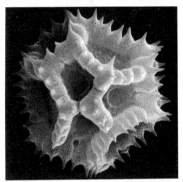

c

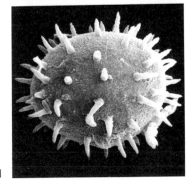

d

Above: Pollen grains of four different wild flowers greatly magnified with a scanning electron microscope: (a) Bindweed (Calystegia *species*), *(b) Timothy Grass* (Phleum pratensis), *(c) Lettuce* (Lactuca sativa), *(d) Yellow Water-lily* (Nuphar lutea).

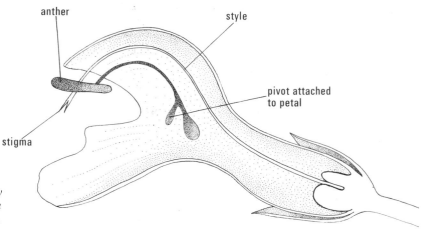

anther

style

stigma

pivot attached
to petal

Right : A flower of Meadow Clary (Salvia pratensis) *cut vertically in half to show the internal structure. One of the pivoting stamens which brushes pollen on to the backs of visiting bees is shown.*

Above : Gorse (Ulex europeaus), *with flowers in various stages, some unopened and others which have been pollinated and have their petals pushed down to uncover the stamens and styles. The plant has a long flowering season with flowers opening at different times.*

This mechanism is so effective that, when the bee is visiting the flower, the anthers brush up and down along its body as if they have a life of their own.

The flowers of the Pea family (Leguminosae) have another method of covering visiting bees with pollen. Here the size and weight of the bee are important in triggering the mechanism. Small flowers of this kind are too small for the larger bees to land on, and the larger flowers need a heavy bee. The back petal, or *standard*, of Pea family flowers is often brightly coloured to attract the bees, but does not act as a landing stage. Instead, the bee lands on the keel and wing petals, which then fold suddenly downwards so that the anthers and stigma are uncovered and a shower of pollen is thrown on to the insect as it feeds. The Clovers (*Trifolium* species) have this type of flower and are often visited by bees, which makes them very important to bee-keepers.

In some flowers the nectar is at the end of long spurs, or otherwise placed so that bees cannot reach it, and these are usually found to be flowers visited by butterflies or moths. Some moths, particularly the Hawk Moths, are able to hover in front of a flower and insert their tongue to obtain nectar without landing. The flowers of the Honeysuckle (*Lonicera periclymenum*) are often visited by Hawk Moths at dusk or in the early night, when the moths locate the flowers by their sweet smell.

Bright colours and sweet scents are not the only things which attract insects to flowers. Many wild flowers are pollinated by flies which are attracted by unpleasant smells. The Carrot family (Umbelliferae) includes many plants pollinated in this way and the names of some, such as the Hogweed (*Heracleum sphondylium*), suggest the smell of their flowers. The unusual-shaped flower of Lords-and-Ladies (*Arum maculatum*) actually traps insects which are attracted by its smell. Once inside the flower, they cannot escape and, in their efforts to fly out of the flower, they transfer pollen from the male flowers to the female ones. The entrance to the flower is ringed by backward-facing hairs through which the insects can force their way into, but not out of, the flower.

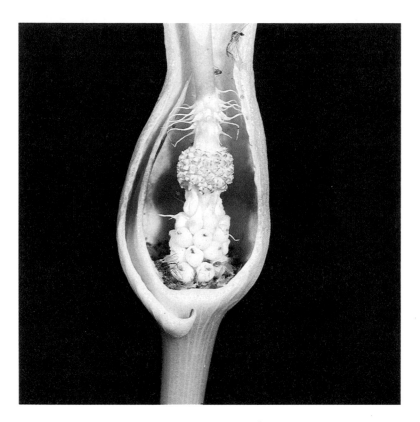

Left : The trap-like flower of Lords-and-Ladies (Arum maculatum) *cut open. Some of the small flies which were trapped in the flower have died and remain inside. The young fruits are starting to develop.*

The Pollination of Orchids

Orchid pollination is often so unusual in its complexity and in the elaborate mechanisms which exist in the flowers that it is worthy of special mention. Descriptions of the ways some Orchids are pollinated sound more like tales of science fiction than botanical fact. Orchid flowers have an unusual and distinctive construction; they are bilaterally symmetrical (see page 41), often with one or more distint spurs, and have special pollen masses instead of anthers. Each flower has two of these pollen masses, which consist of clusters of many pollen grains stuck firmly together in a club-shaped structure. At the base of each pollen mass is a sticky pad which can glue it to the head of an insect visitor to the flower. When the insect flies away, it carries the pollen mass on its head. After a few minutes, the base of the pollen mass starts to curve so that it points forward over the head into the ideal position to touch against the special stigma, all or some of the pollen grains detach from the insect.

In most European Orchids, insects are attracted by the bright colours of the flowers and visit them to obtain nectar from the spurs. Relatively few European Orchids attract insects by means of a strong scent, although the Fragrant Orchid (*Gymnadenia conopsea*) is an appropriately-named exception. Not all Orchid flowers are brightly coloured or strongly scented; some are green-flowered, such as the Common Twayblade (*Listera ovata*). The most remarkable kind of Orchid pollination involves the attraction of insects to the flower in an attempt to mate with it. This phenomenon is known as *pseudocopulation* and occurs in Orchids whose flowers so closely mimic the appearance of a female insect of a particular kind that males attempt to mate with it. In so doing, the pollen masses become

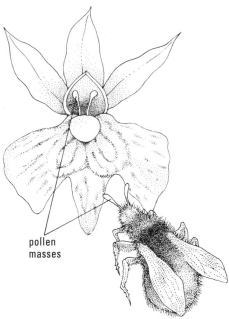

pollen
masses

Above : A bee with two pollinia *(pollen masses) adhering to its head is about to land on an unpollinated Orchid flower, where it may effect pollination and pick up more pollinia.*

49

stuck to their bodies and so make pollination possible. The
attractive Bee Orchid (*Orchis apifera*) is so named because it is
visited by bees in this way.

The Process of Fertilization

Once pollen grains have been transferred to the surface of a stigma
the fertilization of the female egg cell can take place. But before this
happens the pollen grain and stigma of many kinds of flower communicate with each other to find out whether they belong to the same
species. This process of communication is a chemical one and its
mechanism has only been elucidated relatively recently by some
very sophisticated experimental research. Basically what happens is
that when a pollen grain lands on a stigma it absorbs water and
begins to swell, and as it does so it releases a complex mixture of
substances from its surface on to the stigma. If these substances
react with those on the stigma surface the pollen grain and stigma
have recognized one another. Substances are then produced which
cause the pollen grain to germinate and produce a hair-like growth
called the *pollen tube*. If the stigma is of the wrong kind of plant, the
reaction will not take place and the pollen tube will not develop.
After the pollen tube has started to grow, it penetrates the stigma
and passes down through the style to the ovary where fertilization
occurs. The chromosomes from the male sex cell combine with
those of the egg cell to form an embryo, which has the double set of
chromosomes found in the cells of the mature plant. The embryo
grows larger as the number of cells multiplies, and the development
of a seed is the final result.

Above: A close-up of the magnificent flower of the Bee Orchid (Orchis apifera), *which simulates the appearance of a female bee to attract males.*

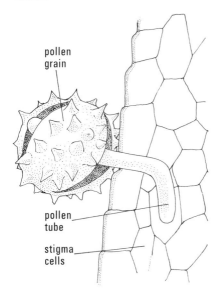

pollen grain

pollen tube

stigma cells

Above: A germinating pollen grain entering the tissues of a stigma, as seen through a microscope. The stigma is shown in sectional view.

Fruits and Seeds

Seeds represent an important stage in the life cycle of wild flowers. Producing seeds gives these plants an enormous advantage over the spore-producing plants, such as Ferns, Mosses and Liverworts, which do not have seeds. A seed makes it possible for a particular kind of wild flower to become more widespread and can also act as a dormant or resting stage which can survive through periods of unsuitable conditions.

The Structure of Seeds and Fruits

An individual seed consists of a fully developed *embryo* inside a protective outer *seed coat*. The embryo has several recognizable parts which will grow into a young rootlet, a young shoot and one or two *cotyledons*. The cotyledons are the first leaves to sprout when the seed germinates and are often quite different in shape from the mature leaves which develop later. In many wild flowers the cotyledons never appear above soil level; they stay underground, where they act as suppliers of stored energy to the growing seedling. If a seedling has a single cotyledon, the plant is a *Monocotyledon*; if it has two, then it is a *Dicotyledon*. This basic distinction between the two groups of plants is, however, rarely seen, and the differences in the fully developed leaves and the flowers are of more practical value in recognizing individual plants.

Seeds develop inside *fruits*, which are made up of the ovary wall with one or more seeds inside. The seeds may be released individually when the fruit splits open or dispersed intact as a whole fruit. When botanists talk about fruits they include all structures formed in this way. The Tomato (*Lycopersicum esculentum*), for example, is a fruit, although it is often thought of as simply a vegetable.

seed coat

cotyledon

shoot

rootlet

Above: A seed cut in half to show the arrangement of the cotyledons, young root and shoot inside. Seeds of various plants differ in the amount of storage tissue and the size of the cotyledons.

Right: Young pods of Broom (Sarothamnus scoparius) *with the developing seeds visible inside.*

Left : The follicles of the Marsh Marigold (Caltha palustris) *splitting open to reveal the seeds. The outer fruits ripen first and many have already lost their seeds.*

Right : The Common Poppy (Papaver rhoeas) *in flower and fruit. Some of the petals are dusted with yellow pollen. The ovary in the centre of the flower already shows the characteristic shape of the ripening capsule.*

Kinds of Fruits and Seeds

There are many different kinds of fruits, each of which has a particular way of dispersing itself or the seeds it contains. The simplest type of fruit is that found in the Buttercups (*Ranunculus* species), which is made up of a single seed inside the dried-out ovary wall. This kind of fruit is known as an *achene*, as are other dry, one-seeded fruits, such as that of the Dandelion (*Taraxacum officinale*), which look quite different. Similar fruits with much harder outer cases are *nuts*, which are mostly found in trees. Smaller versions, called *nutlets*, are found in some wild flowers, such as the Sorrels (*Rumex* species). A fruit similar to an achene but with more than one seed inside is the *follicle*, which is found in plants such as the Larkspur (*Delphinium ambigua*) of the Buttercup family (Ranunculaceae). The seeds are released from a follicle when it dries out completely and splits along part of one side. A fruit which dries out and then splits along all of one or both sides is a *pod*. The fruits of members of the Pea family (Leguminosae) are pods, and many are important as vegetables because of the high protein content in their seeds.

Some fruits are made up of several fused ovaries which develop into a single fruit. Such a fruit is known as a *capsule* if it dries out and then releases the seeds through slits or openings. There are many varieties of capsules, but those of the Poppy (*Papaver* species) are probably the best known. When the Poppy capsule dries out it becomes brown and hardened. The seeds are shaken out through the holes which open around the top of the capsule. The wind blowing against the fruits has the action of sprinkling out the small seeds. This type of capsule has the advantage of releasing the seeds gradually over a period of time. This increases the probability that

Right : Some of the main types of fruits. The two on the left have been cut in half vertically to show their internal structure.

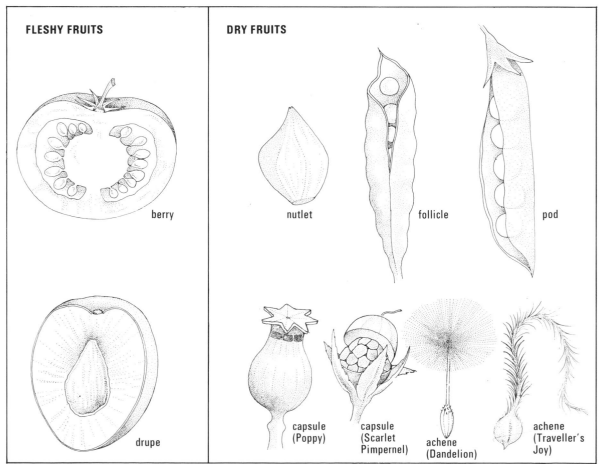

FLESHY FRUITS

berry

drupe

DRY FRUITS

nutlet

follicle

pod

capsule
(Poppy)

capsule
(Scarlet
Pimpernel)

achene
(Dandelion)

achene
(Traveller's
Joy)

some of them will be released when conditions are just right for their growth. The capsules of Orchids are very different and contain millions of minute seeds which look like dust. Each seed is made up of only a few cells, without any special reserve of food to enable the seed to germinate vigorously. The Orchid seeds germinate and develop very slowly, and only when nourished by the fungi with which they form associations.

Not all fruits dry out when fully ripe. Some remain soft and fleshy. There are two main kinds of fleshy fruits: *berries* and *drupes*. A berry is fleshy throughout and often contains a number of seeds; the Bilberry (*Vaccinium myrtillus*) is an example. Fruits such as the Blackberry (*Rubus fruticosus*) are collections of small drupes rather than berries, because their fleshy part is a swollen receptacle rather than the ovary wall. Drupes are fleshy seeds with a hard stone

Below and right: Fruits and seeds dispersed by the wind (this page) and by animals or other means (opposite page).

Poppy capsules releasing seeds in the wind

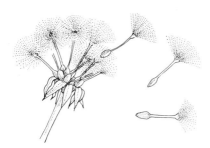

A Dandelion clock with the fruits blowing away

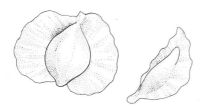

Winged fruits of Mountain Sorrel (*Oxyria digyna*)

Left: The fruits of the Bilberry (Vaccinium myrtillus) *are glossy, bluish-black berries which are eaten by birds and other animals. The resistant seeds can still germinate after passing through the digestive system of the animal.*

54

Right : The Indian Balsam
(Impatiens glandulifera), *which is
naturalized along many stream banks,
has capsules which suddenly twist
open and throw out the seeds quite
violently when the capsules are
touched.*

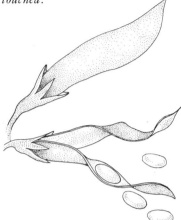

A Vetch pod suddenly splits and throws
out the seeds

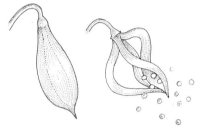

A Balsam capsule bursts and twists to
throw out the seeds

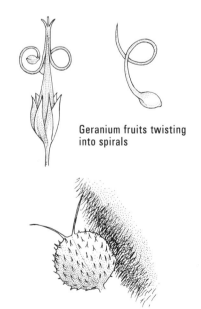

Geranium fruits twisting
into spirals

A fruit of Sanicle (*Sanicula europaea*)
attached to the fur of an animal

inside enclosing the seed. The fruits of the Wild Cherry (*Prunus avium*) and its relatives are good examples of drupes.

The Dispersal of Fruits and Seeds

When the seeds are fully ripened they are shed from the plant either singly or in groups. The seeds of many wild flowers simply fall to the ground around the parent plant and germinate there if they are not too shaded or if the parent is not using up all the available soil water. Many seeds or fruits have some mechanism which deposits them further from the parent plant. When seeds are dispersed in this way it is quite possible that many of them will not land on suitable soil for their growth, but those that do so will increase the range of distribution of the plant. This sometimes establishes new colonies where none grew before. This has the advantage that the plant will be less likely to be wiped out by local changes affecting part of its distribution. The effects of fire or even a gradual increase in shade from surrounding trees may cause a plant to die out in one locality, but if it has an efficient means of dispersal it may survive in other unaffected places. There are several ways in which fruits and seeds become dispersed. They may be actively shed by the parent plant, or be carried away by wind, water or animals.

Fruits whose seeds are dispersed by wind include the Poppy, whose seeds are thrown further from the capsule in a strong wind.

This dispersal is limited to short distances, usually of less than a metre. The seeds of many members of the Pea family (Leguminosae) are thrown similar distances when their pods suddenly burst and their two halves twist into tight spirals. The Balsams (*Impatiens* species) have a slightly more effective method of dispersal. When their capsules are ripe they burst open at the slightest touch and throw the seeds out. The botanical name of Wild Balsam is *Impatiens noli-tangere*, the second part of which comes from one of the plant's common names, Touch-me-not.

Seeds which are dispersed over much greater distances include the plumed fruits of the Daisy family (Compositae) and the similar seeds of the Great Reedmace (*Typha latifolia*). Both have a parachute-like arrangement of hairs called a *pappus*, which carries them on currents of air, sometimes for many miles. The Great Reedmace is one of the most widely distributed plants in the world, and its wind-blown seeds must have been very important in establishing it so widely.

Many seeds and fruits are distributed by animals. Some simply become stuck in the mud on animals' hooves and eventually fall off after being carried some way from the parent plant. Others have hooks or barbs designed to catch in the fur of passing animals. The Burdocks (*Arctium* species) and Cleavers (*Galium aparine*) are two good examples of fruits which become firmly hooked on to fur or clothing. Many fruits are dispersed when animals eat them. Many birds specialize in feeding on fruits and seeds, and often these are capable of surviving through the animal's digestive system. Berries are often eaten by birds and, although their soft, edible outer parts are digested, the hard inner case protects the seeds. Some seeds have such a thick outer case that they cannot begin to grow until they have been broken down by soil organisms or passed through the gut of an animal to soften the outer coat. For this reason, gardeners often scratch the seed coats of some kinds of vegetable seeds before planting them, because this makes them germinate more quickly.

Seeds which Bury Themselves
Some seeds and fruits actually complete their dispersal by burying themselves in the soil. The Meadow Cranesbill (*Geranium pratense*) and related plants have fruits which remain attached to the style by thin strands that twist into spirals and untwist with changes in humidity. When a fruit finally falls to the ground the strands continue to twist and untwist and, if the fruit has landed on soft soil, can bury it as a result.

Similarly, the fruits of the Dandelion (*Taraxacum officinale*), Goat's-beard (*Tragopogon pratensis*) and their relatives have a means of digging into soft soil. As the fruit drops to the ground on its parachute of hairs, it lands seed end first and may become lodged upright in the soil. As the wind blows the pappus hairs, it causes the whole fruit to move from side to side. The small tooth-like projections on the sides of the seed then become more firmly fixed in the ground and eventually bury it. The parachute hairs of the pappus later fall off. If a Dandelion seed is placed between forefinger and thumb and lightly rubbed, it will move along in the same way as it does into the ground.

Above: The Sow-thistle (Sonchus oleraceus) *with a ripe fruiting head of wind-dispersed achenes. The fruits are distributed over a great area in large numbers, so the Sow-thistle is often able to colonize areas of bare ground rapidly.*

Above: The bracts of the Lesser Burdock (Arctium minus) *become hardened as the fruits ripen and act as hooks to attach the entire inflorescence to the fur of passing animals.*

The Growth of Wild Flowers

The growth of a wild flower begins when its seed springs into life in the process known as *germination*. Prior to this, the seed may have been buried in the ground for anything from a few weeks to several years, during which it is in a resting, or *dormant*, state. Dormant seeds are very important in nature because they can survive through conditions which may kill the parent plant. Buried seeds can survive a particularly dry growing season or even fire, and when conditions are suitable again they can germinate and re-establish the plant.

The Germination of Seeds

The germination of seeds is rarely haphazard. They will usually only begin to grow when the surrounding conditions are suitable. How does the seed know when to germinate? The start of germination can be triggered off by a variety of different influences, depending on the kind of plant in question. Some seeds cannot germinate until they have been buried away from light for a certain length of time. Others need to be exposed to a particular temperature for a period of time; in some cases, this means that the seeds must even be frozen before they germinate. In other kinds of plants, freezing would kill the seeds. Despite this variety of conditions which different plants need, there are only two main reasons for seeds to delay their germination. There is often a chemical substance present in the seed which prevents its growth. Until this chemical has been destroyed the seed will not grow. The chemical may be destroyed by exposure to light or frost or some other condition, depending on the season in which the seeds usually grow. Seeds which need exposure to frost are usually those of plants which germinate early in the year after the frosts of winter.

Germination is not always controlled by chemicals within the seed. Before any seed can begin to grow, it must absorb water from its surroundings. Thus some seeds lie dormant in the ground until soaked by the rain. If the seed is provided with a very thick seed coat this will prevent the absorption of water until the seed coat has partly broken down. Once the seed has started to take in water, it swells up and its cells begin to grow and multiply. A small root is usually the first part of the seedling to appear. This establishes the young plant with the supply of water it needs to grow larger.

The energy needed by the seedling for its first period of growth must come from stored reserves of food in the seed, usually in the cotyledons. This food is stored as starch, sugars or oils, and its presence makes seeds a particularly nourishing food source for animals and people. Seedlings of different kinds of plants behave in different ways. In some the cotyledons, which are like embryonic leaves, act only as a food store, but in others they are pushed up above the ground and function like the normal leaves of the mature plant in carrying out photosynthesis. After the small root has grown, a young leafy stem usually develops.

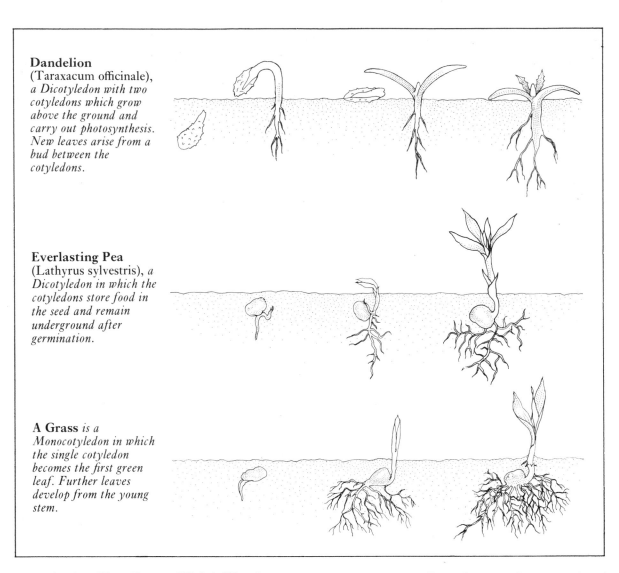

Dandelion
(Taraxacum officinale),
*a Dicotyledon with two
cotyledons which grow
above the ground and
carry out photosynthesis.
New leaves arise from a
bud between the
cotyledons.*

Everlasting Pea
(Lathyrus sylvestris), *a
Dicotyledon in which the
cotyledons store food in
the seed and remain
underground after
germination.*

A Grass *is a
Monocotyledon in which
the single cotyledon
becomes the first green
leaf. Further leaves
develop from the young
stem.*

How the Seedling Knows Which Way is up

Whichever way a seed lands in the soil, it always grows into a plant
the right way up. To be able to do this the seedling must be able to
tell which way up it is. The stem and leaves of the seedling grow
upwards and the roots grow down because they are both sensitive to
light and the pull of gravity. When a house plant is grown on a
window sill, where it receives strong light on one side only, it will
eventually turn towards the light by growing more on the side of the
stem away from the light than on the side facing it. Roots are
affected in the opposite way. If they are exposed to light, the side of
the root which receives the brightest light grows faster than the
shaded side, with an overall effect of causing the root to curve away
from the light, and usually into the soil.

As with the control of germination, this aspect of the growth of the
plant is controlled by chemicals within the plant. These are called
plant hormones because they work in a similar way to the hormones
which control the growth of animals. The hormones control the
direction of growth because they can speed up or slow down the
growth of any part of the plant. Because the hormones become

*Above: Stages in the germination of
seeds of two Dicotyledons and a
Monocotyledon. The cotyledons
themselves may act as reserves of
food and remain underground, or may
be the first green leaves of the
seedling.*

concentrated on the shaded side of stems or roots, and because they accumulate on the lower side of parts of the plant through the influence of gravity, they control the direction in which the plant grows.

Plants with Different Life Styles

Different plants grow and develop at different rates, and there are three categories of plant life style. *Annual* plants complete their whole life cycle in a single year and then die. The plant survives through the harshest time of year, the winter, as a seed. Other plants are *biennials* and take two years to complete their life cycle. The first year is spent growing leaves and stems and building up food reserves. The second year is passed in further growth and then the production of flowers and the completion of the life cycle. A number of garden vegetables, including the Carrot (*Daucus carota*) and the Cabbage (*Brassica oleracea*), are biennials and will not *bolt*, or go to seed, in the first year in which they are planted. Other wild flowers are *perennials* and complete their life cycles over a number of years. Some of the perennials, such as Wild Angelica (*Angelica sylvestris*), are *herbaceous*, or soft-stemmed, and die back in the winter, surviving by means of underground storage organs. Others are *woody*, like the Dog Rose (*Rosa canina*), and may lose their leaves in winter but not their stems. Perennials often produce flowers and seeds every year for a period of years.

These varied ways of life are suited to differing conditions. Many garden weeds are annuals, for example, and spread rapidly by seeds with a usually effective means of dispersal. They then grow rapidly in a single season and set seed. By producing seeds so quickly, they are able to colonize or invade new areas very quickly, before the slower-growing biennials and perennials, which will probably eventually shade out the weeds, have become established. Perennials can become much larger plants; many are small shrubs which have the advantage of growing higher above ground level into brighter light.

The Timing of Flowering

When a plant produces its flowers it is vitally important that it does so at the same time as others of its species, or else there will be no possiblility for cross-pollination. Many wild flowers have quite precise flowering periods when all the buds on every plant burst open together. In such cases the start of flowering can temporarily alter the appearance of the surroundings, as in a Bluebell wood at the end of spring. Other plants, such as the Shepherd's Purse (*Capsella bursa-pastoris*) or the Greater Plantain (*Plantago major*), go on producing flowers in a succession throughout most of the year.

Those plants which have a precise flowering season do so because they are responding to the length of days and nights. As with other events in the life of the plant, plant hormones are involved which encourage the growth of buds when day lengths indicate the right season. Here it is a balance of hormones which builds up by day and breaks down by night which is needed to produce the effect of flowering.

Part Two

Wild Flowers in the Environment

Left: A stream bank provides a moist environment in which many plants flourish. Seen here are Rosebay Willowherb (Epilobium angustifolium) *and Monkey Flower* (Mimulus guttatus).

The Evolution of Wild Flowers

Evolution is a process by which gradual changes appear in living things and are passed on from one generation to the next. The idea of evolution was first put forward by Charles Darwin in his book *The Origin of Species*, which was published in 1859. Darwin developed his theory of evolution as he travelled around the world on the ship *The Beagle*. He suggested that evolution occurred as a result of *natural selection*, by which he meant that those individual plants or animals best suited to survival would be most likely to reproduce and pass on their characteristics to the next generation. A vast amount of time, millions of years, may be needed for sufficient generations to pass, however, before very distinct changes appear.

Fossil Plants

One source of information about the evolution of living things is provided by fossils. Fossils are preserved remains of plants or animals which lived millions of years ago. Unfortunately plants are not often well preserved as fossils because they are made up mostly of delicate, soft parts. Some animals, such as the Dinosaurs, made very good fossils because of their hard bones, which were more likely to become buried and preserved. Surprisingly the part of a plant most likely to be fossilized is its pollen grains, which form *micro-fossils* because they have a hard outer coat. Much of our knowledge about early plants comes from studying fossil pollen. The pollen of flowering plants is very distinctive and can provide information about when the first ones evolved. Unfortunately we do not know whether the first flowering plants had the distinctive pollen grains of their present-day descendants.

Leaves and trunks of trees are the oldest known fossils of flowering plants, apart from pollen grains. These have been found preserved in rocks dating from the Cretaceous period, which began about 141 million years ago and lasted for about 75 million years. This period marked the end of the age of the Dinosaurs and the beginning of the era when Mammals rose to become the main group of large land animals. No one knows why the Dinosaurs became extinct at that time, but there may well have been a sudden change in climate during the Cretaceous period. Many ancient groups of plants became extinct at the same time, leaving seed-producing plants, the Angiosperms and Gymnosperms, as the dominant forms of plants. The Cretaceous period in Europe was the time when most of the chalk rocks were formed. Since these rocks were laid down under the sea they contain fossilized remains of marine life but do not reveal what was happening on land at the time. Elsewhere in the world, however, particularly in North America, there are rock deposits which were formed away from the oceans, and these contain Cretaceous fossil plants. By the end of the Cretaceous period many different kinds of flowering plants had evolved and are found as fossils. Most of these are trees rather than wild flowers, and some

Above: The appearance of extinct plants like this Seed Fern can be reconstructed from their fragmentary fossil remains. Seed Ferns had fern-like leaves, some of which ended in cone-like, seed-producing structures.

Right: A geological time scale showing the groups of plants living in each epoch and period. Before the Devonian period all plant life was in the oceans.

LAND PLANTS THROUGH THE AGES

ERA	PERIOD AND EPOCH	Millions of years Ago	
			Mosses and Liverworts · Clubmosses · Ferns · Conifers · Flowering Plants
CAENOZOIC	QUATERNARY		
	Holocene (Recent)	0·01	
	Pleistocene	1·5	Ice Ages in Europe
	TERTIARY		
	Pliocene	6	Flowering plants became dominant
	Miocene	22·5	
	Oligocene	38	
	Eocene	55	
	Palaeocene	65	Giant Club mosses · Seed Ferns · ?
MESOZOIC	CRETACEOUS	141	First flowering plants appeared
	JURASSIC	195	
	TRIASSIC	230	
PALAEOZOIC	PERMIAN	280	Early seed plants
	CARBONIFEROUS	345	First land plants
	DEVONIAN	395	
	SILURIAN	435	
	ORDOVICIAN	500	
	CAMBRIAN	570	
	PRE-CAMBRIAN	4600	

? The origin of the Flowering Plants remains a mystery even today, despite having attracted the attention of many scientific researchers. For this reason dotted lines have been used to suggest a tentative link between them and the other seed-producing plants.

63

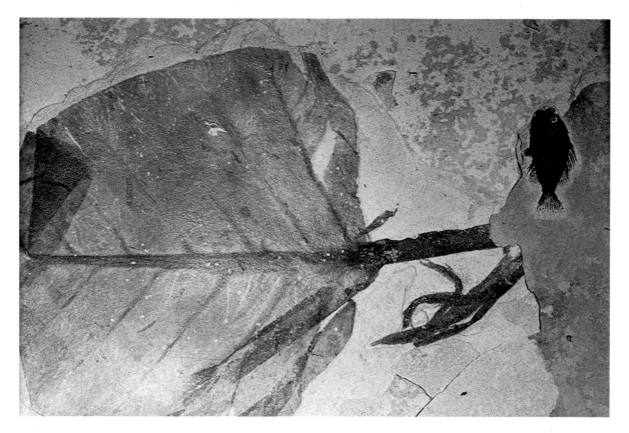

can be recognized as being very similar to certain trees living today. Those plants which grew in wet places such as marshes and ponds are most frequently found as fossils because the conditions in which they grew were ideal for their remains to become buried in mud and preserved as fossils.

The fossil plants of the Eocene epoch (about 55–38 million years ago) show that at that time Europe had vegetation resembling that of the modern tropical regions. A Palm (*Nipa* species) was one of the most abundant plants in Europe during the Eocene, although its relatives today inhabit the tropical mangrove swamps. From the Eocene to the Pliocene epoch (about 6–1½ million years ago) the climate in Europe gradually became cooler, and the plants found as fossils became more like those of present-day Europe. However, there were some plants, such as the Water Chestnut (*Trapa natans*), which grew in Europe during the Pliocene epoch but do not do so now.

The Pleistocene epoch (from 1½ million years ago to about 10,000 years ago) was the time of the Ice Ages, when much of Europe was covered by glaciers and the climate reached its coldest. The Ice Ages greatly influenced the present-day distribution of plants in Europe, as will be explained in the following chapter.

How Wild Flowers Evolve
Darwin's theory of evolution, with his idea of natural selection, accounts for many evolutionary changes in plants but is not the whole story. New kinds of plant can also develop as a result of the formation of *hybrids*. A hybrid is a cross between two different kinds

Above: A rock slab from North America with fossilized remains from an aquatic habitat: a small fish (Priscacaria) and the leaf of a Water-lily-like plant. Plant remains found as fossils rarely show so much detail of venation.

Above: A fossilized flower with five large petals dating from the Miocene epoch which ended about 6 million years ago. Because flowers are delicate, such well-preserved fossil flowers are very rarely found.

Below: The Water Chestnut (Trapa natans) floats on fresh water by means of air-filled, swollen leaf stalks. Although no longer native to northern Europe, it is known to have lived there before the Ice Ages.

of plants, usually two fairly closely-related species. In most cases, hybrids are prevented from being formed because pollen grains will not germinate on the stigma of a different kind of plant. In closely related plants the pollen grains sometimes can develop, and a hybrid may occur. When the Water Avens (*Geum rivale*) grows together with Herb Bennett, or Wood Avens (*Geum urbanum*), hybrids quite commonly form which look intermediate between the two parents. Normally this is prevented from happening because the two plants grow in different types of places, the first in wet places such as stream banks and the second in woods. Where a stream passes through a wood they may grow together. Not all hybrids are able to produce fertile seeds and so they cannot reproduce. However, others do produce fertile seed and may go on reproducing until they have built up a sizeable population of a third plant, different in appearance from its parents. It is thought that many new species of plants have arisen in this way.

The isolation of different populations of a particular plant can eventually result in differences between the individuals of the two populations. These differences are a result of the process of natural selection which acts in different ways on the isolated groups, depending on the conditions in which each is growing.

Occasionally plants change in appearance as a result of the occurrence of *mutations*, or *sports*. Mutations are caused by changes in the chromosomes and may be passed on to successive generations of the plant. If the mutation serves no useful purpose or is actually harmful to the life of the plant, it is unlikely to be passed on because it will not be favoured by natural selection.

The Origin of Wild-flower Habitats

A *habitat* is a place where plants grow with a particular set of environmental conditions prevailing. Woodlands, sea-shores and limestone cliffs are examples of different kinds of habitat. Habitats do not always remain the same, but change over a period of time until they reach a stable form for the climatic conditions. Most of Europe, with its present-day climate, would be covered by forest, except that mankind has modified the vegetation of many places, often creating new kinds of habitat.

The Effect of the Ice Ages

The story of the development of present habitats in Europe begins some. $1\frac{1}{2}$ million years ago with the Ice Ages of Pleistocene times, which brought great changes in climate. These, in turn, caused corresponding changes in the vegetation, which can be traced in surprising detail by studying pollen grains preserved in peat bogs and lake sediments. As with the fossil pollen grains, the resistant outer wall survives intact in peat and some types of mud. The pollen grains of these more recent plants can be identified much more accurately, sometimes to an exact species but often to the family of plant which produced them. By identifying the pollen grains present in a sample of peat formed at the beginning of the Ice Ages and comparing the relative amounts of pollen of different plants, it is possible to build up an idea of the appearance of the vegetation at that time.

When the ice reached its greatest extent, much of northern Europe was covered by glaciers and completely devoid of plant life, except for the tops of mountains that rose above the ice, known as *nunataks*. The level of the sea was much lower at that time because of the vast amounts of water held in the glaciers and the polar ice caps. This meant that Britain and Ireland were joined to continental Europe by land. At this time most of Europe to the south of the ice was covered with a kind of vegetation known as *tundra*. Tundra vegetation occurs nowadays in the most northern parts of Europe and Asia. It has no trees except for dwarf species of Willow (*Salix herbacea*) and Birch (*Betula nana*). Most of the ground cover consists of Lichens and Mosses with a few wild flowers. Some of these, such as the Mountain Avens (*Dryas octopetala*) and the Alpine Crowberry (*Empetrum nigrum*), are also to be found further south in Europe on the tops of high mountains where conditions resemble those of the northern tundra. To the south of the tundra, in Ice Age times, lay extensive areas of evergreen conifer forests of Pine (*Pinus* species) and Spruce (*Picea* species).

The record of the pollen grains shows that about 25,000 years ago the ice began gradually to melt and the glaciers to retreat for the last time. As the ice withdrew, new areas of bare soil were exposed and colonized by tundra vegetation. This general improvement in the climate allowed the coniferous forests to spread northwards,

The Crowberry (Empetrum nigrum) *(above) and* Mountain Avens (Dryas octopetala) *(right) are examples of arctic plants found in tundra. They grow on mountains in more southerly regions and very occasionally at lower altitudes.*

Below: A map of the vegetation of northern Europe during the height of the Ice Ages, when extensive glacial ice sheets covered much of Europe and low-lying land connected Britain to the Continent.

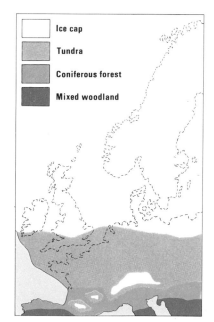

- Ice cap
- Tundra
- Coniferous forest
- Mixed woodland

Below: A simplified map of the present-day vegetation of northern Europe which shows the kind of vegetation which would develop naturally. It does not show cultivated or much-altered habitats.

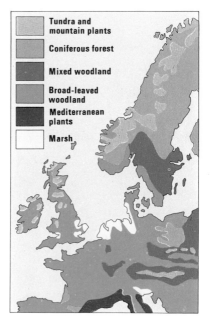

Tundra and mountain plants

Coniferous forest

Mixed woodland

Broad-leaved woodland

Mediterranean plants

Marsh

invading and replacing what had been tundra. Forests of broad-leaved, deciduous trees began to develop in what had been coniferous forest. There was, in effect, a gradual migration of the whole vegetation further north as the climate became milder. This was a slow process taking place over several thousand years.

Eventually the ice stopped retreating as it reached its present position in the polar regions, and the main migrations of vegetation stopped. Without the influence of mankind, the vegetation would have remained essentially the same until today. However, some new kinds of plants have continued to arrive in Europe, without the aid of mankind, by gradually extending their ranges wherever conditions were suitable. There are differences between the kinds of plants found in continental Europe and Britain and Ireland because such later arrivals amongst the plants have not distributed themselves evenly throughout Europe. The main reason for this is the presence of the English Channel, which was flooded when the melting of the glaciers raised the sea level. Britain has fewer species of wild flowers than continental Europe because there was not time for them to spread gradually into Britain before it became an island. Ireland, which was cut off even sooner, has even fewer species of wild flowers, but this is partly compensated for by the presence of some interesting plants of southern Europe which occur along the western coast of Ireland warmed by the Gulf Stream.

The Influence of Mankind

At the height of the Ice Ages people were thriving in Europe. Hunting communities preyed upon the herds of grazing animals which fed upon the tundra vegetation, but these people had little influence on the vegetation. Later, however, when the climate had become warmer and drier and forests of Oak (*Quercus* species), Elm (*Ulmus* species), Birch (*Betula* species) and Alder (*Alnus* species) were widespread, human activity began to change the vegetation. In about 3000 BC Neolithic communities began to establish cultivated areas and villages by clearing the forests. As the people created open spaces so certain plants, which grow best in such conditions, began to thrive. The pollen record shows that weeds such as the Plantains (*Plantago* species) became very common around human habitations. These plants must have been growing in Europe before people began to clear the forests and simply took advantage of the newly created open habitats.

Over the centuries more and more woodland was cleared until most of Europe was open fields, grasslands and heaths, with relatively few large areas of forest intact. Even the remaining woodland areas were modified by such practices as coppicing the trees to obtain poles. The open places created by people only remain open because of continued human activities. The rough pastures cleared for grazing animals were kept open by the continued grazing. The chalk hills which have been grazed by sheep for centuries developed a characteristic short turf rich in wild flowers. On acidic soils heaths often developed when the land was cleared. These usually have a mixture of Gorse (*Ulex* species), Bracken (*Pteridium aquilinum*), Heather (*Calluna vulgaris*) and Heaths (*Erica* species). Traditionally heaths were usually burnt every few years to encourage the growth of fresh shoots for the animals to eat and to prevent shrubs and trees regaining a place.

Eventually the modern landscape developed. In Europe this has almost all been influenced by mankind to a greater or lesser extent. Very few areas of natural vegetation remain, except in the most sparsely populated areas and where the land is unsuitable for agriculture.

The Evolution of Habitats

Some changes in habitats take place without the influence of human beings. Streams may silt up and finally cease flowing, and ponds may dry out and become marshes. When such changes take place a process known as *succession* occurs as different kinds of plants gradually replace one another until a stable vegetation is reached. When a pond dries out, for example, the order of succession might be the spread of Reedmace (*Typha latifolia*) and other rooted plants out into the water, replacing the floating plants that originally grew there. Gradually, on the margins of the area, the Reedmaces themselves might be replaced by Grasses, Sedges and Rushes (*Juncus* species). As the middle of the pond finally becomes covered with rooted plants, a marsh will develop. This might later be colonized by trees such as Alder (*Alnus glutinosa*). Most areas of open ground will eventually develop into woodland. However, in places such as exposed coastal areas or on high mountains, the succession may stop before trees have become established. Thus some open coastal habitats, moorlands and mountains are devoid of trees because of environmental conditions rather than human activity.

Right: A succession of changes (top to bottom) in the vegetation of a pond. As the pond is filled slowly by sediments and plant remains, the area of open water with floating plants becomes reduced and plants of marshy habitats encroach upon what had been water.

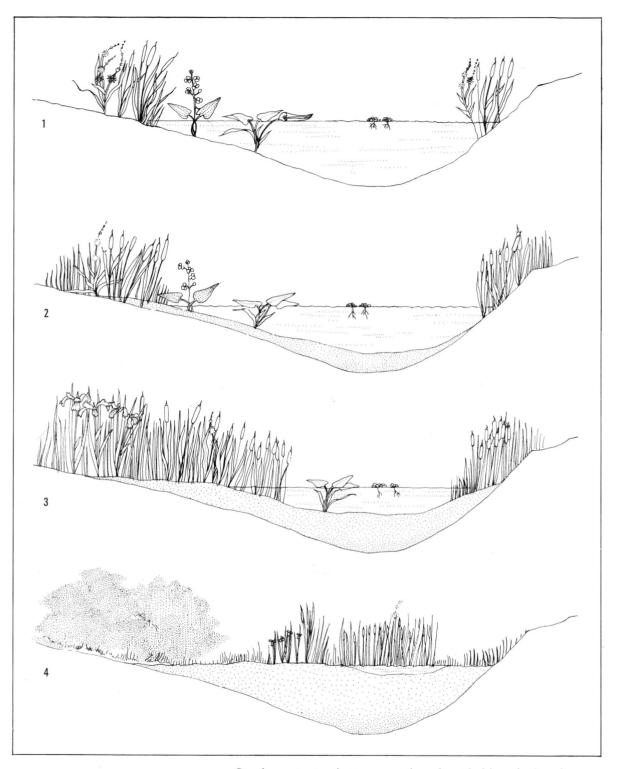

One important point to remember about habitats is that they are not always completely well defined and separate. Depending on the location, mixtures of several different kinds of habitats may be found. Grassland, for example, may merge into heath or bog because of changes in soil or drainage of the land. At the boundary mixtures of plants typical of several kinds of habitat may be found.

Wild Flowers of Woodlands

In the woodland habitat woody plants, trees and shrubs dominate, and wild flowers are mostly found beneath them. The shade of the trees limits the amount of light available for photosynthesis, and for wild flowers to survive in woods they must be able to grow in shade. The trees of the woodland often produce a thick litter of fallen leaves which breaks down into a rich humus producing a very fertile soil for those plants which are able to grow in it. The trees also form a natural windbreak, providing sheltered conditions for smaller plants.

Many woodland plants flower early in the year, and this makes woods one of the most interesting places to look for wild flowers in the spring. The Lesser Celandine (*Ranunculus ficaria*) is one of the first flowers to appear each year, closely followed by the Wood Anemone (*Anemone nemorosa*), both of which are members of the Buttercup family (Ranunculaceae). At about the same time, or sometimes even earlier, Dog's Mercury (*Mercurialis perennis*) begins to flower, although it has such small green flowers that they may go unnoticed.

Kinds of Woodland

Different kinds of woodland are found on different soils; they also vary from place to place depending on the climate. Woods dominated by Oak (*Quercus* species) usually occur on heavy soils or clays. One quite common flower of Oak woods is the tiny Moschatel (*Adoxa moschatellina*), which is sometimes called Clock Tower because of the arrangement of its five flowers. It is the only member of the family Adoxaceae in the world. The Yellow Pimpernel (*Lysimachia nemorum*) also grows in Oak woods, especially in wetter places, but also occurs in other kinds of wood, as do the Primrose (*Primula vulgaris*), Bugle (*Ajuga reptans*) and Ground Ivy (*Glechoma hederacea*).

Left: The Yellow Pimpernel (Lysimachia nemorum) *is a creeping plant of damp woodlands. It belongs to the Primrose family (Primulaceae) and has a long flowering season extending from May until September.*

Right: A diagrammatic representation of part of the edge of a wood. Various kinds of wild flowers grow in the shade of the large trees whilst others are restricted to the lighter parts of the wood.

Left : Ramsons (Allium ursinum) *grows in woods and under shady hedgerows. It often forms large clumps or a continuous carpet over the ground. The plant smells strongly of garlic, especially when the leaves are crushed or trampled.*

Woodland margin
Shrubs, low trees, climbers and light-loving wild flowers

Denser woodland
Ivy and shade-tolerant wild flowers

Woodland clearing
Similar plants to those at woodland margin

Denser woodland
Ivy and shade-tolerant wild flowers

Right: Green Hellebore (Helleborus viridis) *growing amongst fallen leaves in the deepest part of a Beech wood. The green petals of the flowers are easily overlooked and are produced early in the year.*

Below: Wood Sorrel (Oxalis acetosella) *is a common woodland wild flower with trifoliate leaves rather like those of a Clover. Towards the end of its flowering season it has short-stemmed, self-pollinated flowers which never open.*

On limestone and chalk, Beech (*Fagus sylvatica*) woods may grow. The Beech forms a very dense canopy, so that there is even less light available at ground level. Many of the denser parts of Beech woods are without any wild flowers on the ground, which is covered instead by a thick layer of Beech leaves. Ivy (*Hedera helix*) is common in Beech woods, as it is in all woods, growing both on tree trunks and in a mat on the ground. In the deepest shade, the Bird's Nest Orchid (*Neottia nidus-avis*) may be found (see page 16). It lacks chlorophyll because it does not photosynthesize but obtains its food by breaking down the leaf litter and absorbing the products. Another Beech wood plant which behaves in the same way is the Yellow Bird's-nest (*Monotropa hypophegea*), whose species name means 'under Beech wood' although it sometimes grows on sand dunes as well. The two plants are similar in appearance although they belong to quite different families. Wood Sorrel (*Oxalis acetosella*), an attractive flower with Clover-like leaves, and Enchanter's Nightshade (*Circaea lutetiana*) are two common flowers of Beech woods and other shady woods.

On damper soils, Ash (*Fraxinus excelsior*) or Alder (*Alnus glutinosa*) woodland may grow. Alder occurs in wetter places than Ash and often grows with Birch (*Betula pendula*) trees. There are several woodland flowers to be found in such woods. One is Ramsons (*Allium ursinum*), which often forms large colonies and has a distinct smell of garlic. It is in fact related to the Onion and Garlic. Another is Purple Loosestrife (*Lythrum salicaria*).

In the more northern parts of Europe, and elsewhere on sandy soils, grow evergreen Pine (*Pinus sylvestris*) woods. These are shaded all year round because the trees are evergreens. Even in the early spring there is no opportunity for wild flowers to take advantage of direct light as they can in deciduous woodlands. The ground beneath an evergreen wood is usually carpeted with the needle-like leaves, which are tougher than those of deciduous trees and do not decompose easily. The dense shade limits the growth of wild flowers, as it does in Beech woods. In the deepest shade is another leafless Orchid, the Coral Root (*Corallorhiza trifida*), which obtains its nutrition by breaking down the Pine needles. Another wild flower of Pine woods is the Twinflower (*Linnaea borealis*), which is appropriately named as it usually has two flowers on each plant.

Woodland Margins and Hedgerows

The edges of woodlands receive more light than the interior and usually have a much wider variety of wild flowers. The Foxglove (*Digitalis purpurea*) and the Woundwort (*Stachys sylvatica*) are common plants of woodland margins. Paths through woods also have more light and are the home of certain plants. The Wall Lettuce (*Mycelis muralis*) often grows in such places as well as on the shaded walls from which it takes its name. Climbers such as Traveller's Joy (*Clematis vitalba*) and Honeysuckle (*Lonicera periclymenum*) are also often found at the edges of woods or in clearings or along paths.

Hedgerows are like small patches of woodland and often have a selection of woodland wild flowers mixed with some usually associated with more open places. This mixture makes hedgerows very interesting places to look for wild flowers. Often the hedge runs alongside a ditch, in which plants of wet places and streams can also grow. Some plants, such as Garlic Mustard (*Alliaria petiolata*), seem most at home in hedges and are rarely seen elsewhere. The Garlic Mustard, as its name implies, smells of garlic, especially when the leaves are crushed. Unlike Ramsons, this plant is not related to the Garlic or Onions, but is a member of the Cabbage family (Cruciferae). Lords-and-Ladies (*Arum maculatum*) is another plant which thrives in hedgerows and also grows in woods.

It is unfortunate that, despite their great importance as habitats for many wild flowers and animals, hedgerows are often damaged by mechanical cutting machines, sprayed with herbicides if they are near roadside verges, or even uprooted to create more land for farming.

Below: Woodland clearings provide an ideal habitat for the Foxglove (Digitalis purpurea), *which usually grows in slightly shady places such as the margins of woods but cannot thrive in the deepest shade.*

Wild Flowers of Grasslands

Grasslands are open habitats in which there are few shrubs or trees. In most cases these open spaces are the direct result of some form of human activity, such as the burning or felling of trees to clear the land before its use for grazing by animals. However, there are some places in which open grasslands grow naturally without human influence. These are places where conditions prevent the growth of trees, such as exposed coastal areas or on mountains above the so-called *tree line* (see page 78), where only very stunted trees are found. It is mainly the exposure to strong, almost continuous wind that prevents the trees from growing. As with woodlands, the type of grassland which grows in a particular location is largely dependent on the type of soil present and its drainage.

Chalk and Limestone Grasslands

Some of the most interesting of all grasslands are those which develop on chalk or limestone rocks. Such places will often be found to be wooded by Beech (*Fagus sylvatica*) or Ash (*Fraxinus excelsior*) trees, but when these are cleared and the land used for grazing then a very diverse grassland replaces the woods. The effect of constant grazing by sheep and rabbits is that the grass is usually kept very short and the seedlings of trees or shrubs are usually eaten before they become sufficiently established to survive. One of the commonest Grasses is the Sheep's Fescue (*Festuca ovina*) which has very fine leaves and forms a soft, springy turf. This closely cropped turf is an ideal habitat for plants with a basal rosette of leaves. The Mouse-ear Hawkweed (*Pilosella officinarum*) is a common example of a rosette plant of chalk and limestone grassland which also has stolons and reproduces vegetatively. It is one of the most easily identifiable Hawkweeds because of these stolons and its lemon-yellow flowers. The Salad Burnet (*Sanguisorba minor*) and the Stemless Thistle (*Cirsium acaule*) are two other rosette plants common in such places.

Amongst the short Grasses a number of very small wild flowers grow, such as Squinancywort (*Asperula cynanchica*) and the Wild Thyme (*Thymus drucei*). Two attractive Orchids which grow in such habitats are the Pyramidal Orchid (*Anacamptis pyramidalis*) and the Bee Orchid (*Orchis apifera*, page 50). The Bee Orchid also grows in woodlands and is an example of a wild flower which seems equally at home in the two very different habitats. The Common Rock-rose (*Helianthemum chamaecistus*) is one of the few northern European members of the family Cistaceae, which has many members in southern and Mediterranean Europe. The Viper's Bugloss (*Echium vulgare*) sometimes grows in chalk grassland but is often more common on slightly rocky chalk or limestone soil on low cliffs or rock outbreaks in the grassland. The Maiden Pink (*Dianthus deltoides*), which grows on dry grasslands, is a wild relative of the garden Carnation.

Above: The Rock-rose (Helianthemum chamaecistus) *is a low, spreading plant of short grassland and rocky places. Its flowers produce abundant pollen to attract insect visitors.*

Below: The Maiden Pink (Dianthus deltoides), *with its toothed petals, is a plant of dry, grassy places and is related to the cultivated Carnation.*

Above: Viper's Bugloss (Echium vulgare) *growing in short, closely grazed turf. It also grows on dunes and sea cliffs.*

Below: A diagrammatic section through a hillside with chalk grassland. Mole hills are common in such places and often have populations of some of the smallest grassland wild flowers growing on top of them.

Moorlands

The grasslands which develop on acidic soils are known as *moors* and, in complete contrast with those of chalk and limestone, have very few wild flowers. The grasses are much coarser and larger, and are rarely as closely cropped. The fern Bracken (*Pteridium aquilinum*) often grows amongst the thick Grasses. Moorlands do have shrubby plants as well as Grasses, such as the Bilberry (*Vaccinium myrtillus*) and Heather (*Calluna vulgaris*). Many places where moorlands now occur would once have been covered by Oak or Pine woods, but the influence of mankind, through fires, the felling of trees and grazing by herds of sheep, has created the open moorland habitat.

Meadows

Whereas pastures are kept for the grazing of animals, meadows are used to provide an annual crop of hay. The plants of meadows are not exposed to grazing all year round, but the annual harvesting of the hay prevents trees and shrubs becoming established. The lack of grazing means that taller plants can grow, although there are some rosette plants such as the Plantains (*Plantago* species) and the Dandelion (*Taraxacum officinale*).

Some of the most interesting of all meadows are the poorly drained *water meadows* which occur along the banks of low-lying rivers in many parts of Europe, especially in the Netherlands. Unfortunately many of these water meadows have been altered by draining the land and are no longer as rich in wild flowers as they were previously. The Fritillary, or Snake's-head, (*Fritillaria meleagris*) is one of the most beautiful flowers of water meadows. It occurs in a variety of differently coloured forms from pure white to chequered purple, all of which grow together to form a mass of colour in the few places where the plant survives in large numbers. The Wild Daffodil (*Narcissus pseudonarcissus*) is another wild flower which is often abundant in wet meadows, although it also grows quite successfully in the shade of woods. Like the Meadow Saffron (*Colchicum autumnale*), it is a Monocotyledon, with a bulb for surviving over winter. The Daffodil is an early-flowering plant, but the Meadow Saffron, as its botanical name implies, does not flower until the autumn.

Some wet meadows are very water-logged and more marsh-like in nature, but these too have attractive wild flowers such as the King Cup, or Marsh Marigold (*Caltha palustris*). The Cuckoo Flower (*Cardamine pratensis*), Ragged Robin (*Lychnis flos-cuculi*), Meadowsweet (*Filipendula ulmaria*) and several kinds of Buttercup (*Ranunculus* species) are also found in such wet places.

In the high mountains of parts of Europe there are meadows at higher altitudes which are famous for the great profusion of wild flowers which appear in them. These *alpine meadows* would naturally be covered by Pine and other coniferous trees but have been cleared by humans. Growing at higher altitudes, the plants live in a colder climate and have a shorter season in which they can grow. At the beginning of spring most of the species present put on a rapid period of growth and all flower together in a magnificent display of colour.

Above: Red Campion (Silene dioica) *growing on a grassy slope. It is also commonly found on roadside verges and along the edges of woods. The male and female plants are found on separate plants.*

Right: A water meadow, one of the most diverse of all grassland habitats which often supports a profusion of wild flowers. Seen here are Ragged Robin (Lychnis flos-cuculi), *Red Clover* (Trifolium pratense) *and Buttercups* (Ranunculus *species*).

Wild Flowers of Mountains

Mountains are often very interesting places to look for wild flowers. On the lower slopes the vegetation may be moorland or perhaps alpine meadow (see page 76), but higher up there is vegetation which has been influenced by people to a much lesser extent. The tops of mountains are some of the wildest places in Europe, and their appearance is usually shaped by the forces of nature alone.

The Mountain Habitat

As one climbs a mountain the climate becomes colder. Mountains often support plants which would be found at lower levels further north where the climate is similar. The Mountain Avens (*Dryas octopetala*, page 67), for example, is often found on calcareous mountains but also grows in the tundra of the most northern parts of Europe. In fact, the Mountain Avens is typically a tundra plant and is usually found on the high mountains of Europe because it was left behind there after the end of the Ice Ages. It is surprising to find the Mountain Avens growing at sea level in western Ireland and one reason for this may be the presence of calcareous soils there.

Not only is the temperature lower on mountains than in the surrounding low-lying areas, but the rainfall is often higher and the exposure to wind much greater. Furthermore, many of the higher mountains are snow-covered for much of the year. The plants which live on the mountains consequently have to be able to survive in these harsh conditions. They are faced with a very short growth season each year. For those which inhabit the very highest levels there may be as little as two months each year during which the climatic conditions are mild enough to permit the plants to grow and flower.

The lower slopes of most mountains in Europe would have been heavily wooded at one time, and in places there are still woods of such trees as Birch (*Betula pendula*), Larch (*Larix decidua*), Spruce (*Picea abies*) and Pines (*Pinus* species), and stunted trees of the Sessile Oak (*Quercus petraea*). Higher up the mountains there comes a point, called the *tree line*, where constant exposure to strong winds reduces the number of trees to a few wind-swept individuals and low shrubs such as the Alpine Crowberry (*Empetrum nigrum*). Eventually a height is reached where there are only wild flowers or ferns. This may be anywhere between about 700 and 1500 metres in places, depending on the degree of exposure. This point marks the beginning of the habitat of mountain wild flowers, most of which do not grow at lower altitudes except much further north. The Alpine Lettuce (*Cicerbita alpina*) is one such mountain plant. It is extremely rare in Britain, where it is protected by law, but more common elsewhere in Europe.

Higher still up the mountains are found the plants which are known collectively as *alpines* and are often eagerly cultivated by enthusiasts.

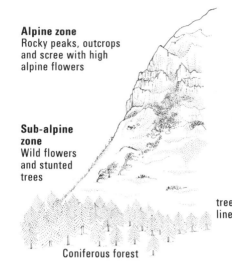

Alpine zone
Rocky peaks, outcrops and scree with high alpine flowers

Sub-alpine zone
Wild flowers and stunted trees

tree line

Coniferous forest

Above: The different zones of vegetation which may be present at various altitudes on a mountain. The altitude at which a particular zone begins depends upon such factors as the latitude and soil type; lower mountains will not usually show the whole range of zones.

Above: The Spring Gentian (Gentiana verna) is a small plant found in exposed mountain habitats. In a few unusual locations it may also be found near to sea level.

High mountains such as the Alps have the full range of mountain habitats and the greatest variety of wild flowers.

Below: A diagrammatic section through part of a mountain showing some of the kinds of habitat in which mountain plants grow.

Alpine meadows and streams
Lush growth of wild flowers in moist conditions

Rocky terrain
Plants liking well-drained conditions

Rock scree
Compact, low-growing plants tolerating harsher conditions

High rocky outcrops
Scattered plants in the most exposed positions

Above: The Alpine Snowbell (Soldanella alpina) *often flowers while the ground is still snow-covered.*

Below: Several kinds of Daffodil (Narcissus *species) are found on high mountains and are also grown in gardens.*

Alpines of the High Mountains

The main attraction of alpines is that they often have flowers which are large in proportion to the plant and that many are challengingly difficult to grow at lower altitudes. The small size of these plants is one of their important characteristics. Larger plants would simply be blown over or lose all their water by evaporation in the strong winds of their harsh habitat. The Saxifrages (*Saxifraga* species) are typical in habit, with their compact mass of leaves growing flat against the ground, often in a rosette. Here the rosette habit offers protection against the wind rather than grazing animals. The Alpine Snowbells (*Soldanella* species) are also low-growing plants whose ability to grow in cold conditions is quite remarkable. They begin to flower even before the snows have melted, forcing their buds up through the snow to burst into flower while the leaves are still below the snow. There are also dwarf species of Daffodil (*Narcissus* species) which survive through the winter as bulbs and sprout when spring arrives, flowering at about the time when the snow thaws. On the highest mountain tops virtually the only plant life to be found consists of Mosses and Lichens. One of the highest-growing wild flowers is the tiny Arctic Buttercup (*Ranunculus glacialis*), which is able to survive on the highest peaks with very short periods of conditions favourable to growth.

A feature shared by many mountain plants is their ability to grow in very shallow pockets of soil or even in cracks in rocks where there is no soil at all. Plants growing in cracks cause a certain amount of humus to build up, mostly from the remains of their own leaves as they die back each year. This humus will hold water for the roots, but without the high rainfall that falls on most mountains many of the plants would be unable to survive in the places where they do.

Mountain plants often have hairy leaves, and this can be seen partly as a protection against cold and partly against water loss through transpiration. The hairs reduce the flow of air blowing across the leaf surface and this reduces evaporation. The closely spaced hairs of some leaves also protect the plants from becoming waterlogged in the melt water from the snow. Air is trapped between the hairs, and this prevents the water from coming in contact with the leaf, which could be especially harmful if it were to freeze.

The Reproduction of Alpine Plants

Most of the high mountain wild flowers are perennials. There is less chance of surviving through a very hard winter for annuals, which, in the mountains, may not set seed every year. A succession of hard winters could wipe out an annual plant, whereas a perennial has other means besides seeds of surviving. One exception is the annual Snow Gentian (*Gentiana nivalis*), which does rely on successfully setting seed for its survival. The perennial plants which grow on mountains mostly survive over winter by means of an underground storage root, but relatively few have bulbs, which are more sensitive to the freezing of the soil in winter.

Because the harsh climatic conditions of mountains prevent wild flowers from producing seeds every year, many of them have some means of vegetative reproduction. Some of the Saxifrages, for example, spread by means of runners. Others, such as the Lesser

Bulbous Saxifrage (*Saxifraga cernua*), have small *bulbils*, which are swollen, bulb-like structures at the base of the stem. There are also a number of mountain wild flowers which can set seed without pollination or fertilization. The Alpine Lady's Mantle (*Alchemilla alpina*), a member of the Rose family (Rosaceae), is an example of such a plant.

Above: Purple Saxifrage (Saxifraga oppositifolia) *growing in a crack in an exposed rock. The low, creeping stems and very small leaves help prevent the loss of water in such wind-swept habitats.*

Wild Flowers of Bogs and Heaths

Bogs and heaths are two types of vegetation which can occur on acid soils. Heaths develop in relatively dry places, whilst bogs only occur in very wet places. Both are fairly open habitats, although there are often Birch trees (*Betula pendula*) and sometimes Pines (*Pinus sylvestris*) on heaths.

Bogs

There are three main types of bog which differ in their appearance and the way in which they are kept wet. *Raised bogs* form only in places with very high rainfall where there is level ground. The high

Left: A heath dominated by Heather (Calluna vulgaris) *with a few Birch trees. In the middle distance is an area of Bracken* (Pteridium aquilinum) *and, beyond, a valley bog.*

Right: Greater Butterwort (Pinguicula grandiflora) *growing on wet rocks in a bog. Several small insects have been trapped by the rolled, sticky leaves and will be digested to provide nutrients lacking in the bog.*

Below: A diagrammatic section through a valley bog surrounded by heathland. Much of the bog surface is covered with water in which Sphagnum *moss grows and provides anchorage for the other plants.*

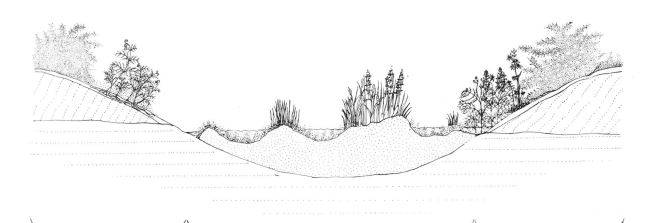

Well-drained land
Heathland vegetation

Valley bog
Mosses and other plants growing in
water-logged peat

Well-drained land
Heathland vegetation

Above: Marsh Pennywort
(Hydrocotyle vulgaris) *is a plant of marshes and bogs which has creeping stems and produces inconspicuous flowers on short stalks. It is an unusual-looking member of the Carrot family (Umbelliferae).*

Below: The flowers of Bog Asphodel
(Narthecium ossifragum) *are bright yellow at first but turn deep orange as the flowers age. The conspicuous hairy, yellow stamens stand up vertically from the spreading petals.*

rainfall permits the growth of the Bog Mosses (*Sphagnum* species) which are an important feature of bogs. If the rainfall is exceptionally high, such bogs can even develop on alkaline soil, although, once it is more established, the surface of the bog itself becomes acidic. In raised bogs the Bog Mosses form hummocks, together with such plants as Heather (*Calluna vulgaris*). *Blanket bogs* also require very high rainfall, but they form on the slopes of hills and are relatively well drained. *Valley bogs* form in stream valleys or around springs in valleys and are kept wet by the flow of water.

In each type of bog the most important environmental factor is the acidity of the soil. This prevents the growth of the usual soil-living organisms, such as bacteria, which carry out decomposition. As a result, the remains of the plants growing in the bog do not decompose but simply become compacted together. If you take a handful of peat out of a bog and pull it apart, you will find that some of the fragments of plants present are recognizable. Because there is little decomposition, the nutrients from dead parts of plants are not re-cycled and made available to growing plants. Consequently bogs are nutrient-deficient places, and the number of kinds of plants which inhabit them is rather limited.

Those few plants which can survive in bogs are interesting ones. Amongst them are the carnivorous wild flowers which trap and digest small animals to make up for the deficiency of nutrients in their habitat. There are several species of Sundew (*Drosera* species), but all are immediately recognizable by their distinctive leaves (see page 35). The plants are small and sometimes go unnoticed until their reddish leaves are seen. They often grow on mats of Bog Moss in the wettest parts of bogs. The other type of carnivorous plant found in bogs is the Butterwort (*Pinguicula* species), which grows on the drier parts of the bog, often on the sides of valley bogs.

The most abundant flowering plants in any bog are Sedges (Cyperaceae), Grasses (Graminae), or Rushes (Juncaceae). These plants often cover most of the surface of the bog, with the Bog Moss growing in-between. A common Orchid of bogs is the Spotted Orchid (*Dactylorhiza fuchsii*), which grows in amongst the Sedges and varies considerably in its flower colour and markings. The Little Bog Orchid (*Hammarbya paludosa*) is a much rarer plant of bogs and has unspectacular greenish-brown flowers.

Another inconspicuous plant of bogs is the Marsh Pennywort (*Hydrocotyle vulgaris*), which has circular, or *peltate*, leaves (see page 33). It is a member of the Carrot family (Umbelliferae), but has its flowers grouped so closely together that they do not look like the typical umbel of that family. One of the most colourful flowers found in bogs is the Bog Asphodel (*Narthecium ossifragum*), which, as its species name suggests, is sometimes called the 'Bone Breaker'. This name comes from the belief that animals which ate the plant were liable to break their bones. There is some justification for this belief, although the Bog Asphodel is not to blame, because animals grazed on bogs would be deficient in calcium, which is lacking in the acidic soil, and this would lead to the development of weak bones. Heather (*Calluna vulgaris*) often grows in the drier parts of bogs and surrounds them, forming a boundary between the bog and the surrounding vegetation, which is usually heath.

Heaths

Heaths are much drier places than bogs and do not develop layers of peat. They are often formed on sand or gravel soils and are usually well drained so that the soil remains dry. They are dominated by members of the Heather family (Ericaceae), including the Heather itself (*Calluna vulgaris*) and the Heaths (*Erica* species). The Bearberry (*Arctostaphylos uva-ursi*) is another member of the same family which is quite common in continental Europe but in Britain is only found in the north. Most of the Heaths (*Erica* species) have the opposite distribution and are commonest in western Europe, in Britain and along the west coast of France, and are much less common in continental Europe. The Gorses (*Ulex* species) are important plants of heaths, and often form dense clumps or thickets, because their spiny stems are not eaten by grazing animals. Very few other plants grow beneath the Gorses and Heaths. The Harebell (*Campanula rotundifolia*) is one wild flower of heaths, but it generally grows in the most open, grassy places. The Common Violet (*Viola riviniana*) and the Scarlet Pimpernel (*Anagallis arvensis*) grow in the shade of the shrubby plants.

Heaths are often kept open by fires, which were traditionally lit to burn back the plants and provide fresh new shoots for grazing animals. This practice is dying out in most of Europe, and the majority of heath fires are now started by accident. When a heath is not burnt for a number of years, the shrubs begin to get much larger and trees may invade it. The Birch (*Betula pendula*) and Pine (*Pinus sylvestris*), both of which favour sandy soils, are often the first to become established.

Below: The Dorset Heath (Erica ciliaris) *has attractive spikes of bell-shaped flowers. The leaves are in whorls of three, which distinguishes it from Cross-leaved Heath* (Erica tetralix), *which has whorls of four leaves.*

Freshwater Wild Flowers

Freshwater habitats include ponds, lakes, streams, rivers, marshes and fens. In each type of habitat there is abundant water, at least for part of the year, and the plants do not need any special adaptations for absorbing or storing water. However, many wet habitats are seasonal and dry out at certain times of year. Some ponds, for example, become more like marshes, whilst marshes may dry out completely. To be able to live in such places the plants must be able to survive the dry period in the form of seeds, storage roots or bulbs. In Europe, many stretches of open water become frozen during the winter, and this also presents a problem to water plants, since the ice may damage or kill them. Water plants differ considerably, depending on whether they grow in still or flowing water.

Ponds and Lakes

Ponds and lakes are areas of still water which are fed by streams and rivers and may also be drained in the same way. The water in the lake or pond may vary in acidity just as the soil does, depending on the underlying rock and the water which is brought into the lake.

Lakes and ponds contain three types of wild flowers, distinguished by their growth habit. First, there are floating plants, which are not anchored to the mud but have their roots hanging in the water; secondly, rooted plants with floating leaves; and, thirdly, plants which grow on the wet banks at the shore. The floating plants include the Duckweeds (*Lemna* species), which often form a continuous layer over the surface of the water (see page 190). Although these plants do produce tiny flowers, they generally reproduce vegetatively; the plants gradually grow in size and the leaves separate into different plants. The Canadian Pondweed (*Elodea canadensis*) also reproduces vegetatively and very rarely flowers in Europe. It is a water weed which arrived from North America in the early 19th century and spread very rapidly, often choking ponds and streams. In more recent years the plant seems to have lost its vigour and is no longer such a problem in waterways and canals.

The Bladderwort (*Utricularia vulgaris*, page 165) is another plant which floats on and just below the surface, usually in places with soft water. Its distinctive leaves have minute traps in which it catches animals and, unlike the Canadian Pondweed, it flowers regularly, producing attractive racemes of yellow flowers held clear of the water. Most aquatic plants, even those which grow under water, hold their flowers above the surface in this way so that pollination can take place. There are plants which are pollinated under water but they are uncommon and mostly occur in the tropics. The Water Violet (*Hottonia palustris*) is pollinated by insects and has racemes of lilac flowers held well above the water and finely divided underwater leaves. It is actually a member of the Primrose family (*Primulaceae*) rather than a true Violet. The Frogbit (*Hydrocharis morsus-ranae*) is a floating plant of hard-water ponds and

Above: Water Violet (Hottonia palustris) *floats in ponds and ditches. It has finely divided submerged leaves and silvery roots. The attractive racemes of pale purple flowers are the only part of the plant to appear above water.*

Left: This slow-flowing stream supports a variety of water plants including Yellow Flag (Iris pseudacorus) (not flowering), Purple Loosestrife (Lythrum salicaria), Bistorts (Polygonum species), Mint (Mentha species) and the yellow-flowered Fleabane (Pulicaria dysenterica).

Below: A diagrammatic section through the edge of a pond showing some entirely floating plants, others with roots in the mud at the bottom of the pond but with floating leaves, and some with leaves held in the air.

Open water
Rooted and floating plants

Water margin
Plants with roots in wet soil

slow-flowing streams. It reproduces vegetatively by means of stolons but also produces white flowers, which, from a distance, can be mistaken for aquatic Buttercups (*Ranunculus* species).

The rooted wild flowers of ponds and lakes include the Water-lilies. The White Water-lily (*Nymphaea alba*) has all its leaves floating, whereas the Yellow Water-lily (*Nuphar lutea*) has thin underwater leaves as well as floating ones. The Arrowhead (*Sagittaria sagittifolia*) also has leaves of different shapes, as indeed do many water plants. The upper leaves of the Arrowhead have the distinctive shape which gives the plant its name; there are also floating leaves which are more rounded, and submerged strap-shaped leaves (see page 183). The Bogbean (*Menyanthes trifoliata*) is a rooted plant which has spreading floating stems (see page 159). The three-lobed pinnate leaves resemble those of the Bean but, as the flowers plainly reveal, the plant does not belong to that family (Leguminosae). It is in fact a member of the Bogbean family (Menyanthaceae), which is related to the Gentians (Gentianaceae).

Plants of the pond and lake shore include the Great Reedmace (*Typha latifolia*) and the Yellow Flag (*Iris pseudacorus*, page 34), which often grow together, forming a thick band of vegetation.

Streams and Rivers

The movement of the water in streams and rivers prevents the free-floating plants from becoming established, except in very sheltered backwaters. However, provided the flow of water is not too fast, a wide variety of rooted plants with floating leaves may be present. There are many species of aquatic plants related to the Buttercup, some of which have different submerged and floating leaves, as in the Water-crowfoot (*Ranunculus aquatilis*). Others have only the

Above: The Flowering Rush (Butomus umbellatus) *grows on stream and pond banks. Each flower has three large pink petals and three smaller pink sepals. The long, narrow leaves are triangular in cross section.*

Above : Water-crowfoot (Ranunculus aquatilis) *has lobed, palmate leaves floating on the water surface and finely divided submerged ones. The flowers are held above the water, but the stalks curve downwards in fruit.*

Left : Frogbit (Hydrocharis morsus-ranae) *is a Monocotyledon with flowers which resemble those of the Water-crowfoot when seen from a distance. The plant survives overwinter as seeds and small bulb-like buds which sink to the bottom of the pond.*

finely divided submerged leaves, as in the River Crowfoot (*Ranunculus fluitans*), which is a plant for faster-flowing water. Larger leaves would cause too much drag in a strong flow of water and the plant might be uprooted. River banks are similar to the edges of ponds, but again the flow of water dictates whether there is a suitable habitat for rooted plants.

Marshes and Fens

Marshes are intermediate between the banks of rivers and ponds and open grasslands. They often contain a variety of Rushes (Juncaceae), Sedges (Cyperaceae) and Grasses (Graminae), together with a variety of water-loving wild flowers. The Marsh Violet (*Viola palustris*) and the Marsh Thistle (*Cirsium palustre*) are common in marshes and other wet places. This habitat is also suitable for many of the water plants of stream and lake edges.

Fens are places which are poorly drained and very wet. Because there is no decomposition of plant remains, peat builds up. Unlike bogs, fens have no Bog Moss (*Sphagnum* species) and the peat builds up from the remains of the Reed (*Phragmites communis*) and the Saw Sedge (*Cladium mariscus*), the two most important fen plants. Fens were traditionally used to provide reeds for thatching and peat for fuel, but in many places they have been drained and trees have colonized the drier soil.

Coastal Wild Flowers

There are many different kinds of coastal habitat ranging from steep, rocky cliffs to sandy beaches. All are affected by the closeness of the sea which, when rough, throws up salt spray which can be blown a long way inland. Coastal places are often very exposed to winds, which may blow constantly for much of the year. Not only does the wind influence the vegetation by carrying salt spray, it also stunts the growth of larger plants, such as shrubs or trees, except in sheltered spots. Salt absorbs moisture, so that when salt spray lands on leaves it can draw the water out of the leaf unless this is protected by a thick, waxy outer layer. For this reason the leaves of many coastal plants have a greyish waxy appearance.

The salt is also washed into the soil and helps to determine which plants can grow in it. If the soil is very salty the root hairs are unable to obtain water from between the soil particles through the normal process of osmosis (see page 20). To the plant a very salty soil is like a desert soil, even if it does in fact contain water. For this reason, many of the coastal plants look rather like miniature versions of the cacti and succulents of deserts.

Plants of Beaches

Some wild flowers actually grow on sand or pebble beaches just above the *strand line*, the level at which the high tides deposit sea-weed and driftwood. There are even a few wild flowers which live under the sea. These are the Eel-grasses (*Zostera* species), which have grass-like leaves and very reduced flowers. Eel-grasses are not common around the coasts of Europe but are an important group of plants in the tropics, where they make up a large part of the diet of turtles. The strand line plants belong to a number of families, and some look similar to their inland relatives. The Sea Rocket (*Cakile maritima*) is a large and attractive member of the Cabbage family (Cruciferae) which has pale pink flowers and thick, waxy leaves. Several species of Orache (*Atriplex* species) grow along the

Left : Sea Rocket (Cakile maritima) *grows just above the high tide line and on beaches and dunes. It is an annual and has seeds which are dispersed in the sea. The fleshy leaves and stems help the plant retain water.*

Left: A sand dune which has been colonized by Marram Grass (Ammophila arenaria) *and Sand Couch Grass* (Agropyron junceiforme), *which have stabilized the sand enough for Bird's-foot Trefoil* (Lotus corniculatus) *to become established.*

Below: A diagrammatic section through a section of beach and adjacent sand dunes. The horizontal scale has been shortened between the strand-like plants and the dune.

Sea

Strand line
Plants tolerating salt water

Beach
Scattered, salt-resistant plants

Newly colonized dunes
Grasses able to grow in moving sand

Older, stabilized dunes
A greater variety of plants growing in an accumulating layer of humus

strand line. They are all rather uninteresting-looking plants with inconspicuous flowers and belong to the Goosefoot family (Chenopodiaceae).

Plants of Sand Dunes

Sand dunes are mounds of sand piled up by the wind. As the wind blows the grains of sand along the surface of a dune, its shape and position gradually change. Any plants which are to grow on this slowly moving surface must be able to grow up through the sand if they are buried or must spread over the surface of the dune and avoid burial. Many sand dune plants have stolons by which they radiate out over the sand. Their growth helps to make the dunes more stable. As the amount of vegetation on a dune increases, so the sand is prevented from blowing away and the dune finally becomes stable. Amongst the first colonizers of dunes are two grasses, the Sand Couch Grass (*Agropyron junceiforme*) and Marram Grass (*Ammophila arenaria*). Both have stolons and both are able to withstand salt spray and to grow up through the sand if they become buried. The Marram Grass has tightly rolled leaves, with all the stomata inside the rolled blade so that little or no water is lost from the leaves by evaporation.

The well-drained sand of a dune contains little fresh water for the plants living there. Only when the dune has become stable and humus begins to accumulate in the upper layers of the sand will moisture be held there. When the dunes have reached this stage, a variety of interesting wild flowers may be found. The Sea Holly (*Eryngium maritimum*) is an attractive member of the Carrot family (Umbelliferae) with Holly-like leaves covered with a thick layer of wax for protection from salt spray. The Sea Bindweed (*Calystegia soldanella*) has showy pink flowers and spreads widely by means of

Above: As sand dunes become more stable due to the colonizing plants a number of characteristic wild flowers are able to grow, including Sea Bindweed (Calystegia soldanella) (pink flowers), Sea Spurge (Euphorbia paralias) (green flowers) and Burnet Rose (Rosa pimpinellifolia).

stolons. The Buckshorn Plantain (*Plantago coronopus*) and the Sea Plantain (*Plantago maritima*) both grow on sand dunes and in other coastal places and have slightly succulent water-storing leaves unlike those of their inland relatives. The Pyramidal Orchid (*Anacamptis pyramidalis*), which grows on chalk hills, seems equally at home amongst the other plants of stable sand dunes.

Plants of Salt Marshes

Salt marshes are very different from inland marshes in the plants which inhabit them. They are low-lying, flat areas of sand and mud which are usually just above the high tide level and often form in the mouth of an estuary. They are sometimes flooded by sea water during the highest tides, so the plants which grow there must be able to withstand being covered by salt water for short periods of time. The roots of these plants are permanently growing in salty water. Amongst the plants found closest to sea level in salt marshes are the Sea Milkwort (*Glaux maritima*) and the Seablite (*Suaeda maritima*). Both plants have succulent stems for water storage and slightly succulent leaves. The Sea Aster (*Aster tripolium*) is a colourful member of the Daisy family (Compositae) which has heads of blue ray florets and yellowish-orange disc florets. The Sea Lavender (*Limonium vulgare*) is another colourful salt-marsh flower whose inflorescences are cymes of closely-spaced blue flowers.

Plants of Sea Cliffs

Sea cliffs provide a suitable habitat for a variety of wild flowers, including some which are also found in other coastal habitats. A few, such as Samphire (*Crithmum maritimum*), are seldom found anywhere except on sea cliffs. Samphire is a member of the Carrot family (Umbelliferae) whose fleshy leaves were once prized as a vegetable and sometimes collected at great risk from cliffs. The Scurvy Grass (*Cochlearia officinalis*) is another cliff plant that was formerly eaten. Its leaves are rich in vitamin C, and it was used as a cure for the disease scurvy. The Thrift (*Armeria maritima*) is one of the best-known wild flowers of the seaside and is often grown in gardens. It grows wild in a variety of coastal habitats but is most abundant on cliffs and cliff tops.

Left: Sea Holly (Eryngium maritimum), *a plant of sand and shingle beaches, has leaves thickly coated with wax to protect against salt spray and to prevent water loss. The fruits have hooked hairs and are distributed by animals.*

Right: Sea Milkwort (Glaux maritima) *has fleshy stems and leaves and grows in salt marshes, on beaches and elsewhere near the sea. Each flower has five colourful pink sepals and no petals.*

Wild Flowers of Waste Land

Nearly all the habitats described in previous chapters have been influenced and altered to some extent by mankind. Even heaths are considered to be disturbed habitats in as much as they are not allowed to change towards their natural ultimate vegetation. The waste-land habitats discussed in this chapter, however, are those which have been greatly modified so that they cease to resemble any other natural habitat – places such as the sites of derelict buildings, factory land, industrial waste heaps and the centres of cities. In these rather artificial habitats a relatively small number of wild flowers grow very successfully. These are all opportunistic plants which grow rapidly and flower profusely, forming as much seed as possible to be able to spread even further. These characteristics apply to the majority of plants which are considered to be weeds; indeed, most of the plants of disturbed places are weeds, since many of them also grow in gardens and arable land.

Rosebay Willowherb (*Epilobium angustifolium*) has attractive pink flowers and grows in dense patches. The flowers are followed by long, narrow capsules, which split open to release thousands of plumed seeds which carry the plant to new places. The Rosebay Willowherb also reproduces vegetatively, and this makes it doubly efficient in rapidly colonizing vacant land. Several closely related members of the Daisy family (Compositae), including the Groundsel (*Senecio vulgaris*), Common Ragwort (*Senecio jacobaea*) and the Oxford Ragwort (*Senecio squalidus*), grow abundantly on waste land. The Oxford Ragwort, originally only a southern European species, was introduced to northern Europe in the last century and, in Britain, spread along railway embankments until it achieved its present wide distribution.

The Bindweed (*Calystegia sepium*) is a familiar sight, even in the centre of towns. It climbs over chain-link fences instead of the hedgerow plants over which it scrambles in more natural habitats. The Nettle (*Urtica dioica*) is another plant of woodland and hedge-

Above: Common Ragwort (Senecio jacobaea) *is a weed which rapidly colonizes bare ground. Each plant has many heads of florets and can produce thousands of seeds in a growing season.*

Right: The Common Poppy (Papaver rhoeas) *growing on a gravel heap, where few but the toughest weeds could begin to grow. Like the Ragwort it produces great numbers of seeds; although each flower lasts only one day there are many of them.*

Above: Derelict sites can support a surprising variety of wild flowers and create valuable refuges for wildlife in urban areas. Buddleia (Buddleia davidii) is one of the most spectacular plants to thrive on waste land.

rows which also commonly invades waste land. A number of small members of the Cabbage family (Cruciferae) are common in city centres, where they grow in cracks between paving stones and in other small pockets of soil. Some of the most frequently seen are Shepherd's Purse (*Capsella bursa-pastoris*), which has distinctive purse-shaped capsules (see page 119), Charlock (*Sinapis arvensis*) and the Wild Radish (*Raphanus raphanistrum*).

Although none of the plants of waste land has any special claim to be conserved or allowed to grow, they are, as a group, very important. They provide food and shelter for a variety of kinds of animals which would not otherwise be able to survive in towns and cities. Butterflies, for example, are often abundant in disturbed places. Many have caterpillars which feed on the Nettle (*Urtica dioica*), and the Buddleia (*Buddleia davidii*), another common plant of waste land, provides an important source of nectar. Where the land is not required for building or other forms of development, it is best left to be colonized by plants which can grow in these conditions.

Wild Flowers and Mankind

Throughout the history of mankind, plants have played a vital part in providing food, fibres for cloth making, pigments, medicines and even charms. Human beings are *omnivores*, eating both plants and the flesh of other animals, but we know relatively little about which wild plants were gathered and used by the earliest people, although some clues come from archaeological discoveries. The best source of information on the uses of plants in more recent times are the books on botany, known as *herbals*, of the 16th century and later. These also furnish information about plant uses almost 1,500 years earlier, since their authors drew heavily on much older traditions and manuscripts for their information.

The Herbals

When the herbals first began to be printed, they contained everything that was then known about the kinds of plants in existence and their properties and powers. Much of their content was derived from sources such as the *De Materia Medica* written by Dioscorides, a Greek physician, in about AD 60. This was a treatise on the medicinal plants of Asia Minor (now Turkey), which provided a large part of the information of the later herbals. The writers of the herbals strove to find plants to fit the descriptions given by Dioscorides so that they could transfer to them the properties of the plants which Dioscorides had known. Sometimes they were successful and probably correct in recognizing close relatives, at least, of the plants, but often they simply selected the plant which came closest to the description. The herbals also included illustrations printed from woodcuts. These were very stylized and were rarely drawn from nature, often being copied from one manuscript to another. Even so, they usually depicted the main characteristics of the plant well enough for it to be recognizable.

Some of the most famous herbals are those by Richard Banckes, written in 1525, Otto Brunfels of 1532 and John Gerard of 1597. John Gerard was a barber-surgeon whose interest in plants came from the fact that they provided the medicines of his craft. Much of medical practice at the time was founded on the Doctrine of Signatures, which held that each plant had a mark or sign which revealed the virtues of the plant and the kinds of ills it could be used to cure. Red plants were associated with blood and diseases of the blood, for example. Many kinds of wild plant, however, were valued simply because they were edible, and many were collected from fields and hedgerows and brought in to the markets to be sold.

Wild Flowers as Food

When gathering wild flowers for use as food, it is necessary to be able to distinguish one kind from another. Such knowledge must have been commonplace in past times and ensured that only edible plants were collected and poisonous ones left undisturbed. Many poisonous

Above: Digging up herbs, an illustration from a 12th-century herbal.

Opposite: Wolfsbane, or Common Monkshood, (Aconitum napellus) from the 1633 edition of Gerard's Herball, *showing the stylized way in which the plants were illustrated. Long descriptions in Latin were used to name the plants. Here an English translation is also given. The roots were usually depicted because they were frequently the useful part of the plant.*

plants can be recognized by an unpleasant or bitter taste, such as that caused by the poisonous chemical substances known as *alkaloids*, which are present in members of the Poppy family (Papaveraceae) and Potato family (Solanaceae). In the Poppy family these poisons are contained in the white or yellow juice, or *latex*, which runs from broken stems and leaves. Drugs such as opium are prepared from the latex of certain kinds of Poppy. Not all plants with latex, however, are poisonous; for example, the Dandelion (*Taraxacum officinale*) and other related plants such as the cultivated Lettuces (*Lactuca* species) are harmless. The latex of some species of Dandelion has been used to make a type of rubber, since the latex is similar to that of the Rubber Tree.

Just as there are certain families of plants with many poisonous members, so there are others which are mostly edible. The Cabbage family (Cruciferae), for example, contains many well-known edible plants such as the Cabbage, Cauliflower, Brussels Sprout and Broccoli, all of which have been derived from the Wild Cabbage (*Brassica oleraceae*), a plant of coastal places. The Water-cress (*Rorippa nasturtium-aquaticum*) is widely cultivated, whereas the Sea Kale (*Crambe maritima*) and Scurvy Grass (*Cochlearia officinalis*) are wild members of the Cabbage family and are less commonly eaten.

The Goosefoot family (Chenopodiaceae) has a number of edible members. A variety of crops including Beetroot, Sugar Beet and Mangolds are derived from plants closely related to the Sea Beet (*Beta vulgaris*). Fat Hen (*Chenopodium album*), a common weed of gardens and fields, was formerly eaten as a vegetable. The seeds of this plant were amongst those recognized in the stomach of the

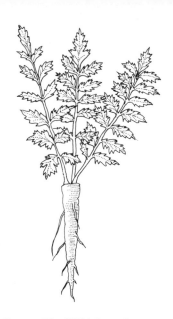

*Above: The Wild Parsnip (*Pastinaca sativa*) was gathered from the wild as an edible root, like the Pignut (*Conopodium majus*) and others in the Carrot family (*Umbelliferae*). Later, through cultivation, the size of the roots was increased.*

*Below: The inconspicuously flowered Sea Beet (*Beta vulgaris*) is a close relative of the plants from which cultivated Beetroots and other crops were derived.*

Tollund Man, who died violently at least 1,500 years ago and lay buried and preserved in a peat bog in Denmark until discovered. He had also eaten two species of Persicaria (*Polygonum* species) and Corn Spurrey (*Spergula arvensis*), which shows that seeds were a commonplace part of the diet.

Seeds are often particularly nourishing because they are usually rich in protein and contain a stored food reserve of carbohydrate. Likewise, storage roots make good vegetables, and before the introduction of the Potato into Europe from the New World many wild roots were eaten. The Silverweed (*Potentilla anserina*) is mentioned in most herbals as a medicinal plant, but also as an edible root. Likewise the Pignut (*Conopodium majus*), a member of the Carrot family (Umbelliferae), was dug up for its tuberous roots. The Wild Parsnip (*Pastinaca sativa*) was used in the same way and is the ancestor of the cultivated varieties now grown as a crop.

Today, many wild flowers are eaten in small amounts as culinary herbs. Originally these were often prized for their real or imagined medicinal properties or to provide flavour in otherwise plain food. The Mint family (Labiatae) and Carrot family (Umbelliferae) include a number of well-known herbs, and most members of both families are distinctly aromatic. The Mints (*Mentha* species) were used as flavourings, but also as remedies for coughs and jaundice, and to drive away fleas. Similarly, Wild Thyme (*Thymus drucei*) was regarded as a cure for headaches and convulsions. Fennel (*Foeniculum vulgare*) and Wild Angelica (*Angelica sylvestris*), both belonging to the Carrot family, have long been used as herbs. Wild Chives (*Allium schoenoprasum*) is a member of the Lily family (Liliaceae) which has a more delicate flavour than the related Onion.

Fibres and Dyes from Wild Flowers

The fibres of wild flowers such as the Nettle (*Urtica dioica*) were formerly used to weave into cloth, a practice which was widespread in Europe and survived into the early part of the present century. The Nettle was also traditionally an important medicinal plant used for treating stomach pains and colic, and the young leaves were valued for making soups and herbal teas. The extraction of fibres from wild plants was finally superseded by the cultivation of crops such as Flax (*Linum usitatissimum*) and more recently by synthetic fibres.

A variety of dyes obtained from wild flowers were used over the centuries to colour cloth, and some were later cultivated especially for this purpose. Woad (*Isatis tinctoria*) is famous as the plant used by ancient British tribes to dye their skin. It was also used as a blue dye for cloth until about 50 years ago, when man-made dyes replaced it. The Dyer's Rocket (*Reseda luteola*) yielded a bright yellow dye, and Dyer's Greenweed (*Genista tinctoria*), when mixed with Woad, produced a green colour. The Gipsywort (*Lycopus europaeus*), a member of the Mint family (Labiatae) which grows near water, was used to prepare a black dye. Many other wild flowers were used on a smaller scale to provide different colours. Heather (*Calluna vulgaris*) was the source of an orange dye, Bog Asphodel (*Narthecium ossifragum*) a yellow, and the Bramble (*Rubus fruticosus*) a purple or reddish colour.

Above: Woad (Isatis tinctoria) *is a yellow-flowered member of the Cabbage family (Cruciferae) from which a blue pigment was formerly extracted. Its present-day distribution is mainly due to its former cultivation.*

Below: Dyer's Rocket (Reseda luteola) *belong to the Mignonette family (Resedaceae) from which a yellow dye can be made. It commonly grows on roadside verges and on waste ground.*

Wild Flowers in Medicine and Magic

Almost all the earliest medicines were prepared from plants, which were either gathered directly from the wild or grown in gardens so that a convenient fresh supply was always close to hand. Some wild flowers were valued as cure-alls for all kinds of minor ailments. Selfheal (*Prunella vulgaris*) was one of these, as its common name indicates. It was used to treat everything from sore throats to wounds. Bugle (*Ajuga reptans*) and Sanicle (*Sanicula europaea*), two common woodland plants, were used in much the same way. One of the most popular cure-alls was Comfrey (*Symphytum officinale*); every part of the plant was employed for some purpose, and it was used to treat wounds, to stop bleeding and to set bones. This most useful of wild flowers is also edible, and the leaves are still popular today in parts of Europe.

Whilst there can be no doubt that none of these plants could cure all the conditions it was used to treat, many of the traditional plant medicines can be shown scientifically to work. The Foxglove (*Digitalis purpurea*) is a good example of this. It used to be regarded as a magical plant which would confer the stealthiness of the fox on those who wore the flowers on their fingers. It was also guaranteed to keep goblins away from houses, as well as being used as a purgative and as a medicine to treat colds and fevers. The doctors of the 18th century found that it did indeed have remarkable effects upon the heart, slowing down the heartbeat. More recently a drug known as digitalin, extracted from the Foxglove, has been used for treating heart conditions. Some of the herbal preparations derived from wild

Above: Selfheal (Prunella vulgaris) *is a common wild flower of woods and grassy places which has opposite, paired leaves on low, creeping stems. It was used to heal cuts, wounds and internal injuries.*

berries

Above: Mistletoe (Viscum album) *was regarded as a magical plant because it remained green when the leaves of the trees it grows on had fallen and because it sometimes grows on Oaks, which were thought by the ancient Druids to be holy.*

Right: Three stages in the preparation of herbal remedies. After selecting the required parts of the plants (right), an extract is distilled (bottom left) and then bottled and carefully labelled (top).

Right: Comfrey (Symphytum officinale) *is another wild flower which had many herbal uses in the past. It was used to treat wounds, broken bones and coughs. The plant is quite common along roadsides and hedgerows and so could be gathered easily.*

flowers in the past and used to treat wounds would also have had a certain effectiveness as antiseptics.

Two of the most magical of all plants are also amongst the most poisonous: the Deadly Nightshade (*Atropa belladonna*) and the Mandrake (*Mandragora officinalis*), both members of the Potato family (Solanaceae). The Mandrake was regarded as magic because its roots are shaped like a human form and because of its great toxicity. The roots could only be collected at night after surrounding the plant with three magic circles for protection. Deadly Nightshade was used as a poison and sometimes as a medicine, although its potency made it difficult to prepare a small enough dosage. Like the Foxglove, the Deadly Nightshade has more recently been used as the source of a useful drug, atropine.

Even such harmless plants as the Plantains (*Plantago* species) were credited with magical properties because of their ability to survive in places where continual trampling kills most plants. The Mistletoe (*Viscum album*) is a strange-looking parasitic plant whose magical associations have survived to the present day. In past times, Mistletoe was used to increase fertility of both man and beast and was hung in the thresholds of houses for good luck and to keep away goblins and evil spirits. Because they were evergreen and kept their leaves when most plants were bare, Holly (*Ilex aquifolium*) and Ivy (*Hedera helix*) had magical associations long before they became associated with the Christian Church.

Below: The flowers of Mandrake (Mandragora officinalis), *a plant prized in the past for its magical properties. The roots were the most potent part because they were said to resemble the human form. Roots of other plants were often sold in imitation of the Mandrake.*

Above: Deadly Nightshade (Atropa bella-donna) *has purplish-brown flowers quite unlike those of the common Woody Nightshade* (Solanum dulcamara) *which is often thought to be Deadly Nightshade. The berries ripen to a shiny, black colour.*

From Herbalists to Botanists

From about the middle of the 17th century the study of plants became more orderly and scientific. The information which had been accumulated and passed on almost without question in the herbals came under careful scrutiny. Many of the remedies which were found to be worthless were no longer used, at least not by the medical profession. The doctors were the most knowledgeable people on the subject of plants because they relied upon them for their medicines. Many of these doctors collected the plants they used themselves and, in doing so added many new records to the kinds of plants known and used. The Doctrine of Signatures (see page 97) came to be replaced by the use of plants whose effects had been carefully observed and tested. More became known about the life of plants, and many botanical books were published. These were written in Latin, because this was effectively an international language by which the educated people of the time could communicate with each other. By the 18th century it became known that plants had male and female parts and their life cycle was understood.

A botanist who was to have a great influence was Carl von Linné, who was born in Sweden in 1707 and wrote many books and scientific papers under the Latinized name of Linnaeus. He became Professor of Practical Medicine at Uppsala, for his background was also as a medical man, and at the height of his fame he would lead groups of more than 200 people on trips to study wild plants in the

MEANINGS OF SOME LATIN PLANT NAMES

Note: the gender of these species names depends on that of the genus name. Here only the Latin masculine form is listed.

acaulis stemless

acris bitter-tasting

albus white

alpinus alpine

anglicus English

annuus an annual plant

aquaticus an aquatic

autumnalis of the autumn

arvensis of fields

biennis a biennial plant

communis a common species

cordatus with cordate leaves

europaeus European

erectus an upright plant

foetidus stinking

fluitans a floating plant

glabrus hairless

hirsutus hairy

lanceolatus with lanceolate leaves

latifolius broad-leaved

maculatus spotted

major a large plant

maritimus a coastal plant

medius medium-sized

minor a small plant

muralis of walls

nigrus black

nivalis of the snow

nemorosus of woods and glades

odoratus scented

officinalis of medicinal use

ovatus with ovate leaves

palustris of marshes

perennis a perennial plant

petiolatus with distinct petioles

pratensis of meadows

pumilus dwarf

repens creeping

rupestris of rocks

sepius black

spicatus with spikes (inflorescence)

sylvaticus of woodland

sylvestris wild

tinctorius used by dyers

vulgaris common

vernus of spring

viridis green

The eminent Swedish botanist Carl von Linné, better known as Linnaeus (above), devised the binomial system, in which each plant has a generic and a specific name. The Twinflower (Linnaea borealis, right) is a plant of Pine woods named in his honour and quite common in his native country. It belongs to the Honeysuckle family (Caprifoliaceae), most members of which are shrubs or climbers.

countryside. These were conducted with great ceremony, and their return was marked by music and an air of festivity.

One of Linnaeus's achievements was a system by which plants could be classified into groups by the number and arrangement of the reproductive parts of the flowers. More important still was his system of giving each plant two names, a *genus name* by which a closely related group of plants would be united, and a *species*, or *specific*, *name* which would indicate precisely which member of the genus was referred to. This way of naming, which is known as the *binomial system*, has become internationally accepted for reasons which are not difficult to understand. Before this, each plant had as its name a short descriptive phrase or sentence in Latin which had to be memorized in order to refer to a particular species accurately (see illustration on page 96). The Lesser Celandine (*Ranunculus ficaria*), for example, was known as *Ranunculus foliis cordatis angulatis petiolatis*, which meant 'the Buttercup with cordate (heart-shaped) leaves and angled petioles'. With the binomial system, the names became much shorter and easier to remember but were still Latinized, although they often contained elements of Greek and other languages. Only by means of these Latinized botanical names is it possible to refer to a plant in a way that can be understood without ambiguity anywhere in the world.

The same is not true of the common names given to plants in

THE CLASSIFICATION OF THE SILVERWEED
(Potentilla anserina)

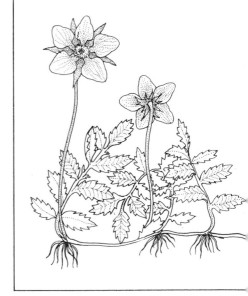

DIVISION	Spermatophytes the seed plants
CLASS	Angiospermae the flowering plants
SUB-CLASS	Dicotyledonae the Dicotyledons
ORDER	Rosales the Rose family and related families
FAMILY	Rosaceae the Rose family
GENUS	Potentilla a genus of 500 species
SPECIES	anserina the Silverweed

different languages. These frequently vary from one place to another within a single country, and some plants have numerous alternative names with no single name that is known everywhere. Lords-and-Ladies, for example, has almost a hundred other common names in English including Cuckoo Pint, Fly Catcher, Priest-in-the-pulpit and Starchwort, besides many names in other languages, but only one botanical name, *Arum maculatum*. Other species of plant, such as some of the Sedges, have no common name at all.

Botanical names often describe the appearance of the plant or the habitat in which it grows, its flowering season, its uses, or even the name of a person who is commemorated, usually for discovering the plant. Linnaeus himself is commemorated in the name of the Twin-flower (*Linnaea borealis*), the specific name of which indicates that it is a plant of *boreal*, or northern, regions. When a botanical name is given to a plant, it must be published in a widely circulating botanical journal, and the name of the author of the publication is given after the name of the plant (in botanical texts). Linnaeus did not name the Twinflower after himself: it was named by his friend Dr Gronovius in his honour. When written in full, the name of the Twinflower is thus *Linnaea borealis* Gronovius. The name of the author is often abbreviated; in the case of Linnaeus, who published many new plant names, it is abbreviated simply to L., as in *Ranunculus acris* L., the Meadow Buttercup. It is a necessary evil that botanical names are sometimes changed to clarify confusing situations, as for instance when a plant has two names. Plant names are governed by a complicated set of rules which are designed mainly to decide which botanical name is correct – usually the oldest – when a particular plant has been named differently by two or more botanical authors.

Wild Flowers in Today's World

Whilst our knowledge of plants continues to grow, certain aspects of modern botanical studies are very complex and may appear daunting to the layman. Nevertheless, there are many gaps in our knowledge and understanding of plants which remain to be filled simply by careful and accurate observation and recording. The distribution of many plants, how they are pollinated and what conditions they grow most favourably in are often simply not known in detail.

Many wild flowers are still used as foods or medicines, although most people no longer have to go out and collect them themselves from the countryside. Many of the medicines now processed and prepared to high standards by pharmaceutical companies contain products derived from plants. Likewise, a great variety of plants, many of them only recently cultivated, are used as food, herbs or spices. We still need wild flowers, and indeed all other plants. Nowadays, plants can be crossed and bred to develop particular attributes more successfully than was ever possible previously. To keep them for future use, we must ensure the survival of wild plants so that they are there when they are needed. In many places today wild flowers are disappearing at an alarming rate. Some represent resources which are being lost before their potential is even discovered. We must now turn to actively conserving the plants from which we have benefited for so long.

The Conservation of Wild Flowers

To many people, conservation means protecting and ensuring the survival of large animals such as the tiger and other big-game animals. It is sometimes forgotten that plants also need conserving, that they will not simply fend for themselves. The fact is that in Europe, and throughout the world, many species of plants and animals are threatened by extinction. Even plants that were common until quite recently are frequently rare or restricted to a few localities now. The reasons why wild flowers are becoming scarcer and some are on the verge of extinction are complicated. Without an understanding of these underlying reasons, it is almost impossible to plan an effective programme of conservation.

The Threat to Wild Flowers

As we have seen in an earlier chapter (pages 66–9), habitats change over periods of time, and the pattern of the landscape in Europe has been shaped by human influence and activity. Through the actions of human beings the countryside has become a very diverse mixture combining such natural habitats as lakes, sand dunes or ancient forests with largely man-made ones such as heaths and meadows. In these different habitats many different kinds of wildlife flourish. Without the influence of people the vegetation of Europe would have been more uniform, with more widespread forests and fewer open places. The activities of people have enriched the countryside over the centuries, providing suitable habitats for more and more species. Why then does this process of enrichment not continue today? One important reason is simply that human populations have now grown to such an extent in Europe that there is an enormous requirement for land to be used for the expansion of towns. In addition, new roads, motorways, railways, industrial sites and reservoirs are all devouring the space that was previously countryside. Much of the countryside in Europe is now farmland and, as the towns and cities expand, more and more new land has to be brought into cultivation to provide food for the growing populations. Another important factor is that agricultural methods have changed greatly in the last century. Many of the changes which have taken place have occurred because of economic pressures upon landowners and farmers.

Many habitats have been drastically altered by the drainage of land to make new fields. By draining bogs, fens and marshes, drier land suitable for agricultural purposes can be created, and areas which were formerly unproductive from the financial point of view can be made to make a profit. Draining such land is often an expensive operation, but in most of Europe there are systems of subsidies to help landowners make such improvements to their land. As the soil becomes drier, the characteristic bog, marsh or fen plants are unable to grow and are replaced by others more tolerant of dry conditions. This means that, even if some parts of the bog or marsh

Above: Edelweiss (Leontopodium alpinum) *and Marsh Orchid* (Orchis maculata) *(pink flowers) growing the the Alps. Both are wild flowers which are often picked because their attractive flowers are so well known.*

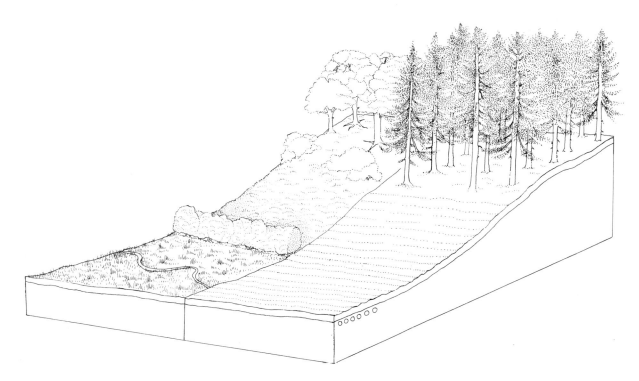

Above: A diagram showing some of the ways in which a habitat (on the left) can be destroyed when the countryside is modified. Underground drainage removes streams and marshes; hedgerow clearance creates more land for crops, but removes a diverse habitat; softwoods replace broad-leaved woodland but do not have the same ground flora. The result is the quite different type of countryside on the right.

are set aside as conservation areas, once they have been drained they will no longer support their original plant and animal communities. When wet places are drained, the rate at which water is carried out of the area is changed and streams may also be affected. The plant and animal life in fast-flowing drainage ditches is not so diverse as that in naturally flowing and meandering streams and rivers.

New land is also being created throughout Europe by the clearing of woods. In Britain, the rate at which woodland is being cleared has accelerated so much in the last 30 years that recent predictions suggest that, at the present rate of clearance, no woodland will remain by the end of the present century. Even where woods are actively being planted, the trees used are often not the native broad-leaved species but fast-growing conifers instead. These new plantations are more profitable than the traditional mixed woodlands but are usually quite lacking in even the commonest woodland plants.

Hedgerows, like woodlands, have recently been cleared on an unprecedented scale in order to produce larger fields more suited to modern farming. Fortunately, the clearing of hedgerows seems to have passed the peak it reached in the 1960s, but perhaps this simply reflects the fact that in many places there are no more hedgerows to clear.

Even the contents of the fields themselves have changed in many places. Hay for the winter fodder of livestock simply used to be cut each year from meadows which contained a great mixture of plants. More recently many meadows are ploughed annually and planted with a mixture of commercial Grass seed which will produce a more consistent type of hay. Some of the meadows recently put under the plough may have existed as meadows since medieval times and may have supported over 100 species of plant. With modern practices, these old meadows may be changed so that they support only a few varieties of cultivated Grasses. Similarly, in arable fields there is now no place for wild flowers as weeds amongst the crops. Purer stocks

Above: Corn Cockle (Agrostemma githago) *is an attractive member of the Stitchwort family (Caryophyllaceae). Once a common weed of cereal crops, it is now quite rare in many places through the use of purer seeds and herbicides.*

Right: The fate of the Cornflower (Centaurea cyanus) *has been similar to that of the Corn Cockle, although it is sometimes found on waste ground. The heads have only disc florets, which are purple with spreading lobes.*

of seed, and the use of herbicides to clear the land before sowing the crop, have eradicated such plants as the Cornflower (*Centaurea cyanus*) and the Corn Cockle (*Agrostemma githago*). Farms cannot be run at a loss, and such new practices are necessary from an economic viewpoint. It is no longer economical to graze downland sheep or coppice woodlands as extensively as in the past. Without sheep to keep the turf short, chalk grassland gradually reverts through scrub to woodland, with the loss of its characteristic flora.

Not all the blame for the loss of plants from the countryside must be taken by landowners and property developers. A number of plants are rare because they have been over-collected by wild-flower enthusiasts. This was particularly commonplace during Victorian times, when many flowering plants and ferns were dug up and transplanted, often unsuccessfully, into private gardens. The wild populations of some of the most spectacular flowering plants were greatly reduced in this way. The Lady's Slipper Orchid (*Cypripedium calceolus*), never a particularly common plant, was ruthlessly collected in this way. Orchids in general were often sought out by amateur botanists and, sadly, this is still true today to a certain extent. The Fen Orchid (*Liparis loeselii*) is now a rare plant in Britain, its numbers having been partly reduced by collecting but more significantly, perhaps, by changes such as the drainage of its fenland habitat. Wild flowers are also valued for other purposes, such as the making of country wines, but, in the majority of cases, the plants used are common enough to cause no alarm. However, new editions of wine-making recipe books continue to recommend making wines from plants such as the Oxlip (*Primula elatior*), which, although locally flourishing where conditions are favourable, is not a common plant.

Why Conserve Wild Flowers?

The countryside, with its wild flowers, is as much a part of our heritage as any ancient monument or celebrated building. Furthermore, it is a part of our heritage which is used and enjoyed by millions of people. Despite this, there is surprisingly little outcry when yet another water meadow is drained and ploughed. How different the situation is when a valued art treasure has to be sold abroad, when it is not even going to be destroyed. Perhaps the reason why the countryside is allowed to slip away with so little fuss is that we always assume there is more of it, just a little bit further down the road. Indeed there often is, but the stage is being reached in many parts of Europe where good examples of water meadows, or bogs or relatively natural woodland are becoming hard to find. When the habitat disappears so do the wild flowers, the birds, insects and other wildlife. In the majority of cases, once they have gone, they are gone for ever. If the importance of wild flowers as part of our heritage were not sufficient reason for preserving them, there are many others.

Wild flowers are an important part of the diversity of habitats, and diversity is the key to the balance of nature. In the wild all living things are interdependent in a complex web of food chains. The wild flowers are at the base of the food chains; they convert the sun's energy to provide their own food and are themselves the food of herbivorous animals. These herbivores, in turn, make up the diet of carnivores. If the base of the food chain is removed, then the organisms at higher levels in the chain are affected. Some herbivores can feed on a variety of kinds of plant but others are more specific and may feed on one kind of plant only. For example, the caterpillars of the Apollo butterfly (*Parnassius apollo*) feed only on plants belonging to the Stonecrop family (Crassulaceae), and this attractive butterfly is protected by law in several European countries. It is now a well-established principle that lack of diversity in natural systems can cause imbalances which may result in the extinction of some organisms and population explosions for others. If the numbers of carnivores or predators, such as insect-eating birds, become reduced, the numbers of the prey, which might be aphids or other kinds of insect pests, can very rapidly increase to a much higher level than usual.

Another argument in favour of conserving as many types of plants and animals as possible is to have them available for use by mankind in the future should any use be found for them. At present people use relatively few plants out of the total number known to exist. Most of these belong to the Grass family (Graminae), Daisy family (Compositae), Pea family (Leguminosae) or Cabbage family (Cruciferae), at least as far as food plants are concerned. There are many wild members of these families which might hold great potential as future food crops. Even if the wild flowers do not actually come to be used as crops, they may be of value for cross-breeding with cultivated plants to produce new strains with particular characteristics. Wild plants represent a vast store of genetic material which may be essential in future plant-breeding programmes. Although to most people the beauty of wild flowers is enough to argue the case for their protection, there are also sound scientific reasons.

Above: The Fen Orchid (Liparis loeselii) *has become quite rare in recent times because of drainage of the fenland where it was once much commoner.*

Below: Oxlip (Primula elatior) *may be locally common but is often reduced by people picking the attractive flowers.*

Left: The Lady's Slipper Orchid (Cypripedium calceolus) *is probably the most spectacular European Orchid, but over-collecting has greatly reduced its numbers in the wild over the past 100 years.*

How Can Wild Flowers Be Conserved?

Several different approaches are used in the conservation of wild flowers, with varying degrees of success. Nature reserves can be created to offer protection to a particularly rare species of plant, or reserves can be established which include good examples of one or more habitats. As another alternative, rare plants can be grown in special botanic gardens. But before any of these measures can be taken, accurate up-to-date information is needed about the distribution of rare plants and whether they are in immediate danger. To provide this kind of information, a number of projects have begun at various institutions in Europe to sift through all available information on plant distribution and abundance in an attempt to produce lists of endangered species. These lists will provide much of the information needed to organize plant conservation in the future.

One category of plants which is given priority in this procedure includes those which are limited in distribution to a particular, restricted area. These plants are known as *endemics* and may be restricted to a single range of mountains, a country, or some other well-defined area. Because of their limited distribution, endemic plants are particularly vulnerable to extinction. Undue emphasis, however, can be placed on conserving a plant such as the Lady's Slipper Orchid (*Cypripedium calceolus*) in Britain, where it is on the brink of extinction. Since the plant is widespread, although not common, in Europe, its extinction in Britain would not mean its complete loss to the world. The Lady's Slipper Orchid is a good example of a plant for which nature reserves have been specially created. The numbers of individual plants in these reserves are so small that their survival is threatened simply by the erosion and trampling caused by the enthusiastic plant lovers who visit the reserves to photograph the plants or simply to see them in the wild.

In 1980 the Society for the Promotion of Nature Conservation appealed to its members and others not to visit the plants during that year.

The problem with many of the reserves which seek to protect a single species of plant is that they are often not established until the plant is already close to extinction in the wild. The reason for the decline in numbers of the protected plant is usually a change in the habitat, and unless the habitat can also be restored there is little prospect of providing the right conditions for the long-term survival of the plant.

On the other hand, those reserves or national parks which are established to protect a particular habitat have considerably more chance of succeeding in saving a wide variety of plants and animals. However, where the habitat was created by human activity, as in the case of chalk grassland, for example, this activity must be continued if the habitat is not to change over a period of time into something much less worth conserving. This means that somehow grazing must be continued in a reserve which seeks to preserve a flora which developed because of grazing. Similarly, coppicing of trees must be continued to preserve the open, airy, coppiced woods which are so often rich in wild flowers. One of the hardest tasks which faces the organizations which have the responsibility of looking after reserve areas of man-made habitats is finding a suitable management programme which will keep the vegetation in a stable condition. Since grazing, coppicing and the other traditional forms of land management which are dying out are uneconomical, the problem of conserving habitats is essentially an economic one.

If the important habitats of wild flowers and animals are to be preserved in Europe, the money must be made available to fund management programmes in the existing reserves and parks and, perhaps even more important, to provide a cash alternative to farmers and land developers so that irreplaceable pieces of the countryside do not have to disappear. The mechanism for recognizing the prime sites which need conserving already exists. Throughout Britain, for example, there are areas which have been designated as Sites of Special Scientific Interest precisely because they are amongst the last good representatives of particular habitats. Their title may be misleading since these are places of special interest to all users and lovers of the countryside, not just to scientists. At present, designation of these sites does nothing to ensure their future, and many are subsequently destroyed. Elsewhere in Europe a similar story can be told. Unless there is legislation soon to protect such sites and provide compensation where necessary or money for their purchase as reserves, then many more of the best of Europe's countryside will be lost. Such legislation is now being discussed in several European countries, but it seems doubtful that sufficient help will be forthcoming.

As a last resort, plants on the verge of extinction could be grown in botanic gardens to preserve their usefulness for future plant-breeding programmes or so that they could be re-introduced into the wild. However, this would seem something of a failure compared to preserving a place where plants can flourish naturally in the countryside of Europe long into the future.

Part Three

Wild Flowers of Northern Europe

Left: Cow Parsley (Anthriscus sylvestris) *is one of the earliest in a succession of members of the Umbelliferae family which flower each year along hedgerows.*

DICOTYLEDONS

The flowering plants are usually divided into two groups. The families up to page 182 are *dicotyledons*. They differ from the *monocotyledons* (page 182 onwards) in normally having net-veined leaves, flower parts in fours or fives, and two seed leaves, or *cotyledons*. There are also differences between their root systems, stems and pollen grains.

BUTTERCUP FAMILY
Ranunculaceae

The structure of certain flowers in the Buttercup family is often regarded as primitive, as in all the examples of the family shown here. There are many stamens. The sepals are sometimes petal-like, as in the Wood Anemone. Many species are acrid-tasting and poisonous to livestock.

WOOD ANEMONE
Anemone nemorosa
A rather delicate, hairless plant of broad-leaved woodland, hedgebank and upland meadow, it grows 6-30 cm high. Like many woodland plants the Wood Anemone makes use of the sunlight of early spring for flowering before the trees come into leaf.
Flower: white or pink-tinged, 2-4 cm across, no petals but 6-7 petal-like sepals; stamens many.
Flower arrangement: solitary, terminal.
Flowering time: March-May.
Leaf: 1 or 2 long-stalked basal leaves of 3 segments, each segment deeply dissected, coarsely toothed, shortly stalked; upper leaves in whorl of 3, smaller with flattened stalks.
Fruit: many downy achenes in nodding heads.

MARSH MARIGOLD
Caltha palustris
Although this stout plant has flowers that look like large Buttercups, its broad, shining, heart-shaped leaves and hollow flower stalks betray its true identity. It grows in marshy ground, often near streams, and may either be erect, to a height of 15-30 cm, or creeping.
Flower: bright golden yellow, 1·5-5 cm across; petal-like sepals, 5 or more; stamens many.
Flower arrangement: few-flowered cyme.
Flowering time: March-July.
Leaf: broadly heart-shaped, teeth blunt or pointed; basal leaves long-stalked, upper often kidney-shaped, stalkless.
Fruit: head of 5-15 follicles, erect or curved back.

Marsh
Marigold

Meadow
Buttercup

Wood
Anemone

lower leaf

MEADOW BUTTERCUP
Ranunculus acris
Commonly found in meadows and pasture, this Buttercup grows up to 100 cm high. The stem is much branched and erect above. The very similar, common Creeping Buttercup (*Ranunculus repens*) has a creeping, rooting stem, furrowed flower stalk and stalked middle leaf segment.
Flower: glossy, bright yellow, 1·5-2·5 cm across; petals 5; sepals lying against petals; stamens many; flower stalk not furrowed.
Flower arrangement: irregular cyme.
Flowering time: April-October.
Leaf: more or less hairy; lower leaf with long stalk, palmate with 2-7 deeply toothed segments, middle segment not stalked; uppermost leaves stalkless, deeply cut.
Fruit: achenes many, hairless, each with short hook, in a round head.

LESSER CELANDINE
Ranunculus ficaria

One of the early spring flowers, Lesser Celandine has more petals than a Buttercup and glossy, heart-shaped leaves. It grows 5-30 cm high on hedgebanks, in woods and streamsides. The roots form tubers.

Flower: bright golden yellow, whitening with age at petal-base, opening only on fine days, 1·5-5 cm across; petals 8-12, more or less pointed; sepals 3; stamens many.

Flower arrangement: solitary.

Flowering time: March-May.

Leaf: broadly heart-shaped, dark green, hairless; basal leaves long-stalked, in a rosette.

Fruit: achenes, many, downy.

Uses: the tubers look like piles and were used in their treatment in the belief that like cures like. Farmers also used Celandine, as they did Buttercups, to charm more milk from cows.

LESSER SPEARWORT
Ranunculus flammula

This is a Buttercup of wet places easily distinguished by its undissected leaves and pale, rather than golden, yellow flowers. Erect or creeping, with a hollow stem, and usually hairless, it grows between 8 and 80 cm high. Irritant poisons are present in larger amounts than in other Buttercups.

Flower: pale yellow, glossy, 8-20 mm across, petals 5; sepals 5; stamens many; flower stalk grooved.

Flower arrangement: solitary or in a cyme.

Flowering time: May-September.

Leaf: lower leaves circular, stalked; upper leaves stalkless, smaller, pointed, parallel-veined, with or without teeth.

Fruit: achenes, hairless, in a round head.

THREAD-LEAVED WATER-CROWFOOT
Ranunculus trichophyllus

This Water-crowfoot has small, white flowers and grows in ponds, slow streams and ditches. There are no floating leaves, and the needle-like segments of the submerged leaves do not lie flat. Several other species of Water-crowfoot grow in N. Europe, some of which have entire, floating leaves in addition to submerged.

Flower: white, petal-base yellow, 8-10 mm across; petals 5, not touching at edges; stamens 5-15.

Flower arrangement: solitary, opening above surface of water.

Flowering time: May-June.

Leaf: all submerged, finely dissected, bristle-like, not lying in one plane, 2-4 cm, shortly stalked.

Fruit: achenes; stalk usually less than 4 cm.

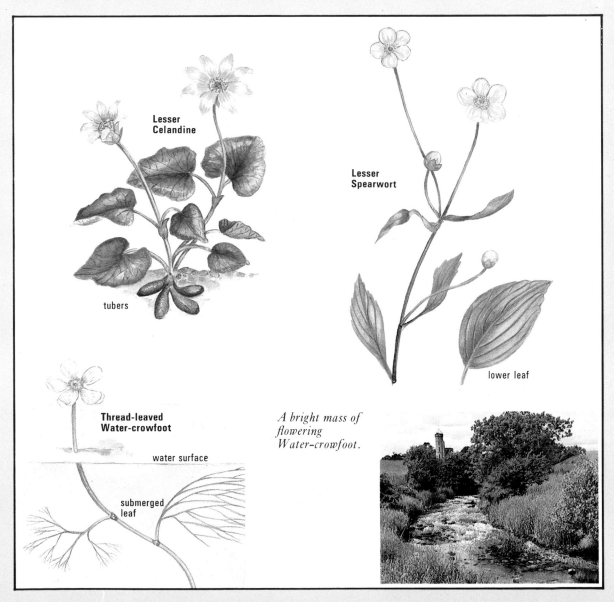

Lesser Celandine

tubers

Lesser Spearwort

lower leaf

Thread-leaved Water-crowfoot

water surface

submerged leaf

A bright mass of flowering Water-crowfoot.

WATER-LILY FAMILY
Nymphaeaceae

Water-lilies grow in fresh water, the flowers and most of the leaves floating on the surface, with their roots in the mud. The leaves may cover large areas of water. As with the Buttercup family, the Water-lilies are considered to have a primitive flower structure.

YELLOW WATER-LILY
Nuphar lutea

Growing in freshwater lakes, ponds and slow streams, the Yellow Water-lily is more widely distributed than the White. The floating leaves are oval compared with the almost circular White Water-lily leaves.

Flower: bright yellow, cup-shaped, smelling of alcohol, 4-6 cm across, rising clear of the water; sepals 4-6, large, petal-like, rounded; stamens many; stigma flat with 15-20 radiating ridges.

Flower arrangement: solitary.

Flowering time: June-August.

Leaf: floating, oval, 12-40 × 9-30 cm, entire with a deep cleft where stalk joins; veins forked, not joined at leaf margin; submerged leaves thin, lettuce-like.

Fruit: bottle-shaped, ripening above water.

Uses: Water-lilies, not surprisingly, were held to have cooling properties. Gerard's *Herbal* of 1597 states, 'the root of the Yellow cureth hot diseases of the kidnies and bladder.'

WHITE WATER-LILY
Nymphaea alba

The White Water-lily grows in standing or slow-flowing water up to a depth of 3 m. It is more tolerant of polluted water than many other water plants. The large, floating flowers are scented.

Flower: white, 10-20 cm across, floating; 20-25 pointed petals; sepals 4; stamens many; stigma flat with 15-20 radiating ridges.

Flower arrangement: solitary, on long stalks arising from root.

Flowering time: June-September.

Leaf: floating, more or less circular, 10-30 cm, entire with deep cleft where stalk joins, veins joined around edge of leaf.

Fruit: flask-shaped, sometimes spherical, ripening underwater; seeds float, aiding dispersal.

Uses: the roots were sometimes eaten in parts of N. Europe, and Elizabethans ate seed and root to promote chastity.

POPPY FAMILY
Papaveraceae

Several species of Poppy are weeds of cultivated fields, especially fields of grain. They are now more common at field edges and on waste land than among crops, due to the use of herbicides and the removal of weed seed from crop seed.

GREATER CELANDINE
Chelidonium majus

There seems little resemblance between this plant, with its small, yellow flowers, and its flamboyant relatives, the Poppies. Despite the common name, it is not related to Lesser Celandine. It has surprising bright-orange sap and grows 30-90 cm high on hedgebanks and walls, usually near buildings.

Flower: bright yellow, 2-2·5 cm across; petals 4; stamens many.

Flower arrangement: umbel of 2-6 flowers.

Flowering time: May-August.

Leaf: pinnate, leaflets 5-7, glaucous, blunt-toothed.

Fruit: a capsule 3-5 cm, straight, opening from below by 2 valves.

Uses: an escape from herbalists' gardens where it grew for many centuries. The bitter, orange sap was used to treat poor eyesight.

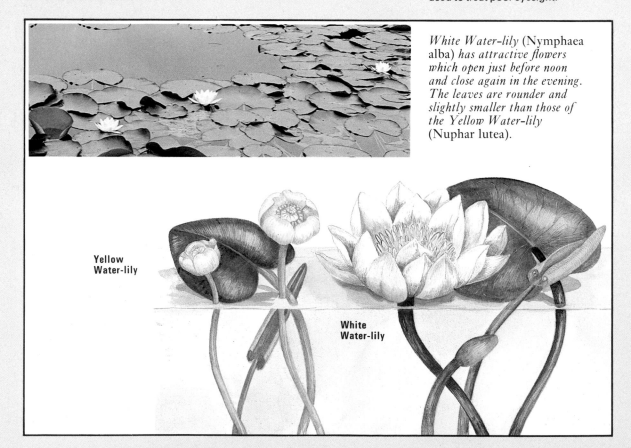

White Water-lily (Nymphaea alba) has attractive flowers which open just before noon and close again in the evening. The leaves are rounder and slightly smaller than those of the Yellow Water-lily (Nuphar lutea).

Yellow Water-lily

White Water-lily

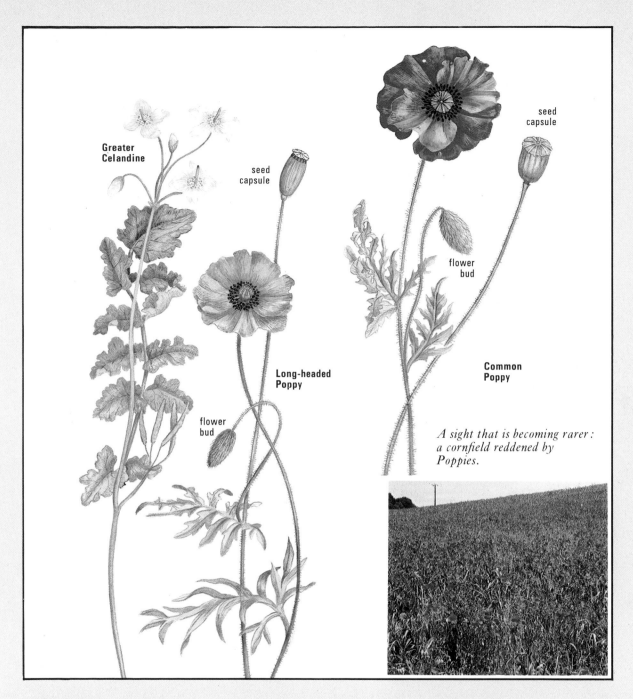

Greater Celandine

seed capsule

seed capsule

flower bud

Long-headed Poppy

flower bud

Common Poppy

A sight that is becoming rarer: a cornfield reddened by Poppies.

LONG-HEADED POPPY
Papaver dubium
The flowers are smaller and more orange than those of the Common Poppy. The stem is stiffly hairy. The plant grows 20-60 cm high, in waste places and as a weed of cultivation.
Flower: orange-pink, sometimes with a dark spot at petal-base; 3-7 cm across; petals circular, overlapping at base; stamens many, purple; stigma disc flat with 7-9 radiating ridges.
Flower arrangement: solitary.
Flowering time: June-July.
Leaf: greyish green, shortly hairy; basal leaves deeply lobed, end lobe not enlarged.
Fruit: long, narrow capsule, 1.5-2 × 0.5-0.75 cm, tapered at base, hairless, often ribbed.

COMMON POPPY
Papaver rhoeas
The Common Poppy, with its large, scarlet flowers and covering of stiff hairs, grows 25-90 cm high. If cut, it exudes milky-white latex.
Flower: scarlet, often with dark blotch at petal-base; 7-10 cm across; petals thin; stamens many; stigma disc more or less flat with 8-12 radiating ridges.
Flower arrangement: on long stalks in the leaf axils.
Flowering time: June-August.
Leaf: stiffly hairy, 1- to 2-pinnate; segments coarsely toothed.
Fruit: capsule, rounded at base, top flat, length 1-2 cm, hairless, opening by pores under top.
Uses: Poppies were thought to cause headaches and thunderstorms, but were also used to treat headaches. Although slightly poisonous, the red Poppy does not contain the opium of the Opium Poppy (*P. somniferum*).

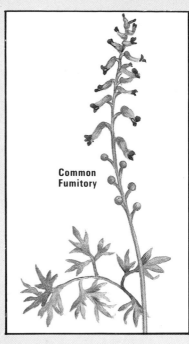

Common
Fumitory

FUMITORY FAMILY
Fumariaceae

Fumitories are sprawling weeds of cultivated or disturbed ground. The leaves are finely cut, reminiscent of Maidenhair Fern. The small flowers are tubular and 2-lipped.

COMMON FUMITORY
Fumaria officinalis
Common Fumitory is a slender, glaucous, long-stemmed plant, climbing or almost erect. It is a weed of arable land and prefers light soils.
Flower: purplish pink, tips blackish red; tube-like corolla 7-9 mm long, spurred behind, 2-lipped; sepals 2, irregularly toothed.
Flower arrangement: raceme, usually of more than 20 flowers, longer than its stalk.
Flowering time: May-October.
Leaf: all arising from stem, finely divided into flat segments.
Fruit: more or less spherical, 2-3 mm.

CABBAGE FAMILY
Cruciferae

Members of this family characteristically have flowers with 4 petals resembling a cross, hence the Latin name. The flowers are often yellow or white and usually have 6 stamens. The seed cases are arranged along the stem, which lengthens as the seeds ripen, and are commonly narrow, elongated capsules which point upwards like candelabra. There are numerous representatives of this family in northern Europe, many of which are weeds of disturbed ground. Others are the wild relatives of important cultivated crops such as Cabbage, Swede, Cauliflower, Mustard and Oilseed Rape. There are also many garden flowers in the family, including Wallflower and Candytuft.

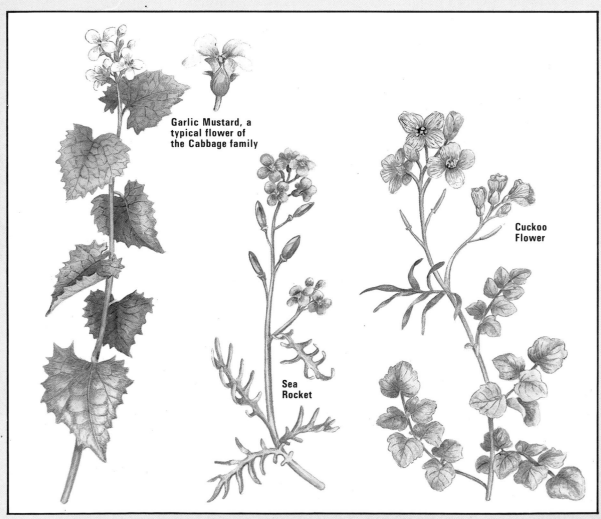

Garlic Mustard, a typical flower of the Cabbage family

Sea Rocket

Cuckoo Flower

GARLIC MUSTARD
Alliaria petiolata
A rather tall, upright plant, un-branched, up to 120 cm, Garlic Mustard smells faintly of garlic when crushed. The plant can be seen along hedgerows, walls and wood margins.
Flower: white, 6 mm across.
Flower arrangement: compact raceme.
Flowering time: April-June.
Leaf: pale, rather bright green, heart-shaped, toothed; basal leaves long-stalked, shape reminiscent of nettle leaf.
Fruit: long, very narrow capsule, 2-7 cm long, opening by 2 valves from below.
Uses: a sauce was formerly made from the leaves to accompany salted fish. An old name for the plant is Sauce Alone.

SEA ROCKET
Cakile maritima
This is a good-looking seaside plant of sand and shingle. The plant is succulent, pale bluish-green and 15-45 cm high. The fruits are dispersed by sea water.
Flower: pale lilac, occasionally purple or white, 1-2 cm across; petals narrowed at base; sepals 4, erect not spreading; stamens 6.
Flower arrangement: many flowers, closely spaced at end of branches.
Flowering time: June-August.
Leaf: deeply pinnately lobed or not; lower leaves 3-6 cm with short stalk; upper leaves stalkless.
Fruit: 1-2·5 cm, bulbous, narrowed at tip.

CUCKOO FLOWER
Cardamine pratensis
A very pretty plant of damp places and stream sides, the Cuckoo Flower grows 30-55 cm high, usually un-branched. The clustered flowers are pale lilac and open in the spring. Seeds are catapulted up to 2 m.
Flower: lilac, rarely white, 12-18 mm across; petals may be slightly notched.
Flower arrangement: clusters of 7-20 flowers.
Flowering time: April-June.
Leaf: pinnate, up to 7 oval or circular leaflets usually with widely spaced teeth; end leaflet enlarged; basal leaves in rosette.
Fruit: 2·5-4 cm, thin, on long stalks pointing upward, opening from below by 2 valves.
Uses: the plant may be eaten in the same way as Water-cress.

SHEPHERD'S PURSE
Capsella bursa-pastoris
Hardly a walk can be taken, whether in town or country, without seeing Shepherd's Purse, a plant 3-40 cm high, of wayside, cultivated land and waste places. It is distributed through-out the world, having followed man as a weed of agriculture.
Flower: white, about 2·5 mm across.
Flower arrangement: flowers crowded at the top of a raceme, becoming less dense in fruit.

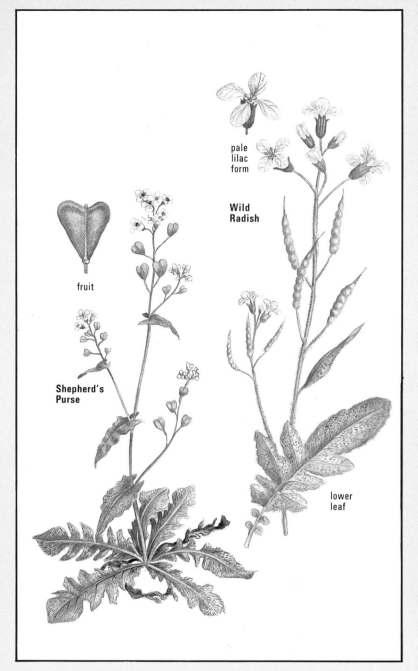

pale lilac form

Wild Radish

fruit

Shepherd's Purse

lower leaf

Flowering time: all the year.
Leaf: basal leaves in rosette, deeply lobed or not; base of upper leaves clasping stem.
Fruit: heart-shaped, 6-9 mm across, the 2 valves breaking apart to disperse pale brown seeds — the 'money' in the 'purse'.

WILD RADISH
Raphanus raphanistrum
This arable weed is bristly, erect, branched and grows 15-150 cm high. The cultivated Radish (*R. sativus*) has the well-known edible swollen root and occasionally escapes from gardens.

Flower: yellow, lilac or white with dark veins, 2·5-4 cm across; petals narrowed at base, twice as long as sepals; stamens 6.
Flower arrangement: raceme.
Flowering time: May-September.
Leaf: lower leaves deeply lobed; end lobe rounded, enlarged; upper leaves lobed or toothed.
Fruit: long, narrow, abruptly narrowed into long spike at tip; contracted between each of the 4-7 seeds, breaking readily into 1-seeded units.

CHARLOCK
Sinapis arvensis
Charlock grows up to 80 cm and often has stiff hairs on the base of the stem. It is a serious weed of arable land.
Flower: bright yellow, 1·5-2 cm; petals narrowed at base; sepals 4; stamens 6.
Flower arrangement: dense raceme.
Flowering time: May-July.
Leaf: up to 20 cm, alternate, roughly hairy; lower leaf stalked, deeply lobed; end lobe large, coarsely toothed; upper leaves stalkless, without lobes.

Fruit: 2·5-4·5 cm long, narrow, abruptly narrowed at tip, indented between seeds, smooth or stiffly hairy, containing dark reddish-brown seeds.

HEDGE MUSTARD
Sisymbrium officinale
Hedge Mustard, familiar if not pleasing to the eye, grows in waste places in town and country to a height of 90 cm. The plant is stiffly erect and branched above, like candelabra.
Flower: pale yellow, small.
Flower arrangement: in small clusters on ends of branches.
Flowering time: June-July.

Leaf: lower leaves in a rosette, deeply lobed; end lobe larger than rest.
Fruit: very thin, cylindrical, 10-20 mm, straight, pressed to the stem, which elongates in fruit.

WATER-CRESS
Rorippa nasturtium-aquaticum
Water-cress grows in masses in wet places where there is fresh, moving water. It is 10-60 cm high, hairless, creeping, often rooting and ascending at the tip.
Flower: white, 4-6 mm across, petals about twice as long as sepals.
Flower arrangement: clustered at the top of a raceme.
Flowering time: May-October.
Leaf: pinnate, lower leaves with 1-3 circular or broadly ovate leaflets; upper leaf with 5-9.
Fruit: 13-18 mm, curving slightly upward.
Uses: commercial cultivation as a salad crop started at the beginning of the 19th century.

VIOLET FAMILY
Violaceae

The flowers are of 5 unequal petals, the lowest spurred. The sepals have small flaps or appendages. After producing normal flowers in spring, Violets often produce flowers which do not open and are self-fertilizing. Many tropical members of this family are shrubs.

SWEET VIOLET
Viola odorata
Although cultivated in gardens and often escaping, the scented Sweet Violet is also a native of Europe. It grows in hedgebanks, scrub and woods, and is 5-15 cm high, with a rosette of leaves and creeping, rooting runners.
Flower: deep violet or white with lilac spur, about 1·5 cm, scented; petals 5, unequal, lower petal forming spur behind; spur longer than sepal appendages; sepals rounded at tip.
Flower arrangement: solitary, on long stalks.
Flowering time: February-April.
Leaf: heart-shaped, rounded or pointed at tip, blunt-toothed, sparsely hairy, long-stalked.
Fruit: capsule, spherical, downy.
Uses: a flower prized for its sweet scent, it may also be candied for cake decoration.

COMMON DOG-VIOLET
Viola riviniana
This Violet can be very variable in size. It lacks creeping stems and grows in woods, on hedgebanks or in grassland.
Flower: usually blue-violet though

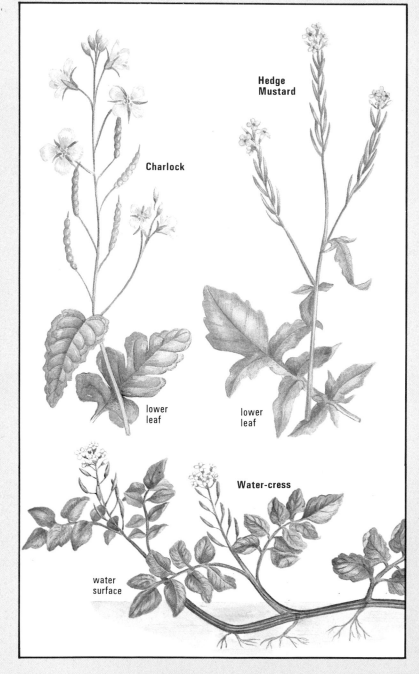

Charlock

lower leaf

Hedge Mustard

lower leaf

Water-cress

water surface

Violets can often be seen on damp shady banks and under hedgerows.

Wild Pansy

seed capsule

Common Dog-violet

Sweet Violet

white form

varying; spur paler; lower petal with many long, dark veins; unscented, 1-2·5 cm; spur 2-5 mm, stout, often curved up, notched at tip; sepals with appendages about 2-3 mm.
Flower arrangement: solitary, on axillary branches.
Flowering time: April-June.
Leaf: in loose rosette; stalked, heart-shaped, blunt-toothed, up to 8 cm; stipules toothed.
Fruit: capsules opening by 3 valves; explosive.

WILD PANSY
Viola tricolor
The Violet from which the older garden Pansies were bred is found on cultivated and waste ground and short grassland. It is 15-45 cm high and usually branched. A low-growing form (3-15 cm) occurs on dunes and grassland near the sea.
Flower: blue-violet or yellow, or both colours combined; scentless, 1-3 cm vertically; petals 5, unequal, usually longer than sepals, lower

petal forming spur behind; sepals pointed, rather shorter than spur with appendage immediately below each sepal.
Flower arrangement: solitary, several arising from each stem.
Flowering time: April-September.
Leaf: alternate; lower leaf ovate or heart-shaped, blunt-toothed; upper leaf narrower; stipules leaf-like deeply lobed.
Fruit: 3-valved capsule.

flower

Common Milkwort

MILKWORT FAMILY
Polygalaceae

This world-wide family includes shrubs and small trees but all the North European members are small plants growing in short grassland. The 3 true petals of the flowers are enclosed within the 5 petal-like sepals.

COMMON MILKWORT
Polygala vulgaris
This is a rather low, much branched plant, 10-30 cm high, to be found in short grassland, heaths and dunes. The tiny flowers are almost enclosed by 2 enlarged, coloured sepals.
Flower: blue, pink or white, 6-8 mm; sepals 5, the two inner enlarged, coloured, petal-like.
Flower arrangement: many-flowered raceme.
Flowering time: May-September.
Leaf: alternate, narrow, entire, more or less pointed; lower leaves 5-10 mm, upper leaves longer.
Fruit: flat, heart-shaped capsule, about 5 mm.
Uses: herbalists formerly prescribed this little plant for nursing mothers, to increase the flow of milk.

ST JOHN'S WORT FAMILY
Guttiferae

A family mainly of temperate regions. Glands, appearing as black or translucent dots on the plants, are characteristic of this family. There are 5 petals, and the many stamens are joined at their bases into bundles.

PERFORATE ST JOHN'S WORT
Hypericum perforatum
There are tiny translucent dots (seen if the plant is held to the light) and black dots to look for on this plant. Running down the stem are 2 raised lines. The plant is hairless, erect and 10-100 cm high, growing in grassland and scrub.
Flower: yellow, about 2 cm across; petals 5, tiny black dots around margins; sepals 5, pointed, with or without black dots; stamens many.
Flower arrangement: branched cyme.
Flowering time: June-September.
Leaf: alternate, with many translucent dots; 1-3 cm, elliptic to linear, shortly or not stalked.
Fruit: capsule, seeds pitted.
Uses: once an important protective and healing plant, it was smoked over fires lit on 23rd June, St John's Eve, thus strengthening its powers. The ceremony included leaping over the flames, and may date from pre-Christian times.

SQUARE-STALKED ST JOHN'S WORT
Hypericum tetrapterum
The square cross-section of the stem, flanged at each angle, is the main feature of this St John's Wort. The plant is hairless, 10-100 cm high and grows in damp places. It is absent from Norway and the greater part of Sweden.
Flower: pale yellow, 1 cm across; petals 5; sepals pointed, occasionally with 1-2 black dots; stamens many.
Flower arrangement: many-flowered, branched cymes.
Flowering time: June-September.
Leaf: opposite, ovate, stalkless, weakly clasping stem at base, with some small, translucent and black dots.
Fruit: capsule, seeds pitted.

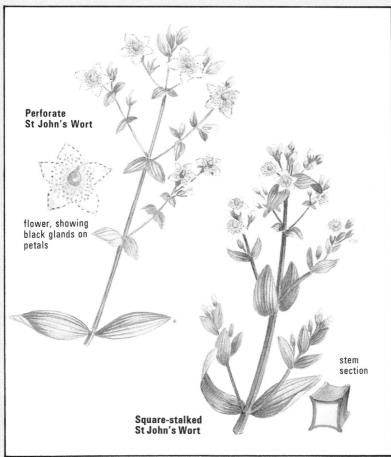

Perforate St John's Wort

flower, showing black glands on petals

stem section

Square-stalked St John's Wort

STITCHWORT FAMILY
Caryophyllaceae

This large family includes Carnations, Pinks and many other garden plants, as well as widespread weeds such as the Chickweeds. The flowers have 4 or 5 petals, which are notched, except in the case of Sandworts and Spurreys.

PROCUMBENT PEARLWORT
Sagina procumbens

As a result of its moss-like size and creeping habit, this common plant is easily overlooked. The stems spread out from a central rosette of needle-like leaves. It is found in lawns, grass verges and paths.
Flower: white, minute; petals 4 or 5; sepals much larger than petals.
Flower arrangement: solitary on long stalks.
Flowering time: May-September.
Leaf: 5-12 mm, needle-like, in tufts along stem.
Fruit: capsule.

THYME-LEAVED SANDWORT
Arenaria serpyllifolia

The lower parts of this small plant are often more densely branched than the upper. It is 3-30 cm high, with scattered hairs, and is slightly rough to the touch. Its habitat is arable and bare ground and walls. It seems to be ignored by rabbits and is common around their burrows.
Flower: white, 5-8 mm; petals 5, shorter than sepals; sepals hairy; anthers yellow.
Flower arrangement: cyme.
Flowering time: June-August.
Leaf: opposite, ovate; lower leaves shortly stalked, upper stalkless.
Fruit: capsule, flask-shaped; seeds tiny, black.

SEA SANDWORT
Honkenya peploides

The Sea Sandwort is a small, fleshy plant, 5-25 cm high, partly creeping on sand and shingle by the sea. It can withstand brief immersion in salt water.
Flower: greenish white, 6-10 mm; petals 5, rounded, as long as or shorter than the sepals.
Flower arrangement: solitary, in leaf axils and forks of branches.
Flowering time: May-August.
Leaf: opposite, ovate, fleshy, stalkless.
Fruit: capsule, spherical, opening by 3 teeth; seeds large, pear-shaped, reddish-brown.
Uses: in Yorkshire the whole plant was used as a pickle.

The conspicuous flowers of a member of the Stitchwort family.

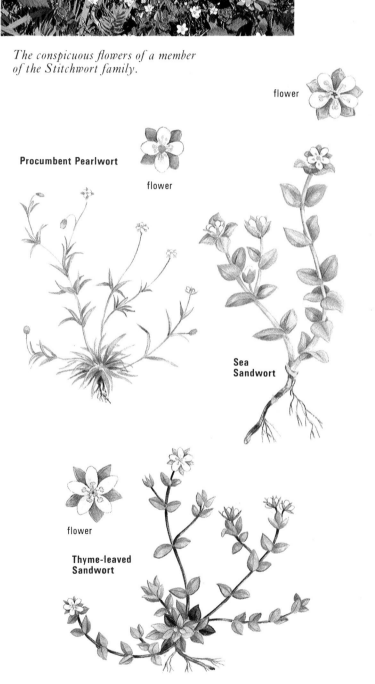

flower

Procumbent Pearlwort

flower

Sea Sandwort

flower

Thyme-leaved Sandwort

CORN SPURREY
Spergula arvensis

Corn Spurrey is a pale green plant, 5-70 cm high, slightly to very sticky, with weak, branched stems and whorls of leaves. It is a weed of cultivated land, preferring sandy soils.
Flower: white, 4-7 mm across; petals 5, rounded, slightly longer than sepals.
Flower arrangement: forked or umbel-like panicle, the stalks turning down in fruit.

Flowering time: June-August.
Leaf: 1-3 cm long, needle-shaped, in whorls, slightly fleshy, channelled beneath, sticky.
Fruit: capsule, 5 mm, opening by 5 teeth; seeds blackish, warty.
Uses: various forms of this weed are grown in Germany and the Netherlands as a nutritious fodder crop for sheep and cows. When cultivated it may grow 90 cm high.

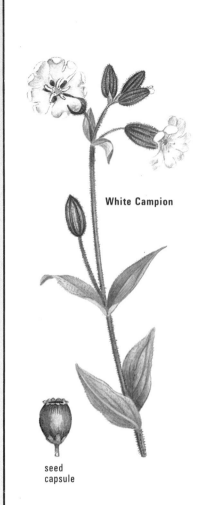

White Campion

seed capsule

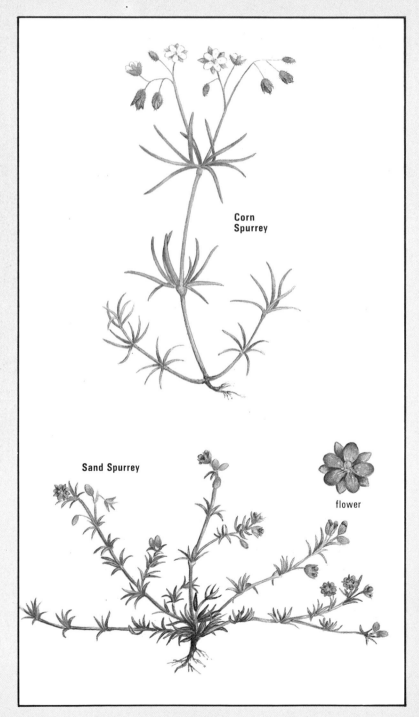

Corn Spurrey

Sand Spurrey

flower

SAND SPURREY
Spergularia rubra

Sand Spurrey, with its tiny, pink flowers, is a straggling plant, 5-25 cm high, found on sandy soils in open ground. The upper parts of the plant have slightly sticky hairs.
Flower: pink, paler at base of petals, 3-5 mm, petals 5; sepals longer than petals.
Flower arrangement: few-flowered cyme.
Flowering time: May-September.
Leaf: in clusters along stem, very narrow, tapering to stiff, sharp point, not fleshy; stipules silvery, conspicuous.
Fruit: capsule, 4-5 mm, opening by 3 teeth; seeds tiny, dark brown.

WHITE CAMPION
Silene alba

The White Campion is a branched, softly hairy weed of cultivated land and grows to 80 cm. As with the Red Campion, the flowers are unisexual. They open in the evening

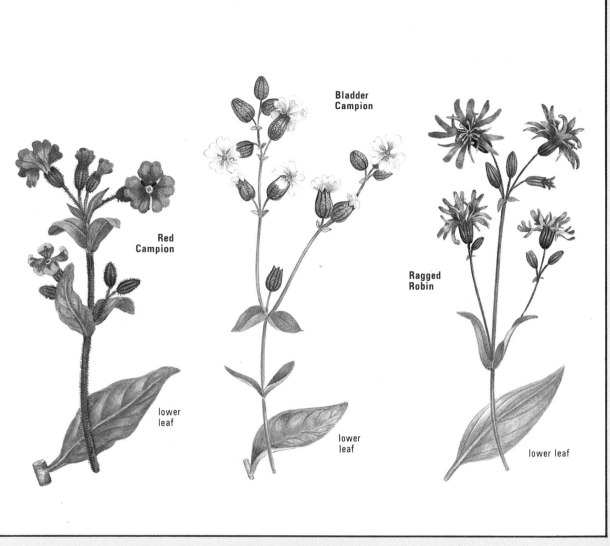

Bladder Campion

Red Campion

Ragged Robin

lower leaf

lower leaf

lower leaf

when they are slightly scented to attract moths as pollinators.
Flower: white, 2·5-3 cm across; petals 5, deeply cleft, narrowed at base; calyx-tube hairy, sticky.
Flower arrangement: cyme.
Flowering time: May-September.
Leaf: opposite, ovate, stalked; stem leaves stalkless.
Fruit: capsule 1·1·5 cm, ovoid, opening by 10 teeth.

RED CAMPION
Silene dioica
The Red Campion grows in woods and hedgerows. The whole plant is softly hairy and grows up to 80 cm high. There are separate male and female flowers. Red Campion interbreeds readily with White Campion, the offspring having pale pink flowers.
Flower: bright rose, 18-25 mm across; petals 5, deeply cleft, narrowed at base; calyx-tube hairy, slightly sticky.
Flower arrangement: cyme.

Flowering time: May-June.
Leaf: opposite, broadly ovate; the basal leaf blade continuous as thin border down each side of stalk; upper leaves stalkless.
Fruit: capsule 1-1·5 cm, spherical or ovoid, opening by 10 teeth which curve back.
Uses: Campions were associated with snakes, the pounded seed being used to treat snake bite.

BLADDER CAMPION
Silene vulgaris
This erect, often grey-green, branching plant is usually without hairs and grows up to 90 cm high. The 'bladder' is the inflated calyx-tube. It is found in grassland and arable land, and along roadsides.
Flower: white, about 1·5 cm across; petals 5, deeply cleft, narrowed at base; calyx-tube inflated, net-veined; bracts papery.
Flower arrangement: loose cyme.
Flowering time: June-August.
Leaf: often greyish-green, opposite,

ovate; lower leaves short-stalked, upper stalkless.
Fruit: capsule, with 6 erect teeth, enclosed by persistent calyx.

RAGGED ROBIN
Lychnis flos-cuculi
The rose-red, finely dissected flower petals of the Ragged Robin are striking. The stem and leaves are slightly rough to the touch. The height of the branched stem is 20-90 cm. The plant is a lover of damp places.
Flower: rose-red, 3-4 cm across; petals deeply cut into thin segments; calyx-tube 5-toothed; stamens 10.
Flower arrangement: cyme.
Flowering time: May-June.
Leaf: opposite; basal leaves ovate, stalked, slightly rough to touch; upper leaves stalkless.
Fruit: capsule 6-10 mm, opening by 5 teeth.

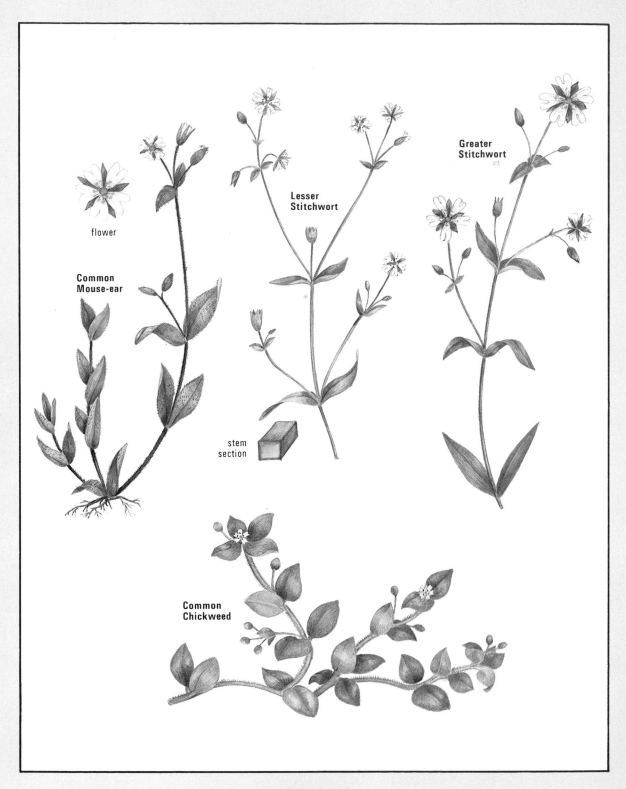

flower

Common
Mouse-ear

Lesser
Stitchwort

stem
section

Greater
Stitchwort

Common
Chickweed

COMMON MOUSE-EAR
Cerastium holosteoides
The flowering stems of this very common little plant, up to 45 cm high, are longer than the non-flowering stems. It is found almost everywhere, growing in loose, straggling tufts. The leaves and stem are hairy.
Flower: white; petals 5, deeply notched, equalling sepals; sepals with narrow, papery margins and showing between petals of open flower; stamens 10 or 5.

Flower arrangement: loose clusters.
Flowering time: April-September.
Leaf: 10-25 × 3-15 mm, stalkless, tip pointed or rounded.
Fruit: capsule, curved; seeds warty.

LESSER STITCHWORT
Stellaria graminea
Lesser Stitchwort is 20-90 cm high, and the 4-angled stem is smooth to the touch. The leaves are a bright green and the flowers smaller than those of Greater Stitchwort. It grows in woods and grassland and on heaths.
Flower: white, 5-12 mm, long-stalked; petals 5, notched to more than half their length (looking like 10 petals); sepals with narrow, papery margins; stamens 10.
Flower arrangement: loose clusters.
Flowering time: May-August.
Leaf: bright green, opposite, 1·5-4 cm long, lanceolate, tapering to sharp point, stalkless.
Fruit: capsule, ovoid; seeds reddish-brown.

GREATER STITCHWORT
Stellaria holostea
The slender, flowering stems are 15-60 cm high and 4-angled, the angles being slightly rough to the touch. The plant is slightly greyish-green and grows in hedgerows and woods.
Flower: white, 2-3 cm, long-stalked; petals 5, notched to about half their length; sepals with narrow, papery margins; stamens 10.
Flower arrangement: loose clusters.
Flowering time: April-June.
Leaf: rather greyish-green, opposite, 4-8 cm long, lanceolate, tapering to sharp point, stalkless.
Fruit: capsule, spherical; seeds reddish-brown, warty.
Uses: seed of Stitchwort was powdered, added to wine and used against pains or 'stitches' in the side.

COMMON CHICKWEED
Stellaria media
The straggling, branching stems of this world-wide weed are 5-40 cm long. The tiny flowers are inconspicuous and there is a single line of hairs running down the stem.
Flower: white, 8-10 mm; petals very deeply cleft; sepals same length as petals with narrow, papery margins, showing between petals of open flower.
Flower arrangement: loose clusters.
Flowering time: all year.
Leaf: opposite, ovate; lower leaves stalked, upper stalkless.
Fruit: capsule, stalk curved down.
Uses: young plants can be eaten in salads and sandwiches. Small birds love the seed.

GOOSEFOOT FAMILY
Chenopodiaceae

Economic crop plants in this family include beetroot and spinach. Flowers are inconspicuous and clustered into small spikes, and are wind-pollinated. The pale mealiness on the leaves is composed of minute, bladder-like hairs. Many of the species grow in dry, salty conditions, either in coastal areas or inland.

FAT HEN
Chenopodium album
Growing 10-150 cm high, Fat Hen often has a red tinge to the grooved stem. The plant is deep green with a mealy covering and grows on cultivated and waste land. It is very variable and there are several other similar species.
Flower: green, inconspicuous, bisexual.
Flower arrangement: spikes, arising from leaf-axils.
Flowering time: July-October.
Leaf: alternate, mealy, diamond-shaped to narrowly ovate, stalked, toothed, sometimes nearly 3-lobed or entire.
Fruit: black.

COMMON ORACHE
Atriplex patula
The plant is branched, up to 150 cm high and slightly mealy. The stems are ridged and striped white and green or red and green. This is a weed of waste places and cultivated ground. Although similar to Fat Hen, Common Orache can be distinguished by its separate male and female flowers.
Flower: green, inconspicuous, unisexual, males with 5 green 'petals' and 5 stamens, females with 2 stigmas and enclosed by 2 diamond-shaped bracts.
Flower arrangement: spikes arising from leaf-axils.
Flowering time: July-September.
Leaf: alternate, diamond-shaped, base tapering into leaf-stalk, toothed or entire; upper leaves narrow, entire, stalkless.
Fruit: black, enclosed by 2 bracts.

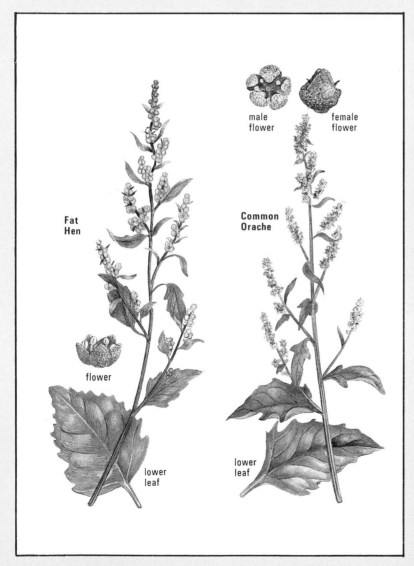

Fat Hen

flower

lower leaf

male flower

female flower

Common Orache

lower leaf

PURSLANE FAMILY
Portulacaceae

Plants belonging to this family are hairless and more or less fleshy. The pairs of opposite leaves are without teeth and may be joined into a cup shape surrounding the stem. There are 5 flower petals and only 2 sepals. Many of the species are natives of North America.

BLINKS
Montia fontana
A small and straggling plant, Blinks grows up to 50 cm high in fresh water. When growing on mud, the plant is more compact and tufted. The often reddish stem and green to yellow-green leaves are hairless and slightly fleshy. The plant is absent from most of N. France.
Flower: white, very inconspicuous, about 2 mm across, long-stalked; petals 5; sepals 2; stamens 3.
Flower arrangement: cyme.
Flowering time: May-October.
Leaf: 3-20 mm long, opposite, oval, entire, base tapering into stem.
Fruit: capsule, 1·5-2 mm, spherical; seeds usually 3.

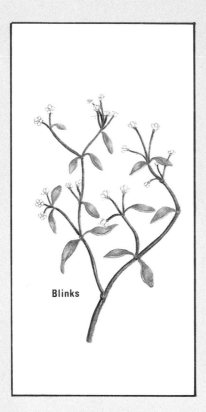

Blinks

FLAX FAMILY
Linaceae

Members of this small family are often slender and hairless. Flax is the most important member, from which comes linseed oil and a fibre used for good-quality paper.

PURGING FLAX
Linum catharticum
Slender, hairless and not usually more than 15 cm high, the Purging Flax is found in grass or on rocks, especially on limey or sandy soils.
Flower: white, yellow at petal-base, 4-6 mm across, nodding in bud, on thin stalks; petals 5, round-tipped; sepals 5, pointed at tip, with a few glandular hairs on margin; stamens 5.
Flower arrangement: loose cymes.
Flowering time: June-September.
Leaf: opposite, oval, stalkless, single-veined; the pairs widely spaced, pointing up.
Fruit: capsule, spherical.
Uses: as the common name suggests, this particular Flax was commonly used as a purge.

MALLOW FAMILY
Malvaceae

Mallows, Cotton and Hollyhock are all members of this family. The 5 flower petals are twisted in bud, and the many stamens are bunched centrally on a single stalk. Seen through a hand lens, the hairs on most of the species are branched in a star shape.

COMMON MALLOW
Malva sylvestris
This plant is erect or straggling, up to 150 cm high, and the stem is woody at the base. The habit, hairiness and leaf shape are all variable. The plant favours dry, open places on waste and cultivated land.
Flower: rose-purple, dark-striped, 2·5-4 cm across; petals 5, thin, narrowed at base, notched, 3 or 4 times as long as sepals; 5 sepals joined at base, with 3 smaller beneath; stamens many, clustered on a single stalk.
Flower arrangement: several stalked flowers arising from each leaf-axil.
Flowering time: June-September.
Leaf: palmately lobed, blunt-toothed, often folded along main veins; basal leaves long-stalked.
Fruit: nutlets, arranged in circle, covered by network of ridges, sharp-angled.

nutlets

Common Mallow

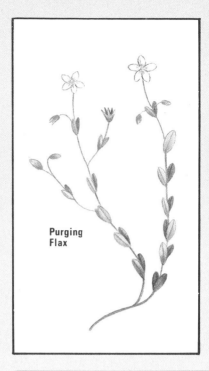

Purging
Flax

GERANIUM FAMILY
Geraniaceae

Many species in the Geranium family have long, soft hairs, and the flowers are usually brightly coloured, with 5 petals. The seeds of the characteristic fruit are arranged around the base of the stiff, persistent style.

HERB ROBERT
Geranium robertianum
The stem and leaves of Herb Robert are hairy and often turn bright red. The plant grows 10-50 cm high, is branched and erect or straggling. If bruised, it smells unpleasant. It is most often found in hedgerows but also grows among rocks, on walls and in woodland.
Flower: bright pink-mauve, 2 cm across, long-stalked; petals 5, narrowed at base; sepals erect, with bristle-like tips; stamens 10, anthers orange or purple.
Flower arrangement: in pairs.
Flowering time: May-September.
Leaf: in 3 main segments, each deeply and repeatedly dissected; long-stalked.
Fruit: arranged around base of stiff, persistent style to which fruits are attached by thin strands.

COMMON STORK'S-BILL
Erodium cicutarium
This plant looks rather similar to Herb Robert but differs in the clustered flowers, the pinnate leaf-segments and the spiralling strands attached to the fruits. The stem and leaves are slightly to very hairy. The plant grows up to 60 cm high in dry, open places, particularly near the sea.
Flower: bright rose-purple; petals 5, 12-14 mm across, upper 2 sometimes with black spot at base, especially on plants growing inland; sepals spreading, not erect, with bristle-like tips.
Flower arrangement: 3-12 flowers in umbel-like cluster.
Flowering time: June-September.
Leaf: doubly pinnate.
Fruit: arranged around base of stiff, persistent style to which fruits attached by thin, spiralling strands.

Herb
Robert

Common
Stork's-bill

Right: Herb Robert (Geranium robertianum) *was formerly used as a medicinal plant to treat disorders of the blood and to heal cuts. Because of the Doctrine of Signatures, the red colour of the plant was associated with blood.*

WOOD SORREL FAMILY
Oxalidaceae

The flowers in this family have 5 petals and 10 stamens. The family is mainly distributed in the tropics. Some *Oxalis* species are grown as ornamentals in gardens, and a few have edible tubers. The leaflets of the Clover-like leaves often fold down at night or in cold weather.

WOOD SORREL
Oxalis acetosella

A small plant of woodland and shaded hedgebanks, Wood Sorrel has leaves composed of 3 leaflets, like Clover leaves but a paler, more delicate green. In cold weather and at night the leaves fold down. The stem creeps, bearing the long-stalked leaves and flowers in small clusters. Although Wood Sorrel contains oxalic acid, livestock rarely eat sufficient quantities for it to prove fatal.
Flower: white, lilac-veined, bell-shaped, nodding; petals 5, 8-15 mm long; sepals 5.
Flower arrangement: solitary.

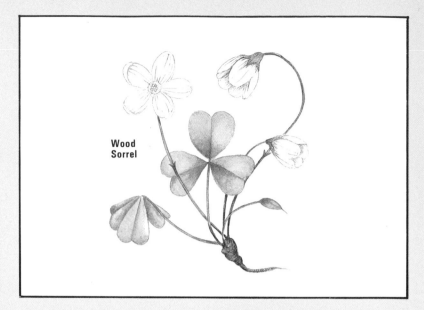

Wood Sorrel

Flowering time: April-May.
Leaf: in 3 rounded, notched leaflets, pale yellow-green.
Fruit: capsule, rounded, 5-angled, 3-4 mm long; seeds light brown.

BALSAM FAMILY
Balsaminaceae

The Balsams are hairless plants with juicy, easily broken, translucent stems often with stalked, sticky glands. The flowers are irregular in shape, with 5 petals forming a broad lip, a hood and a curved spur behind. Typically the flower dangles from the flower stalk. The fruits explode on being touched. The house plants known as Busy Lizzies (*Impatiens* species) are in this family.

INDIAN BALSAM
Impatiens glandulifera

Introduced as a garden plant from the Himalayas in 1839, and naturalized along waterways and in waste places, this tall, stout-stemmed species grows 100-200 cm high. It is hairless and the stems reddish. There is no mistaking the rather Orchid-like, mauve, dangling flowers.
Flower: purplish pink, 2·5-4 cm, petals 5, forming a broad, lower lip and hood; sepals 3, lower forming a mauve, spurred bag.
Flower arrangement: long-stalked racemes arising from leaf-axils.
Flowering time: July-October.
Leaf: opposite or in threes, 5-18 cm long, elliptic, toothed; reddish glands along basal margins.
Fruit: capsule, club-shaped, opening by 5 valves which spring into coils, shooting out seeds.

Indian Balsam

PEA FAMILY
Leguminosae

The flowers in this very large family are easily recognizable, being composed of an upright 'standard' petal, 2 side 'wing' petals and a pair of fused, boat-shaped petals under the standard, as in the Sweet Pea. The 5 sepals are fused into a calyx tube, and stamens and style are usually enclosed by the petals. The flowers are loosely clustered or in small, dense heads. Leaves are usually alternate and pinnate, sometimes with a tendril, or with 3 leaflets. The fruit is typically a pod and many important food crops such as soybeans and peas belong to this family. Clover and Lucerne are very widely grown as fodder and green manure. The roots form nodules which contain nitrogen-fixing bacteria and act as a natural fertilizer.

GORSE
Ulex europaeus

Gorse is a spiny shrub which can cover large areas of heath and rough grassland. Its golden, scented flowers are favoured by bees. On being touched, the flowers explode pollen onto the visiting insect.
Flower: golden yellow, about 1·5 cm, on short, velvety stalks; calyx yellowish, 2-lipped, hairy.
Flower arrangement: in leaf-axils toward ends of shoots.
Flowering time: mainly in spring or late winter.
Leaf: a stiff, branched spine, 1·5-2·5 cm long, deeply grooved, slightly grey-green.
Fruit: pod, black, 11-20 mm long, hairy, barely longer than the calyx, bursting open when ripe to expel seeds.
Uses: an old use for Gorse was as a fuel and, after crushing, as fodder.

BROOM
Sarothamnus scoparius

A shrub similar to Gorse but without spines, the Broom grows up to a height of 2 m. The twigs are 5-ridged and hairless. The flowers respond to the landing of visiting insects by expelling pollen onto their undersides. The shrub is found on heaths, mountains and dunes, and in woods.
Flower: golden-yellow, about 2 cm, on stalks up to 1 cm; style forming loop; calyx 2-lipped, hairless.
Flower arrangement: solitary or in pairs in leaf-axils.
Flowering time: May-June.
Leaf: composed of 3 elliptic leaflets, short-stalked or stalkless, slightly hairy.
Fruit: pod, black, 2·5-4 cm long; hairs on margins only.
Uses: the shoots are still used to stimulate urine production, and the long, supple branches were made into brooms for sweeping.

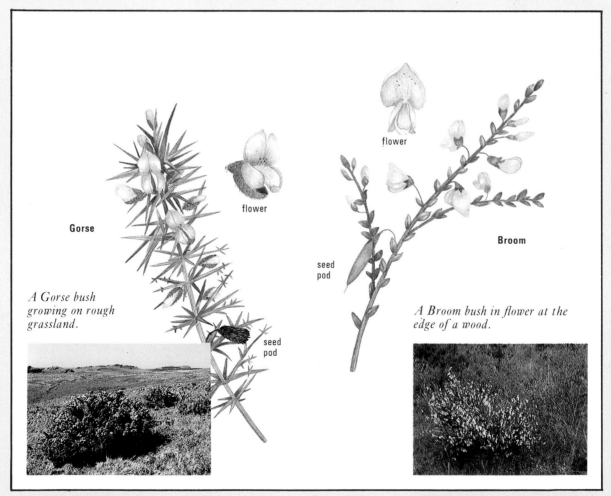

Gorse

flower

seed pod

A Gorse bush growing on rough grassland.

flower

Broom

seed pod

A Broom bush in flower at the edge of a wood.

COMMON REST-HARROW
Ononis repens
A shrubby, hairy plant of 40-70 cm, this species is prostrate, often with upturned tips bearing the pink flowers. The stems are hairy all round and the roots are long and very tough. The plant grows in rough grassland and dunes.
Flowers: pink, 1·5-2 cm long, on shortly hairy stalks; wing petals as long as keel; calyx tube with 5 long teeth, densely hairy.
Flower arrangement: in the leaf-axils.
Flowering time: June-September.
Leaf: 1-3 leaflets, oval, finely toothed, hairy, short-stalked; stipules 3-5 mm, finely toothed, clasping stem at base.
Fruit: pod, hidden by calyx.

COMMON BIRD'S-FOOT TREFOIL
Lotus corniculatus
This plant is usually almost hairless and grows in grassland. Plants growing on the coast may have small, fleshy leaves. The stems, 5-35 cm long, are prostrate, turning up at the tips.
Flowers: yellow, often tinged or streaked with red, 1-1·5 cm long; petals 2 or 3 times as long as calyx-tube.
Flower arrangement: 2-7 flowers in outward-facing ring on erect stalk up to 8 cm.
Flowering time: June-September.
Leaf: of 5 elliptic or almost circular leaflets, each 3-10 mm long, rounded at tip or with a short point; short leaf-stalk often between lower and upper leaflets.
Fruit: pod, 1·5-3 cm long, cylindrical, straight; seeds many.

BLACK MEDICK
Medicago lupulina
The leaves of Black Medick are Clover-like and the flowers yellow. The plant is sprawling, 5-50 cm high and downy, growing in open places such as roadsides, cultivated fields and at the coast.
Flower: bright yellow, 2-3 mm.
Flower arrangement: grouped into small, round heads 3-8 mm across, on stalks longer than the leaf-stalks.
Flowering time: April-August.
Leaf: of 3 leaflets, each narrowed towards base, finely toothed, often shallowly notched at tip in which is a minute bristle; stipules finely toothed.
Fruit: tightly curved disc, about 2 mm across, containing 1 seed, covered by network of ridges.
Uses: this Medick is sometimes grown for fodder.

RED CLOVER
Trifolium pratense
Red Clover grows erectly 5-100 cm high in grassland, and is more or less hairy.
Flower: pink-purple; individual flowers 15-18 mm long.
Flower arrangement: in compact,

Common Rest-harrow

Common Bird's-foot Trefoil

Black Medick

rounded or ovoid heads of 2-4 cm.
Flowering time: May-September.
Leaf: of 3 elliptic leaflets, each 1-3 cm long, often with pale crescent, usually rounded at tips; leaf-stalk up to 20 cm; pair of short-stalked leaves immediately below flower head; stipules conspicuous, joined up the leaf-stalk, with 2 free points, each ending in bristle.
Fruit: pod, about 2 mm.
Uses: a variety with hollow stems is widely grown for fodder.

WHITE CLOVER
Trifolium repens
A very familiar little plant of grassland, including lawns and verges. The stems of White Clover creep along the ground rooting at intervals. The plant is hairless and may grow as long as 50 cm.
Flower: white or pink-tinged, scented, individual flowers 8-13 mm, turning down and becoming brown from base of head upwards; calyx-tube white, green-veined with narrow, pointed teeth.
Flower arrangement: round head on long, grooved stalk.
Flowering time: June-September.
Leaf: of 3 rounded leaflets, minutely toothed, each 1-3 cm long, each often with pale crescent; stipules joined, sheathing stem, with 2 free points.
Fruit: pod, hidden by dead flower.
Uses: bees use the nectar to produce clover honey, and several varieties are grown for fodder.

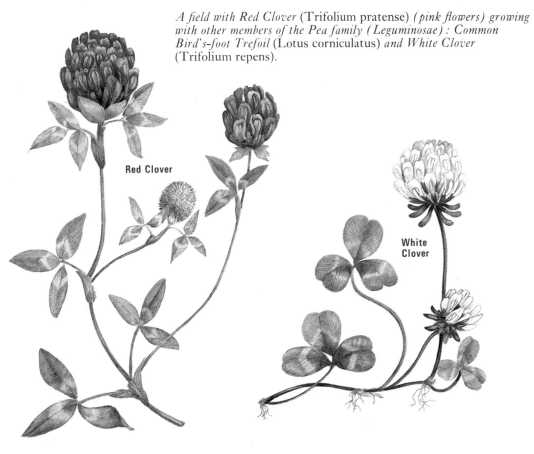

A field with Red Clover (Trifolium pratense) *(pink flowers) growing with other members of the Pea family (Leguminosae): Common Bird's-foot Trefoil* (Lotus corniculatus) *and White Clover* (Trifolium repens).

Red Clover

White
Clover

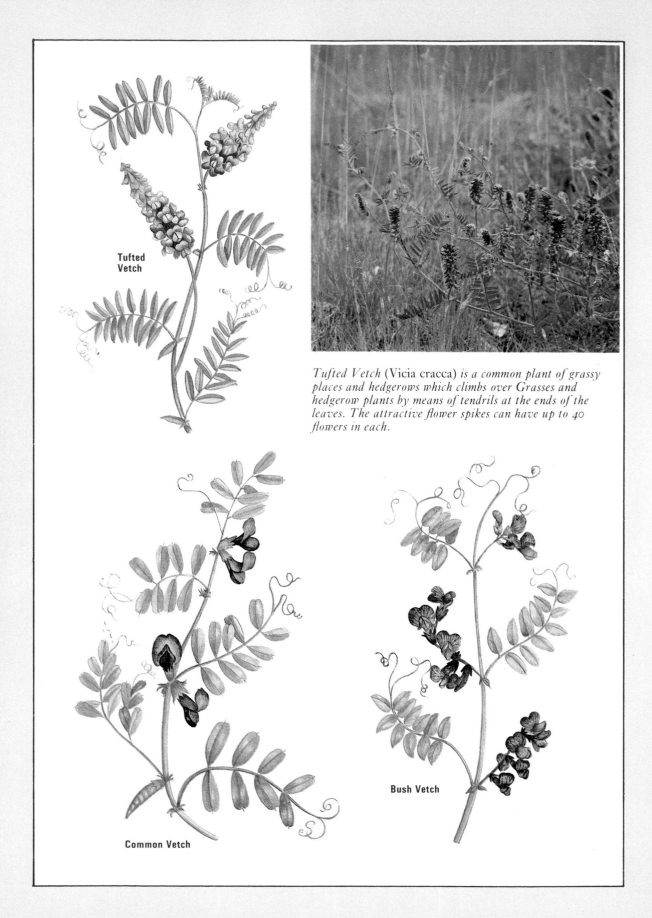

Tufted Vetch

Tufted Vetch (Vicia cracca) *is a common plant of grassy places and hedgerows which climbs over Grasses and hedgerow plants by means of tendrils at the ends of the leaves. The attractive flower spikes can have up to 40 flowers in each.*

Bush Vetch

Common Vetch

TUFTED VETCH
Vicia cracca

Tufted Vetch is a weak-stemmed plant which gains support by clambering over other vegetation. It is 60-200 cm long, slightly hairy and grows in hedges and bushy places. The long, crowded racemes of flowers are characteristic of this species.

Flower: blue-purple, 8-12 mm long, each drooping on short stalk; style equally hairy all round; upper teeth of calyx-tube minute; lower teeth about as long as calyx-tube.

Flower arrangement: dense raceme of 10-40 flowers on stalk 2-10 cm long.

Flowering time: June-August.

Leaf: pinnate, with 6-15 pairs of narrow leaflets, each 1-2·5 cm long, pointed or with minute bristle; leaf ends in branched tendril; stipules untoothed.

Fruit: pod, brown, hairless, 1-2·5 cm long; seeds 2-6.

COMMON VETCH
Vicia sativa

The Common Vetch is a slightly hairy plant, scrambling or climbing in hedges or grassy places. It can grow up to 120 cm.

Flower: purplish red, 1-3 cm long; calyx teeth about equal.

Flower arrangement: solitary or in pairs, on very short stalks or stalkless.

Flowering time: May-September.

Leaf: pinnate, with 3-8 pairs of narrow leaflets, each 1-2 cm long, often wider at tip than base, with minute bristle, notched or pointed; tendrils branched or not; stipules toothed or not, often with dark spot.

Fruit: pod, 2·5-8 cm long, yellow-brown to black, hairless or slightly hairy; seeds 4-12.

Uses: a form of this Vetch is often grown as a fodder crop.

BUSH VETCH
Vicia sepium

Climbing or scrambling in grassy or bushy places, the Bush Vetch grows 30-100 cm long. The leaves and stem have short hairs or are almost hairless.

Flower: pale purple, 1-1·5 cm; lower calyx teeth much shorter t han calyx-tube, and tips curving toward each other.

Flower arrangement: raceme of 2-6 flowers, very shortly stalked.

Flowering time: May-August.

Leaf: pinnate, with 3-9 pairs of leaflets, each 1-3 cm long, variably shaped; tips rounded or pointed, with or without minute bristle at centre of slight notch at leaflet-tip; tendrils branched; stipules sometimes toothed, with black spot.

Fruit: pod, 2-3·5 cm long, black, hairless; seeds 3-10.

MEADOW VETCHLING
Lathyrus pratensis

This Vetchling, with or without short hairs, scrambles over vegetation in grassy or bushy places. It is 30-120

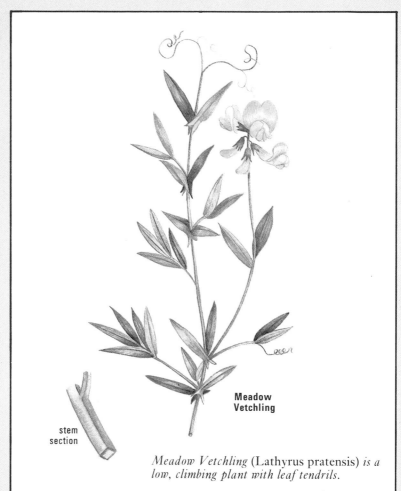

Meadow
Vetchling

stem
section

Meadow Vetchling (Lathyrus pratensis) *is a low, climbing plant with leaf tendrils.*

cm in length and has a sharply angled stem.

Flower: yellow, 10-18 mm long; teeth of calyx-tube narrowly tri-angular.

Flower arrangement: raceme of 5-12 flowers on long stalk.

Flowering time: May-August.

Leaf: 1-2 pairs of narrow, pointed leaflets, 1-3 cm long; tendril branched or not; stipules leaf-like, 1-2·5 cm, arrow-shaped.

Fruit: pod, 2-4 cm long, black; seeds 5-12.

Dog
Rose

A Dog Rose adds colour to a hedgerow on chalk downland.

ROSE FAMILY
Rosaceae

This ancient family is among the more primitive of the flowering plant families. The flowers are often conspicuously coloured, but very rarely blue. The regular, unspecialized flowers attract a wide range of insects. There are 5 petals and many stamens. The fruits are varied and include achenes, follicles and the commercially very important tree fruits – apples, pears and plums. The popular modern roses of gardens are complicated hybrids, far removed from their wild ancestors.

DOG ROSE
Rosa canina
The Dog Roses are extremely variable shrubs, 1-3 m high, with stems that arch and scramble in hedgerow and scrub. The prickles are hooked.
Flower: pink or white, 4-5 cm across; petals 5, notched; sepals 5, lobed, falling before fruit ripens; stamens many; stigmas in a head.
Flower arrangement: cluster of 1-4 flowers, stalks hairless.
Flowering time: June-July.
Leaf: pinnate, with 2-3 pairs of elliptic, toothed, usually hairless leaflets; stipules joined to leaf-stalk.
Fruit: rose hip, scarlet, about 1·5-2 cm long, spherical or ovoid.
Uses: jelly and syrup may be made from the fruit, which is rich in vitamin C. More than 500 tons of hips were collected in Britain in 1943 as part of the war effort, to provide children with rose-hip syrup.

BRAMBLE
Rubus fruticosus
The stems of these woody shrubs often arch over, rooting at the tip and bearing hooked prickles, some of which may be straight. The Brambles are extremely variable. About 2,000 micro-species may be recognized in the *Rubus fruticosus* group. This huge number is thought to have arisen by a combination of hybridization and self-fertilization.
Flower: pink or white, 2-3 cm across; petals 5; stamens many.
Flower arrangement: solitary or clustered.
Flowering time: May-September.
Leaf: of 3-5 toothed leaflets.
Fruit: the 'blackberry'.
Uses: blackberries have been eaten and enjoyed for thousands of years. Healing powers were associated with the leaves and stems, mainly for relieving burns and swellings.

Bramble

A Bramble (Rubus fruticosus), *showing the curving branches which climb over surrounding shrubs or give the characteristic domed shape to bushes which grow in the open.*

137

Water Avens

flower

lower leaf

Wood Avens

lower leaf

WATER AVENS
Geum rivale

A plant of shady, wet places and cleared woodland, the Water Avens is 20-60 cm high and shortly hairy. The flowers may easily be overlooked due to their nodding habit.

Flower: orange-pink, nodding; petals 5, 1-1·5 cm long, shallowly notched, abruptly narrowed at base; sepals purple, 5 as long as petals alternating with 5 shorter; stamens many; styles many, in central tuft.
Flower arrangement: few-flowered cyme.
Flowering time: May-September.
Leaf: pinnate, with 3-6 pairs of toothed leaflets; end leaflets enlarged, more or less rounded; leaf-stalk long; upper leaves smaller with fewer leaflets.
Fruit: head of achenes; styles persistent, becoming hooked; dispersed by clinging to fur of passing animals.

WOOD AVENS or HERB BENNETT
Geum urbanum

Growing erect in shady places, the Wood Avens is 20-60 cm tall and shortly hairy. Where Wood Avens and Water Avens grow together, hybrids between the two often occur.

Flower: yellow, 10-18 mm across; petals 5, oval; sepals 10, 5 as long as petals, alternating with 5 shorter; stamens many; styles many, in central tuft.
Flower arrangement: long-stalked, few-flowered cyme.
Flowering time: June-August.
Leaf: basal leaves pinnate, stalked, with 2-3 pairs of toothed leaflets, 5-10 mm long; end leaflet enlarged; stipules leaf-like.
Fruit: head of hooked achenes, dispersed by catching on clothing of passers-by and fur of animals.
Uses: the roots are said to smell and taste of cloves and were used to flavour ale.

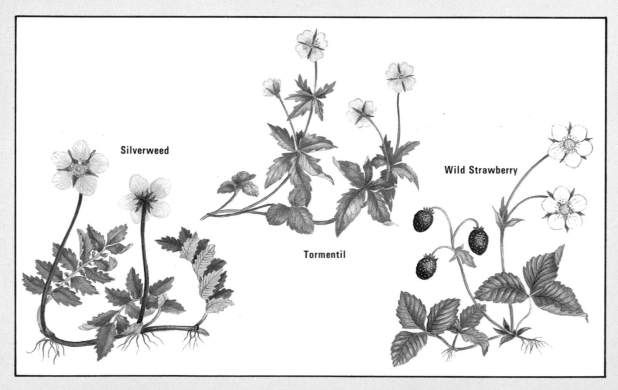

Silverweed

Wild Strawberry

Tormentil

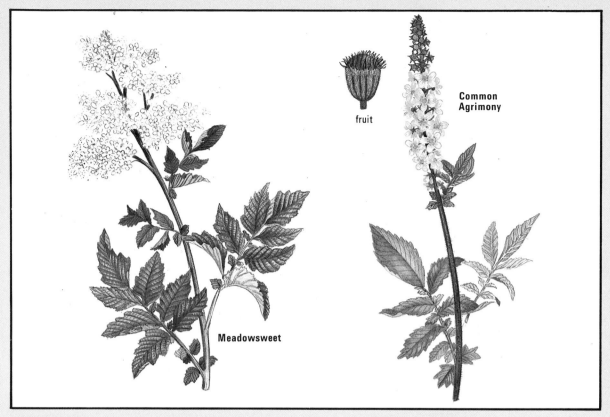

fruit

Common Agrimony

Meadowsweet

SILVERWEED
Potentilla anserina
The name describes the silvery, silky hairs with which this plant is covered. The leaves form a rosette from which creep rooting runners up to 80 cm long. The plant grows in damp roadside places and meadows.
Flower: yellow, 1·5-2·0 cm across; petals 5, rounded; sepals 10, in 2 layers, outer layer toothed and half as long as petals; stamens many.
Flower arrangement: solitary, on long stalk.
Flowering time: June-August.
Leaf: pinnate, 5-25 cm, with 7-12 pairs of deeply toothed leaflets, alternating with much smaller leaflets; dense, silver, silky hairs beneath or silky both sides.
Fruit: achenes hairless, in a head.
Uses: the fleshy roots were eaten in the poorer parts of Britain as a vegetable or made into meal for bread and porridge.

TORMENTIL
Potentilla erecta
Erect or creeping but not rooting, Tormentil is 10-30 cm high. It grows in grassland and may be found on mountains to a height of about 1,000 m.
Flower: yellow, 7-11 mm across; petals 4, shallowly notched, longer than sepals; sepals 8; stamens many.
Flower arrangement: on long slender stalks in loose cymes.
Flowering time: June-September.

Leaf: of 3 toothed segments; stalked basal leaves in rosette, often withering before flowering; stem leaves stalkless with large, toothed, leaf-like stipules (leaf appearing 5-segmented).
Fruit: achenes, hairless, in a head.

WILD STRAWBERRY
Fragaria vesca
This plant grows 5-30 cm high, with long runners which root and form new plants. It grows in woods and on hedgebanks. The Alpine Strawberry is a form of the Wild Strawberry.
Flower: white, 12-18 mm across; petals 5, rounded, not notched, edges touching or overlapping; sepals 10, in 2 layers; stamens many.
Flower arrangement: long-stalked cyme; stalk hairs lie flat.
Flowering time: April-July.
Leaf: divided into 3 toothed segments, each 1-6 cm long, ovate, bright green, paler with silky hairs beneath; leaf-stalks long, hairy.
Fruit: strawberry.
Uses: although the fruits are smaller than the cultivated strawberry, their flavour makes them very good to eat.

MEADOWSWEET
Filipendula ulmaria
This is a rather tall, erect plant, 60-200 cm high, of wet places, including damp meadows. The small, cream-coloured flowers with long stamens are in frothy, irregular masses. The stems are often reddish.
Flower: cream, scented, 4-10 mm across; stamens many, twice length

of petals.
Flower arrangement: in loose, irregular masses.
Flowering time: June-September.
Leaf: pinnate, with 2-5 pairs of large, ovate, toothed leaflets with small leaflets between; usually white, downy beneath.
Fruit: carpels becoming twisted together to form achene about 2 mm.
Uses: Meadowsweet was formerly used against malaria when forms of that disease were common in undrained lowland areas.

COMMON AGRIMONY
Agrimonia eupatoria
This is an erect plant, 30-60 cm high, with a slender spike of yellow flowers above and densely leafy below. The reddish stems have long hairs, and the plant favours dry roadsides and field edges.
Flower: yellow, 5-8 mm across; petals 5; sepals 5, hairy; ring of hooked bristles immediately below; stamens many.
Flower arrangement: slender spike.
Flowering time: June-August.
Leaf: pinnate, with 3-6 pairs of toothed, elliptic leaflets, 2-6 cm long; hairy, greyish beneath, not glandular; smaller leaflets between; stipules leaf-like.
Fruit: grooved; top covered with hooked bristles which point forward; dispersed by catching onto clothing, or fur of passing animals.

STONECROP FAMILY
Crassulaceae

Members of this family are adapted to dry habitats such as walls and stony places, and have fleshy, hairless stems and leaves. The leaves are often closely spaced, and regeneration from fallen buds or leaves is common. The small flowers are of 5 pointed petals and sepals, and the fruits are clusters of follicles containing tiny seeds.

BITING STONECROP
Sedum acre
Growing in mats on dry, stony or sandy ground or on walls, the Biting Stonecrop gets its name from the burning taste of its small, fleshy leaves.
Flower: bright yellow, star-shaped, about 12 mm across; petals 5, pointed; sepals 5; stamens 10.
Flower arrangement: at the ends of the branches.
Flowering time: June-July.
Leaf: very fleshy, hairless, rounded, 3-6 mm long, overlapping on non-flowering shoots.
Fruit: group of spreading follicles.

ORPINE
Sedum telephium
Orpine is a fleshy, hairless, upright plant, 20-60 cm tall, with slightly grey-green leaves and a stem often tinged red. Although native in European woods and hedges, it may also be found as a garden escape.
Flower: red-purple, star-shaped, 9-12 mm across; petals 5, pointed; sepals 5; stamens 10.
Flower arrangement: in dense clusters at the top of the stems.
Flowering time: July-September.
Leaf: fleshy, oval, alternate, up to 8 cm long, stalkless or shortly stalked, irregularly toothed.
Fruit: group of follicles.

GRASS-OF-PARNASSUS FAMILY Parnassiaceae

There is only one European species in this family. The plant name was first used by a Flemish botanist in the 16th century, who identified it as the Grass-of-Parnassus of Dioscorides, the founder of medicine according to ancient Greek mythology.

GRASS-OF-PARNASSUS
Parnassia palustris
The habitat of this very pretty, slightly grey-green plant is wet moorland and bogs. The plant is hairless, growing in a loose tuft and 5-40 cm high, the white, veined flowers smelling faintly of honey.
Flower: white, 1·5-3 cm across; petals 5, clearly veined, oval; sepals 5; fertile stamens 5; infertile stamens fan-shaped, lying against petals.
Flower arrangement: solitary.
Flowering time: July-October.
Leaf: all basal, heart-shaped, stalked, except for single, stalkless leaf about a third of the way up flower stem.
Fruit: capsule, opening by 4 valves.

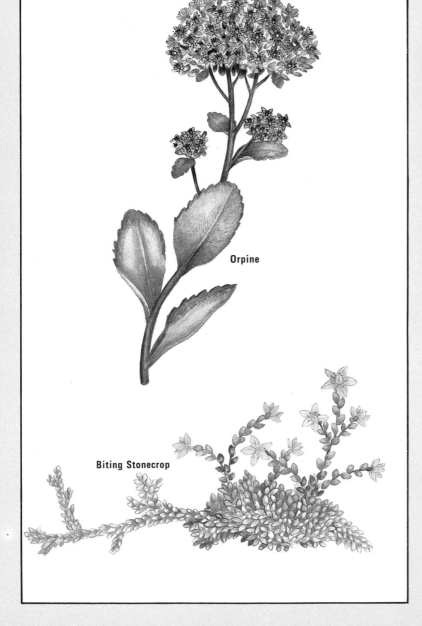

Orpine

Biting Stonecrop

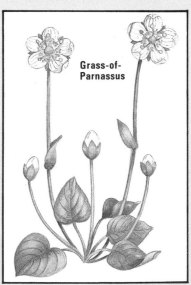

Grass-of-Parnassus

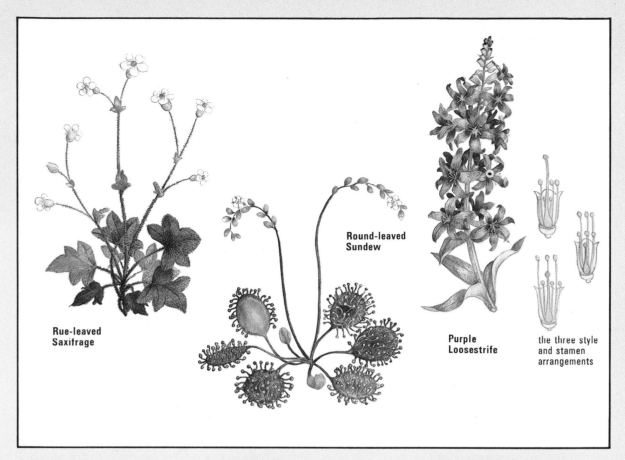

Rue-leaved
Saxifrage

Round-leaved
Sundew

Purple
Loosestrife

the three style
and stamen
arrangements

SAXIFRAGE FAMILY
Saxifragaceae

Many species of Saxifrage are short, mountain plants and several are commonly grown in gardens. The flowers have 5 petals and sepals and 10 stamens. The alternate leaves often form rosettes.

RUE-LEAVED SAXIFRAGE
Saxifraga tridactylites
This is a slender, often red-tinged plant of 3-8 cm, though sometimes taller, often branched and covered in sticky hairs. In sunshine the ring-shaped nectaries at the flower centres exude glistening nectar. Although this Saxifrage inhabits mainly dry walls in lowland areas, many others are mountain-dwellers.
Flower: white, 4-6 mm across; petals 5, rounded; sepals 5, joined at base, erect; stamens 10; nectary yellow, ring-shaped.
Flower arrangement: loose cyme.
Flowering time: April-June.
Leaf: 3-5-lobed; basal leaves not forming rosette, often withered at flowering time.
Fruit: 2-lobed capsule; seeds brown.

SUNDEW FAMILY
Droseraceae

As well as the Sundews, this family of insectivorous plants includes the Venus Fly Trap. Sundews have long, sticky glands on the leaves, which trap insects and digest them with secreted enzymes. This may be a response to a lack of nitrogen in the boggy, waterlogged conditions in which these plants grow.

ROUND-LEAVED SUNDEW
Drosera rotundifolia
Stalked, sticky red glands on the leaves of this little plant often lend a red tinge to the ground of bogs and wet moors where it grows. Insects stick to the glands which slowly bend toward the leaf centre, further enmeshing the insect. Eventually the prey is digested and the glands return to their former positions.
Flower: white, 5 mm across; petals 5 or 6.
Flower arrangement: spike, slender, on long stalk.
Flowering time: June-August.
Leaf: circular, long-stalked, in a rosette, upper surface covered in sticky, red, stalked glands.
Fruit: capsule.

LOOSESTRIFE FAMILY
Lythraceae

This is a small family of plants which favour damp places. The flowers have 4-6 petals which are crumpled in bud. Some species in this family produce dyes, one of the best known being henna.

PURPLE LOOSESTRIFE
Lythrum salicaria
This is an erect plant, 50-150 cm tall with a 4-angled stem and varying from almost hairless to densely hairy. It is found in damp places such as river banks. The flowers are insect-pollinated and are of 3 kinds, differing in the relative lengths of their styles and stamens. Each plant bears only one kind of flower.
Flower: red-purple, 1-1·5 cm across; petals 6, flimsy; calyx tubular, ribbed, with 12 teeth; stamens 12.
Flower arrangement: in whorls on a tall spike.
Flowering time: June-August.
Leaf: opposite or in threes; narrow, pointed, without teeth, 4-7 cm long, stalkless.
Fruit: capsule, ovoid, enclosed by calyx.

WILLOWHERB FAMILY
Onagraceae

This family is widespread throughout the world and includes some shrubs and water plants as well as such garden ornamentals as the Evening-primroses (*Oenothera* species). The flowers have 4 petals, which may be formed into a tube as in Fuchsias. There are commonly 8 stamens and the stigma is 4-lobed or undivided. Many are pollinated by moths. The fruit is usually a capsule.

ROSEBAY WILLOWHERB
Epilobium angustifolium
The tall, almost hairless plants are up to 120 cm high. In Britain a century ago this species was confined to certain localities but has since spread widely. It has a preference for burnt ground, and covered bombed sites in World War II.

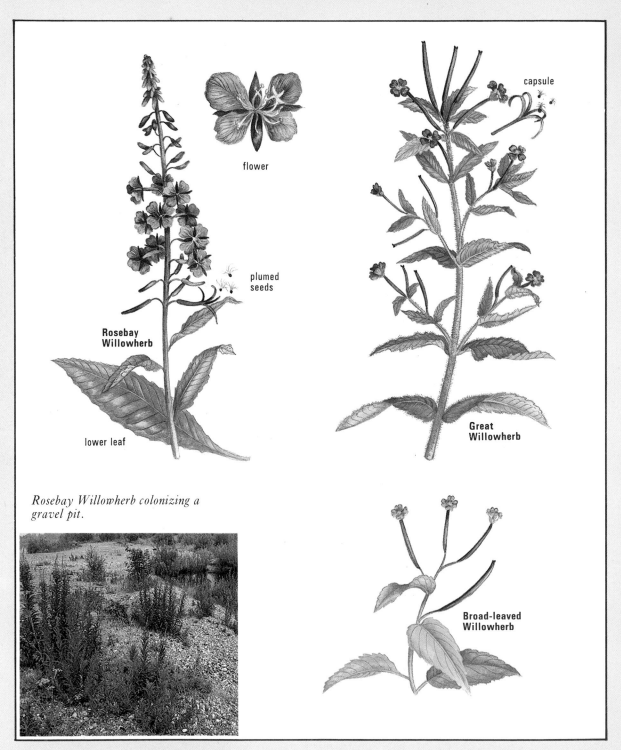

flower

plumed seeds

Rosebay Willowherb

lower leaf

capsule

Great Willowherb

Rosebay Willowherb colonizing a gravel pit.

Broad-leaved Willowherb

Flower: rosy-purple, 2-3 cm across; petals 4, upper 2 slightly larger; sepals 4, narrow, purple; stamens 8; stigma 4-lobed.
Flower arrangement: raceme, long, many-flowered.
Flowering time: July-September.
Leaf: narrow, pointed, alternate, 5-20 cm long, entire or with small, widely spaced teeth.
Fruit: capsule, long (2·5-8 cm), narrow, opening by 4 long slits, downy; seeds with plume of hairs.

GREAT WILLOWHERB
Epilobium hirsutum
This Willowherb is tall, up to 150 cm, erect and densely covered in soft hairs. It often forms stands in moist places such as marshes and stream-sides. It is absent from N.W. Scotland and most of Sweden and Norway.
Flower: deep purplish pink, 1·5-2·5 cm across; petals 4, notched; sepals 4, erect, pointed; stamens 8; stigma cream-coloured, 4-lobed; buds erect.
Flower arrangement: raceme, flower stalks arising from leaf-axils.
Flowering time: July-August.
Leaf: rather narrow, opposite, pointed, teeth curved forward; stalkless, leaf base weakly clasping stem.
Fruit: capsule, long (5-8 cm), narrow, opening by 4 long slits, downy; seeds with plume of hairs.

BROAD-LEAVED WILLOWHERB
Epilobium montanum
This is a small, sparsely hairy plant. The stems are erect, 20-60 cm high and reddish. It is found in gardens as a weed, and in woods, hedges and stony places.
Flower: pale mauve, 6-9 mm across; petals 4, notched; sepals 4, erect, pointed; stamens 8; stigma 4-lobed; buds nodding.
Flower arrangement: raceme, flower stalks arising from leaf-axils.
Flowering time: June-August.
Leaf: ovate, opposite, toothed, shortly stalked.
Fruit: capsule, long (4-8 cm), narrow, opening by 4 longitudinal slits, downy; seeds with plume of hairs.

ENCHANTER'S NIGHTSHADE
Circaea lutetiana
Standing 15-70 cm high, this shade-loving plant of woods and gardens often grows in patches. The stem and leaves have scattered glandular hairs.
Flower: white or pink-tinged, 4-8 mm; petals 2, deeply notched, appearing as 4; sepals 2, glandular, hairy; stamens 2.
Flower arrangement: raceme.
Flowering time: June-August.
Leaf: opposite, ovate, sparsely toothed, 4-10 cm long, stalked, dull above, shiny beneath.
Fruit: rounded, covered with hooked bristles, 2-4 mm; stalks turning down; dispersed by clinging to fur of small animals, especially cats.

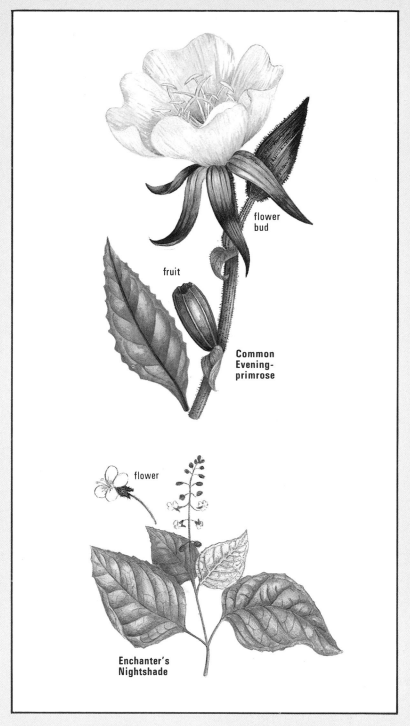

flower bud

fruit

Common Evening-primrose

flower

Enchanter's Nightshade

COMMON EVENING-PRIMROSE
Oenothera biennis
This species grows 50-150 cm high. The stems are stout and often shortly hairy. The flowers open at dusk and exude scent to attract pollinating moths. Evening-primroses were originally introduced from N. America. This one occurs on dunes and in dry, waste places.
Flower: yellow, 5-6 cm across; petals 4, broadly heart-shaped; sepals 4, narrow, tapered to point, bent sharply down; stamens 8; stigma deeply 4-lobed.
Flower arrangement: raceme, flower stalks arising from leaf-axils.
Flowering time: June-September.
Leaf: elliptic, alternate, sparsely toothed, stalkless or shortly stalked, main vein becoming reddish.
Fruit: capsule, 3-3·5 cm long, opening by 4 valves; seeds angled.

IVY FAMILY
Araliaceae

This is a family of mainly tropical herbs, shrubs and trees. The small flowers are green or white. The fruits are small drupes borne in clusters. Many climbing species have modified aerial roots. Ginseng *(Panax quinquefolium)*, a tropical plant, is one of the few commercially important members of this family.

IVY
Hedera helix
The familiar, evergreen Ivy climbs to 30 m on trees, cliffs and buildings. Short, thick roots up one side of the stem help it to cling to a support. It may also be found carpeting the ground in woods.
Flower: yellow-green; petals 5, 3-4 mm long, pointed; calyx with 5 tiny teeth; stamens 5; style surrounded by nectar-secreting disc.
Flower arrangement: in rounded, umbel-like clusters on unshaded, high parts of plant.
Flowering time: September-November.
Leaf: glossy, stalked, of 2 kinds: those on non-flowering branches 3-5-lobed, those on the flowering not lobed, ovate or more or less diamond-shaped.
Fruit: black, berry-like, 8-10 mm.

MARE'S TAIL FAMILY
Hippuridaceae

There is only one species, *Hippuris vulgaris,* in this family. Despite being distributed throughout the wet parts of the northern temperate regions of the world, it varies very little from one locality to another. The flower has a single stamen and one carpel.

MARE'S TAIL
Hippuris vulgaris
Growing 25-75 cm high in still or slow-moving fresh water, the unbranched shoots of Mare's Tail bear many whorls of narrow leaves. The leaves are flattened, not tubular as in the superficially similar Horsetails, which are relatives of the ferns.
Flower: inconspicuous, without petals, greenish, wind-pollinated.
Flower arrangement: in the leaf-axils of aerial shoots.
Flowering time: June-July.
Leaf: very narrow, 1-7·5 cm long, in whorls, stalkless; submerged leaves very thin, pale, limp.
Fruit: nut, green, 2-3 mm.

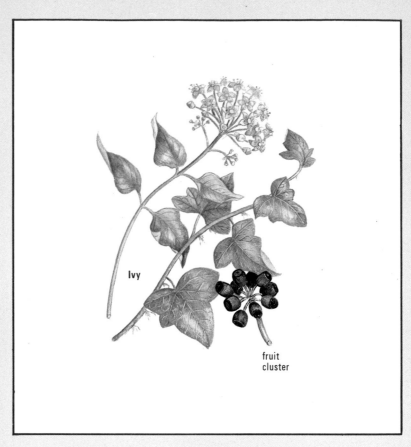

Ivy

fruit cluster

Mare's Tail

Water-starwort

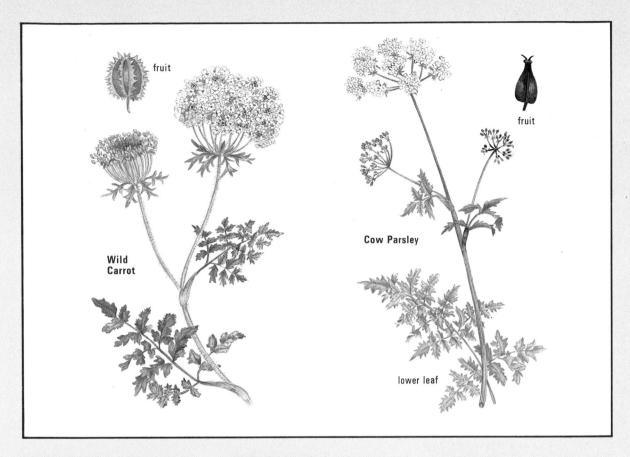

fruit

Wild Carrot

Cow Parsley

fruit

lower leaf

STARWORT FAMILY
Callitrichaceae

The Starwort family consists of one genus of 17 species. They are small, slender water plants. Some species grow and are pollinated underwater, some grow in or beside water and others only on wet mud. The flowers are minute and unisexual.

WATER-STARWORT
Callitriche stagnalis
These small, hairless water plants may be found creeping and rooting on wet mud, or floating or submerged in ponds, streams or lakes. The stems grow 1-25 cm long on land and to 100 cm in water. The species in this aggregate group are extremely variable and difficult to separate. Leaf shape depends on whether the plants are submerged or not and on water depth and movement.
Flower: inconspicuous, green, without petals, unisexual.
Flower arrangement: in leaf-axils.
Flowering time: April-October.
Leaf: oval or strap-shaped, opposite, often forming rosettes at tips of emerging shoots.
Fruit: 4-lobed.

CARROT FAMILY
Umbelliferae

Among the most easily recognizable features of this large family is the arrangement of tiny flowers in umbels. These are flat-topped clusters of flowers, with the bases of the stalks (*rays*) all joining at one point. Many species have compound umbels. These are umbels formed, in turn, of smaller umbels. Bracts may be present at the base of a compound (*primary*) umbel and smaller bracts (*bracteoles*) at the bases of the individual (*secondary*) umbels. The fruits and bracts are important for identification.
There are many herbs and spices in the family, including parsley, fennel and dill, as well as many poisonous plants.

WILD CARROT
Daucus carota
The Wild Carrot usually has stiffly hairy stems, ridged, not hollow and 30-100 cm high. It grows in grassy places, and at the coast. The middle flower of each umbel is often red. The widely cultivated carrot with a swollen edible tap root is a form of the Wild Carrot.
Flower: white, middle flower of umbel often red; petals 5, tips incurved; petals of outer flowers enlarged.
Flower arrangement: compound umbel, 3-7 cm across; rays many; bracts conspicuous, each of 3 or more long points; bracteoles similar.
Flowering time: June-August.
Leaf: finely dissected, often fleshy if growing by the sea.
Fruit: ovoid; ridges spiny; 2-4 mm; umbel becoming hollow in fruit.

COW PARSLEY
Anthriscus sylvestris
One of the commonest white-flowered umbels, Cow Parsley is also among the earliest to flower. A tall, slightly downy plant, it grows up to 150 cm high in hedges and wood borders. The stems are hollow, grooved and may be tinged red.
Flower: white, 3-4 mm across; petals 5, tip often slightly notched and curved inward.
Flower arrangement: in compound umbels, 2-6 cm across; no bracts; bracteoles 5 or 6.
Flowering time: April-June.
Leaf: 2- or 3-pinnate, up to 30 cm long, shortly hairy beneath, leaf-stalk sheathing stem at base.
Fruit: of 2 oblong, joined carpels, black, smooth, 5-10 mm, each bearing short, persistent style.

BURNET SAXIFRAGE
Pimpinella saxifraga

This species has a downy and tough but slender stem, weakly ridged. It grows 30-100 cm high in dry grassland, very often on chalk or limestone. The seed of a Mediterranean species of Pimpinella is the aniseed of seed cake and sweets.
Flower: white, 2 mm across; petals 5, tips incurved.
Flower arrangement: compound umbel, 2-5 cm across, flat-topped; rays 10-20; no bracts or bracteoles.
Flowering time: July-August.
Leaf: pinnate; leaflets ovate, coarsely toothed, stalkless; upper leaves doubly pinnate, leaflets narrow.
Fruit: ovoid, 2-3 mm.

HEMLOCK
Conium maculatum

Hemlock is extremely poisonous in all parts. It can be recognized by the smooth, purple-spotted stem and a 'mousy' smell if the plant is crushed. The hairless plant grows up to 2·5 m in damp habitats, near water and on waste land.
Flower: white, 2 mm across; petals 5, tips shortly incurved.
Flower arrangement: compound umbel, 2-5 cm across; rays 10-20; bracts 5-6; bracteoles on outer sides of secondary umbels.
Flowering time: June-July.
Leaf: finely dissected, up to 30 cm.
Fruit: spherical, 2·5-3·5 mm, ridges bumpy.
Uses: traditionally this was the drug used to poison Socrates. Medicinal use of Hemlock was revived in the late 18th century but discontinued due to the uncertain effects.

WILD ANGELICA
Angelica sylvestris

Often stout and up to 200 cm or more high, this Umbellifer is almost hairless. It favours damp, shady places. The hollow, grooved stem is often purple with a whitish cast or bloom.
Flower: white or pink, 2 mm across; petals 5, incurved.
Flower arrangement: compound umbel, rounded, 3-15 cm across; rays many, slightly hairy; few or no bracts; bracteoles few, bristle-like.
Flowering time: July-September.
Leaf: doubly or trebly pinnate; leaflets 2-8 cm, ovate, toothed, leafstalks deeply grooved on upper side, widely sheathing stem at base.
Fruit: ovoid, 4-5 mm, flattened, winged; persistent styles curved.

LESSER WATER-PARSNIP
Berula erecta

These hairless plants, 30-100 cm high, grow in shallow fresh water, often forming sprawling masses. The stems are hollow and ridged. Fool's Water-cress (*Apium nodiflorum*) is similar to this species. They cannot easily be told apart unless flowers or fruit are present.
Flower: white, 2 mm across; petals 5, tips incurved.
Flower arrangement: compound umbel, 3-6 cm across, on long stalk; rays 10-20; bracts and bracteoles many, often with a few teeth.
Flowering time: July-September.
Leaf: pinnate, up to 30 cm long; 7-14 pairs ovate, toothed leaflets; dull, blue-green.
Fruit: 2-lobed, 1·5-2 mm, a little wider than high; persistent styles curved.

GROUND ELDER
Aegopodium podagraria

The leaves of Ground Elder have broad, undissected leaflets, unlike the finely dissected leaves of many other Umbellifers. The plant is hairless, with hollow, grooved stems, and grows in shady places and gardens, where it can be a stubborn weed.
Flower: white, sometimes pink, 1 mm across; petals 5, tips incurved.
Flower arrangement: in compound umbels, 2-6 cm across; rays 15-20; few or no bracts or bracteoles.
Flowering time: May-July.
Leaf: of 3 leaflets, each 4-8 cm, ovate, toothed, on long, 3-angled leaf-stalk sheathing stem at base.
Fruit: ovoid, 4 mm, ridged; persistent styles curved down.

HOGWEED
Heracleum sphondylium

The stout stem of Hogweed is grooved, hollow and stiffly hairy, the hairs bent sharply down. The plant is found in grassland, hedges and woods, growing 50-200 cm high. The Giant Hogweed (*H. mantegazzianum*) is up to 3·5 m and has a red-blotched stem.
Flower: white or pink, 5-10 mm across; petals 5, incurved, enlarged in outer flowers.
Flower arrangement: compound umbel, 5-15 cm across; rays 7-20, few or no bracts; bracteoles bristle-like.
Flowering time: June-September.
Leaf: pinnate, 15-60 cm; leaflets broad, toothed and lobed, stiffly hairy; bases of stalks widely sheathing stem.
Fruit: ovoid, flattened, whitish, 7-8 mm; persistent styles short, curved.
Uses: the leaves are fed to pigs.

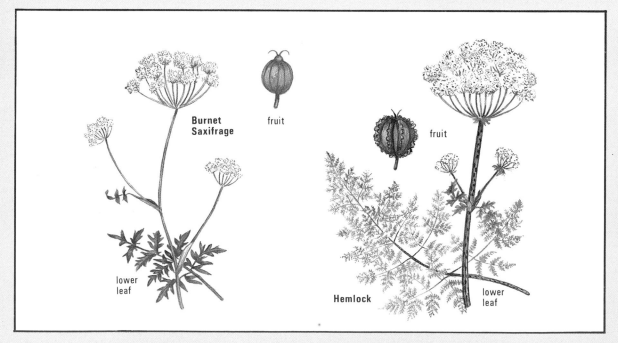

Burnet Saxifrage · fruit · lower leaf · Hemlock · fruit · lower leaf

fruit

Wild Angelica

fruit

Ground Elder

lower leaf

lower leaf

fruit

Hogweed

fruit

Lesser Water-parsnip

lower leaf

147

Sea Spurge (Euphorbia paralias) *sharing a stony beach with other seaside plants.*

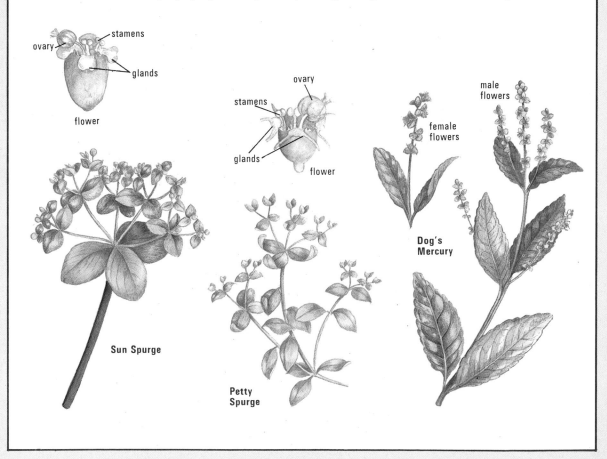

male flowers

Hop

fruit

female flower

A Hop (Humulus lupulus) *climbing on Hawthorn* (Crataegus monogyna) *in a hedge. The stems are covered with hooked hairs, which help the plant to climb since it has no tendrils. Male and female flowers are on separate plants.*

SPURGE FAMILY
Euphorbiaceae

This large, mainly tropical family includes species which produce rubber and castor oil. The Spurges have very distinctive flowers without petals, consisting of a little cup in which are several stamens and a single style and ovary. Glands around the rim attract insects. Poisonous, sometimes milky, sap is characteristic of the family.

SUN SPURGE
Euphorbia helioscopia
The whole plant is hairless, 10-50 cm high and erect. The characteristic yellowish bracts of the flowers lend a yellow-green look to the plant. The stem is often red and if broken exudes white latex containing irritant poison. Disturbed ground is the habitat of this Spurge.
Flower: minute; glands on rim green; kidney-shaped, surrounded by yellowish, leaf-like bracts.
Flower arrangement: in umbel-like, 5-stalked clusters.
Flowering time: May-October.
Leaf: rounded, lower leaf often tapering at base; minutely toothed, alternate.
Fruit: capsule, smooth, 3-5 mm, stalked, nodding over rim of flower; seeds brown, wrinkled.

PETTY SPURGE
Euphorbia peplus
Growing 10-30 cm high in cultivated ground, the Petty Spurge is hairless and light green. The minute flowers are surrounded by leaf-like bracts. If broken the plant oozes white latex, which can irritate the skin.
Flower: minute; glands on rim crescent-shaped with long, pointed tips, surrounded by opposite, leaf-like bracts.
Flower arrangement: flower stalks repeatedly dividing in two.
Flowering time: April-November.
Leaf: oval, not toothed, alternate.
Fruit: capsule, ridged, 2 mm, stalked, nodding over rim of flower; seeds pale grey, pitted.

DOG'S MERCURY
Mercurialis perennis
Poisonous to humans and livestock, Dog's Mercury is erect, up to 40 cm, unbranched and shortly hairy. The plant smells unpleasant if crushed, and grows in woods and shady places. The spikes of inconspicuous flowers open in spring, each plant bearing either all-male or all-female flowers. The very similar species, Annual Mercury (*M. annua*), differs by being hairless and summer-flowering.
Flower: inconspicuous, green; male and female on separate plants.
Flower arrangement: males in slender spikes, females in small, stalked clusters.
Flowering time: February-April.
Leaf: elliptic, blunt-toothed, opposite, 2-8 cm long, shortly stalked.
Fruit: spherical, hairy, 6-8 mm.

HEMP FAMILY
Cannabiaceae

There are two main divisions in this family. One contains the Hops. The other contains species used for their plant fibre (hemp) and the drug cannabis. The flowers are either male or female, borne on separate plants.

HOP
Humulus lupulus
The Hop is found climbing with rough stems in hedges and, although native in N. Europe, is often an escape from cultivation. The 'cones' of pale bracts on the female plants are easy to recognize.
Flower: males and females on separate plants; females enclosed by yellow-green bracts; males tiny, green; petal-like lobes 5.
Flower arrangement: female bracts in hanging 'cone'; male flowers in branched clusters.
Flowering time: July-August.
Leaf: 3-5 lobed, coarsely toothed, roughly hairy, opposite, 10-15 cm, yellow glands dotting underside.
Fruit: enclosed by enlarged bracts dotted with yellow resin glands.
Uses: the female 'cones' are used to flavour beers. Cultivation of Hops began in Britain in about 1520, earlier in the rest of Europe.

ochrea

fruit

Black
Bindweed

Knotgrass

land
form

Amphibious
Bistort

Redshank

water surface

DOCK FAMILY
Polygonaceae

Most members of this large family are from northern temperate areas. Useful species include Rhubarb and Buckwheat. The leaves have a characteristic papery sheath called an *ochrea* encircling the stem at the leaf-base. The small flowers have no true petals and are white, green or pink. The fruit, enclosed by the persistent flower, is important in identification.

AMPHIBIOUS BISTORT
Polygonum amphibium
The stems and leaves of this water plant float on the surface of still or slow-moving water. The stems grow 30-75 cm long and root along their length. A slightly differing form, with short, stiff hairs on the leaves and ochreae, grows at the water's-edge and in damp grassland.
Flower: pink; petal-like lobes 5; stamens 5, red.
Flower arrangement: dense, short spike, 2-4 cm long, stalked.
Flowering time: July-September.
Leaf: long—ovate, hairless, shiny stalked, alternate; ochreae hairless (leaves and ochreae hairy in land form).
Fruit: nut, shiny, brown.

KNOTGRASS
Polygonum aviculare
Knotgrass is a ragged-looking species, erect (up to 2 m high) or straggling in mats on trampled ground and at the coast. The plant is hairless and branched, and the ochreae are ragged and silvery.
Flower: pink or white; petal-like lobes 5.
Flower arrangement: 1-6 flowers in the leaf-axils.
Flowering time: July-October.
Leaf: elliptic to very narrow, tips more or less pointed, almost stalkless; leaves on main stem larger than branch leaves; ochreae silvery, torn.
Fruit: nut, 3-angled, hidden by dead flower.

BLACK BINDWEED
Polygonum convolvulus
The grooved stem of the climbing Black Bindweed twines clockwise around its support to a height of 30-120 cm. It grows on waste or cultivated land.
Flower: greenish white; petal-like lobes 5, 3 outer with ridge; each flower stalk 1-2 mm, jointed above middle.
Flower arrangement: loose spike or raceme in the leaf-axils.
Flowering time: July-October.
Leaf: spear-shaped, stalked, powdery white beneath, usually alternate; ochrea rim at an angle.
Fruit: nut, dull, black, enclosed by persistent flower.

REDSHANK
Polygonum persicaria
The stem, often reddish, is more or less erect, branched and 25-80 cm high. There are dense spikes of tiny pink flowers, and the leaves often bear a dark blotch. The whole plant is almost hairless and grows on waste and cultivated ground.
Flower: pink; petal-like lobes 5.
Flower arrangement: compact spike, up to 3·5 cm long.
Flowering time: June-October.
Leaf: narrow, tapering to point, often dark-blotched, alternate, margin fringed with hairs; ochreae brownish, fringed with hairs.
Fruit: nut, black, shiny.

COMMON SORREL
Rumex acetosa
Growing up to 100 cm but usually much smaller, this almost hairless plant grows in grassland, to which the flowers and fruits can give a reddish tinge.
Flower: green and red, tiny; male and female flowers on separate plants; wind-pollinated.
Flower arrangement: in whorls on branched raceme.
Flowering time: May-July.
Leaf: spear-shaped, basal lobes pointing down, acid-tasting, up to 10 cm long; upper leaves almost stalkless; ochreae fringed.
Fruit: 3-4 mm, with 3 papery wings, tinged red, enclosing 3-angled nut.
Uses: a sharp-tasting sauce, to be eaten with fish or pork, can be made from the leaves simmered in butter with salt and black pepper.

BROAD-LEAVED DOCK
Rumex obtusifolia
This is a very common Dock, 50-120 cm high, of waste places and cultivated land. There are several similar species of dock which can be distinguished by their fruits.
Flower: green, tiny, wind-pollinated.
Flower arrangement: in whorls, on branched raceme.
Flowering time: June-October.
Leaf: oblong, broad, tip pointed or rounded, lobed at base, alternate, up to 25 cm long, minutely blunt-toothed, often hairy on underside.
Fruit: 5-6 mm, with 3 green, deeply toothed wings alternating with 3 unequal red swellings enclosing 3-angled nut.
Uses: traditionally Dock leaves are rubbed on Nettle stings to reduce irritation.

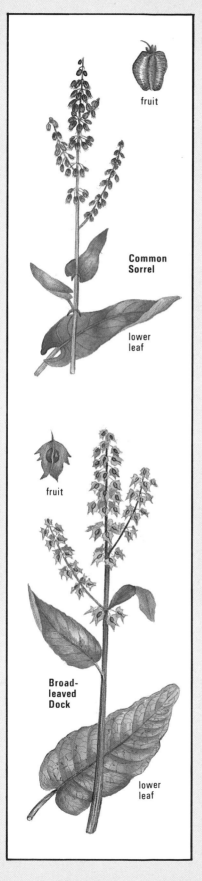

fruit

Common Sorrel

lower leaf

fruit

Broad-leaved Dock

lower leaf

Common
Nettle

NETTLE FAMILY
Urticaceae

Stinging hairs crop up in many members of this family, including some Australian tree species. The flowers are inconspicuous and without petals. The stamens are flicked out as the flowers open, expelling pollen in puffs.

COMMON NETTLE
Urtica dioica
Notoriously covered in stiff, stinging hairs, the Common Nettle grows 30-150 cm high in waste places and woods. When touched, the hair-tip breaks off. The remaining hollow hair injects the skin with fluid containing an irritant poison. It is a major foodplant for the caterpillars of many butterflies.
Flower: green, tiny; male and female flowers on separate plants; wind-pollinated.
Flower arrangement: in loose hanging spikes in leaf-axils.
Flowering time: June-August.
Leaf: ovate, toothed, opposite, 4-8 cm long; lower leaves longer than their stalks.
Fruit: achene.
Uses: this unpromising plant has been made into nettle beer and in World War II the tough plant fibres were made into textiles.

THRIFT FAMILY
Plumbaginaceae

Many members of this family, such as the Thrifts and Sea Lavenders, grow on the coast and elsewhere in dry or salty conditions. The remainder are alpine and arctic species. The flowers are surrounded by papery bracts and have parts arranged in groups of 5 – 5 sepals, 5 petals, 5 anthers and 5 fused ovaries.

THRIFT
Armeria maritima
Thrift forms cushions of narrow leaves and pink flowers mainly in rocky places at the sea-side, in salt marshes, or inland on mountains and sandy places.
Flower: pale to deep pink; petals 5.
Flower arrangement: in dense, rounded head, 1·5-2·5 cm across; bracts below, greenish; flower stalk 5-30 cm high, surrounded by brown, papery sheath above.
Flowering time: April-October.
Leaf: grass-like, slightly fleshy, hairy or not, 2-15 cm long, up to about 4 mm wide.
Fruit: surrounded by papery calyx.

Thrift

Thrift (Armeria maritima) growing in a dense clump at the top of a coastal cliff. The fleshy leaves appear bluish-green because they have a thick coat of wax to protect against salt spray. Thrift is often grown in gardens, and the dried flower heads are used in flower arranging.

Lowland heaths and upland moors often support a thick, springy carpet of Heath and Heather.

flower

Heather

Bilberry

flower

berries

HEATHER FAMILY
Ericaceae

Members of this large family are found throughout almost the entire world. As well as the Heathers and Heaths, the family also includes the Rhododendrons. The members range from small to large shrubs with evergreen, often needle-like leaves. Many are partly dependent on soil fungi, which grow within their roots and help the plants to absorb nutrients from the acidic soils in which they usually grow. The flowers have 4 or 5 petals fused along part or all of their length, often forming a bell-shaped flower.

HEATHER
Calluna vulgaris
This low-growing, wiry shrub grows 15-80 cm high, preferring acid soil and carpeting large tracts of heath, moor and open woods. Heather differs from the similar species of Heath in that the flower petals are not joined into a bell and the leaves are opposite, not whorled.
Flower: mauve, scented; petals 4, hidden by 4 petal-like sepals, about 4 mm long.
Flower arrangement: spikes, 3-15 cm.
Flowering time: July-September.
Leaf: needle-like, opposite, pressed to stem, 1-3·5 mm long, overlapping on short, side shoots.
Fruit: capsule.
Uses: hives of bees are kept on Heather moors in late summer, the resulting honey being particularly good. Heather also feeds sheep and shelters red grouse.

BILBERRY
Vaccinium myrtillus
A low, hairless shrub 15-35 cm high, the Bilberry is known for its sweet, black berries. It grows in woods, and on moors and mountains to an altitude of over 1,200 m. The twigs are 3-angled and green.
Flower: pink, tinged green; petals joined into a globe shape, 4-6 mm.
Flower arrangement: solitary or paired.
Flowering time: April-June.
Leaf: ovate, tip pointed, minutely toothed, bright green, short-stalked, alternate, 1-3 cm long.
Fruit: berry, blue-black, edible.
Uses: the berries are worth the labour of gathering. If too bitter for eating raw then they make good tarts and jam.

Lesser
Periwinkle

PERIWINKLE FAMILY
Apocynaceae

Members of this large family are mainly tall rain-forest trees of the tropics, some of which have buttresses at the base of the trunk. The rest are shrubs and woody climbers, or herbs in northern Europe, with a milky, often poisonous latex, used in the tropics to tip arrows for hunting.

LESSER PERIWINKLE
Vinca minor
This species has long been grown in gardens. It has escaped and become naturalized in shady places and is truly native only in part of N. Europe. It is an evergreen plant with long, rooting stems of 30-60 cm covering the ground.
Flower: blue-purple or white, 2·5-3 cm across; petals 5, wide and blunt at tip, joined at base; calyx tube 5-toothed, hairless.
Flower arrangement: solitary, stalked, in leaf-axil.
Flowering time: March-May.
Leaf: elliptic, opposite, glossy, hairless, short-stalked.
Fruit: pair of follicles, rarely ripening in Britain, forked at tip.
Uses: Periwinkle wreaths were used in ancient ceremonies, especially at the funerals of children.

PRIMROSE FAMILY
Primulaceae

This is a large family, mainly from the northern hemisphere, in which are many garden ornamentals, such as the Primulas. Many species have flowers with either long styles (*pin-eye*), where the stigma shows in the throat of the flower, or short styles (*thrum-eye*), where the stigma does not show (see facing page).

COWSLIP
Primula veris
Cowslip is only locally common and is decreasing owing to the ploughing of old pasture where it grows. The plants are 5-30 cm high.
Flower: pale or deep yellow, orange in throat, nodding; petals joined at bases into tube with 5 notched lobes; calyx tubular, pale green, 5-toothed.
Flower arrangement: 1-30 flowers in umbel-like cluster on shortly hairy stalk, 10-30 cm high.
Flowering time: April-May.
Leaf: oblong, rounded at tip, abruptly narrowed into stalk, wrinkled, shortly hairy all over.
Fruit: capsule, ovoid, hidden by calyx.

PRIMROSE
Primula vulgaris
Less common in some areas than formerly, the well-loved Primrose has suffered much uprooting by 'gardeners'. The plants grow in grassy places, woods and hedges, flowering before the trees come into leaf and shade the ground.
Flower: pale yellow, deep yellow in throat, 2-3 cm across; petals joined at bases into tube with 5 spreading, notched lobes; calyx tubular, 5-toothed.
Flower arrangement: solitary on long, softly hairy stalks.
Flowering time: December-May.
Leaf: oblong, tip rounded, tapering gradually at base into stalk, wrinkled, shortly hairy beneath.
Fruit: capsule, ovoid, enclosed by calyx.

SCARLET PIMPERNEL
Anagallis arvensis
One of the very few scarlet-flowered plants native to N. Europe, the Scarlet Pimpernel grows 6-30 cm on cultivated ground. The stems are square in section and prostrate.
Flower: scarlet or salmon pink, rarely blue, up to 14 mm across; petals 5, more or less rounded; sepals 5, sharply pointed.
Flower arrangement: on thin stalks, longer than leaves, arising from each leaf-axil.
Flowering time: June-August.
Leaf: ovate, pointed, opposite, stalkless, black glands beneath.
Fruit: capsule, spherical, with persistent style, splitting around middle.
Uses: the flowers can be used to tell the time and approaching weather. They open from about 8 am to 3 pm and close in the damp, cool air of impending rain.

YELLOW LOOSESTRIFE
Lysimachia vulgaris
The tall, erect, shortly hairy plants of Yellow Loosestrife grow 60-150 cm high. They are found along riversides and other damp places. This species is absent from N. Scotland, Sweden and much of Norway.
Flower: yellow, about 1·5 cm across; petals 5; sepals 5, orange-margined.
Flower arrangement: in loose, branched heads.
Flowering time: July-August.
Leaf: long, narrow, pointed, in pairs or whorls of 3 or 4; stalkless, dotted with black glands.
Fruit: capsule, spherical, opening by 5 valves.

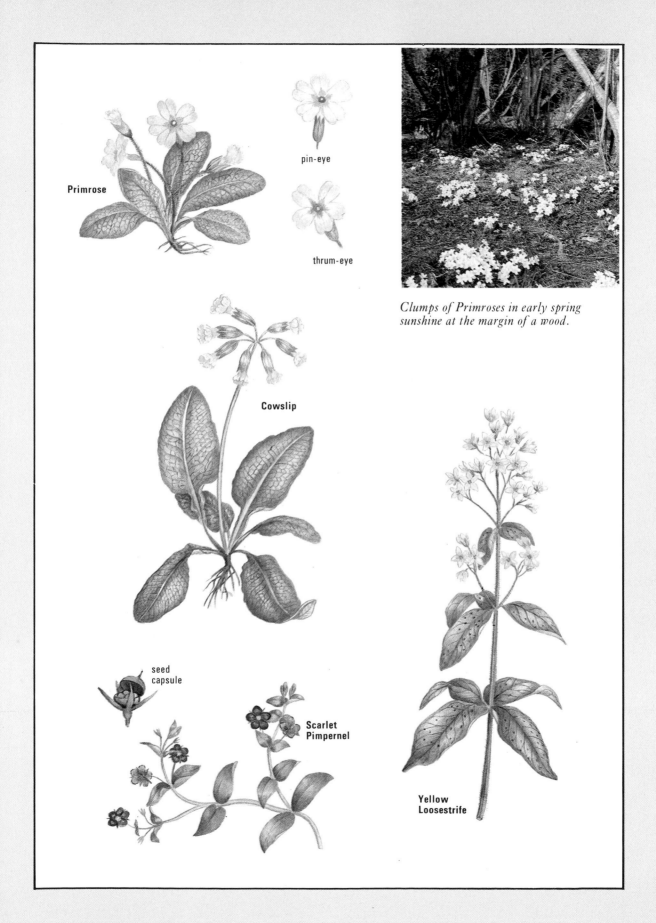

Primrose

pin-eye

thrum-eye

*Clumps of Primroses in early spring
sunshine at the margin of a wood.*

Cowslip

seed
capsule

**Scarlet
Pimpernel**

**Yellow
Loosestrife**

GENTIAN FAMILY
Gentianaceae

Many of the species in this family grow in arctic regions and on mountains. The flowers, of 5 joined petals, are often blue, bell-shaped and erect. The Gentian family is one in which a fungus commonly lives within the roots, benefitting both plant and fungus. The bitter roots have been much used medicinally and in the French aperitif, Suze.

COMMON CENTAURY
Centaurium erythraea
Common Centaury varies between 2 and 50 cm high, with a branched stem bearing flat clusters of pink flowers. It is a hairless plant growing in dry grassland and dunes. It is absent from much of Scotland and Scandinavia.
Flower: rose-pink, 1-1·5 cm across; petals joined into tube below; lobes 5, spreading flat; calyx with 5 long, narrow teeth.
Flower arrangement: in more or less flat-topped clusters.
Flowering time: June-October.
Leaf: opposite, basal leaves in rosette; elliptic, tip rounded or pointed, stalkless.
Fruit: capsule.
Uses: Common Centaury has been called Gall of the Earth due to its bitterness. A tonic can be made from an infusion of dried plants.

FIELD GENTIAN
Gentianella campestris
Absent from much of southern Britain and the Low Countries, the Field Gentian inhabits grassland and dunes. The erect, sometimes branched stem is 10-30 cm high.
Flower: blue-purple; tube yellow-green, 1·5-2·5 cm long; petals joined into 4-lobed tube, fringed within; calyx of 4 unequal lobes, larger pair almost enclosing smaller.
Flower arrangement: clustered on stalks arising from leaf-axils.
Flowering time: July-October.
Leaf: ovate, opposite, stalkless, hairless.
Fruit: capsule, narrow.
Uses: this Gentian has been used in Sweden as a substitute for hops in beer-making.

FORGET-ME-NOT FAMILY
Boraginaceae

Members of this family are almost always hairy, often stiffly so. The blue or mauve, sometimes white, flowers are very often pink in bud and arranged in one-sided racemes which uncoil as the flowers open.

FIELD FORGET-ME-NOT
Myosotis arvensis
The particular characteristics of this shortly hairy Forget-me-not are the concave petals and small flowers (5 mm or less). The plant grows 15-30 cm high in drier places than most other Forget-me-nots, such as roadsides and fields.
Flower: pale blue, yellow in throat, up to 5 mm across; petals joined into tube at base; lobes 5, concave; calyx 5-toothed with hooked hairs; buds pink.
Flower arrangement: cyme, uncoiling as flowers open, without bracts.
Flowering time: April-September.
Leaf: ovate to lanceolate, tips rounded or pointed; lower leaves shortly stalked, forming rosette; upper leaves stalkless.
Fruit: 4 nutlets, brown, shiny, enclosed by calyx.

WATER FORGET-ME-NOT
Myosotis scorpioides
Growing in damp or wet places, this Forget-me-not has a slightly ridged, hairy stem, 15-45 cm high, the base of which often creeps and roots. The important characteristics of this species are the flower size and the notched petal-lobes.
Flower: sky-blue, yellow in throat, 4-10 mm across; petals joined into tube at base; lobes 5, shallowly notched; calyx 5-toothed with straight hairs; buds pink.
Flower arrangement: cyme, uncoiling as flowers open, without bracts.
Flowering time: May-September.
Leaf: oblong, usually rounded at tip, stalkless, shortly hairy or almost hairless.
Fruit: 4 nutlets, black, shiny, enclosed by calyx.

VIPER'S BUGLOSS
Echium vulgare
An erect, stout plant, 20-90 cm tall and densely covered in stiff, whitish hairs with swollen bases, Viper's Bugloss has bright blue flowers, pink in bud, forming an exciting colour combination. It grows in dry places.
Flower: bright blue, 1-2 cm; petals joined into tube at base; 5-lobed; calyx 5-toothed; stamens 5, 4 protruding.
Flower arrangement: a spike of short, curved or coiled cymes.

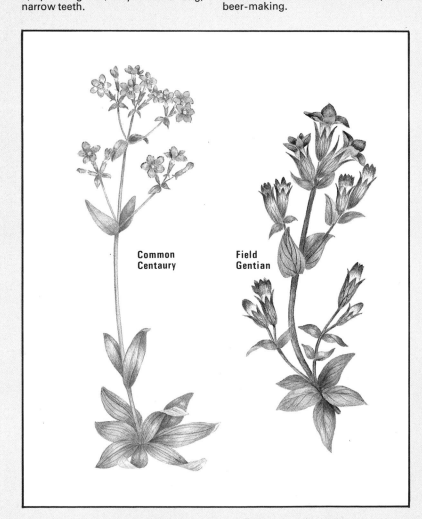

Common
Centaury

Field
Gentian

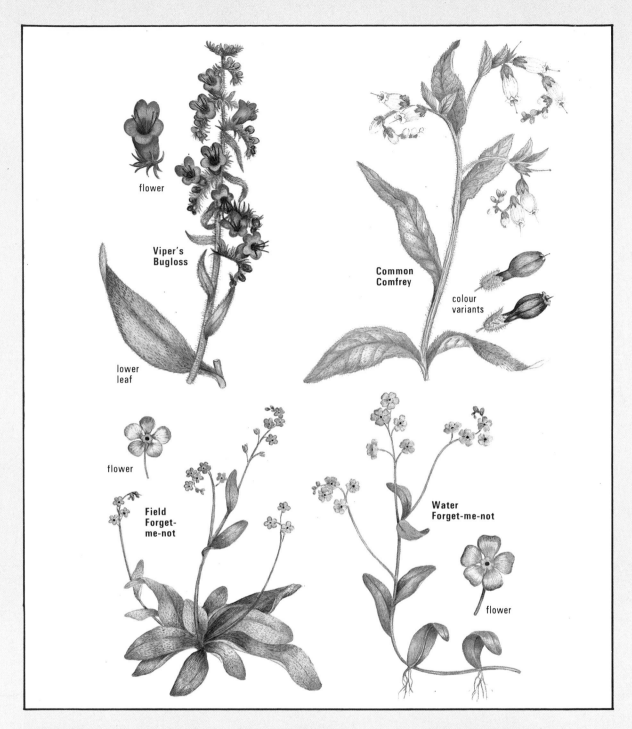

flower

Viper's Bugloss

lower leaf

Common Comfrey

colour variants

flower

Field Forget-me-not

Water Forget-me-not

flower

Flowering time: June-September.
Leaf: lanceolate, tapering gradually to base, up to 15 cm long, stalkless, lowest shortly stalked.
Fruit: 4 nutlets, enclosed by calyx.
Uses: this plant was linked from ancient Greek times with snakes. The nutlet, supposed to resemble a snake's head, was consequently used to treat snake bite.

COMMON COMFREY
Symphytum officinale
Common Comfrey is a branched, stout, stiffly hairy plant of 30-120 cm. The stem has thin prominent ridges, and the plant grows in damp places.
Flower: cream, white, pink or purple, 15-17 mm long; petals joined into tube with 5 short lobes at rim; calyx 5-toothed; style protruding from petal-tube.
Flower arrangement: in nodding cymes, uncoiling as flowers open.

Flowering time: May-June.
Leaf: ovate to lanceolate, tip pointed, bases running down stem in thin, often wavy ridges.
Fruit: 4 nutlets, black, shiny, enclosed by calyx, style persistent.
Uses: in Bavaria the young leaves are fried in batter. Manure water to feed tomato or marrow crops can also be made by soaking Comfrey plants in water for a week. The resulting water is rich in potassium.

Field
Bindweed

Hedge
Bindweed

Sea Bindweed

BINDWEED FAMILY
Convolvulaceae

The flowers in this family are bell- or trumpet-shaped on stems which often climb by twining. The sap is quite often milky and, in some cases, has been used medicinally. The fruits are usually capsules which split open to release the seeds.

FIELD BINDWEED
Convolvulus arvensis
The invasive roots make this little creeping or climbing plant a stubborn weed of farm and garden. The stem coils anti-clockwise around other plants.
Flower: pink or white, striped darker outside, trumpet-shaped, 1·5-3 cm across, scented; sepals 5, rounded.
Flower arrangement: 1-3 flowers on long stalk with 2 small bracts half-way up.
Flowering time: June-September.
Leaf: arrow-shaped, 2-5 cm long, stalked, shortly hairy or not.
Fruit: capsule, spherical.

HEDGE BINDWEED
Calystegia sepium
This climbing Bindweed covers such supports as railings and hedges with a blanket of arrow-shaped leaves and large, white trumpet-shaped flowers. These are visited at dusk by hawk moths. The stems grow 1-3 m long, twisting anti-clockwise, and contain milky sap.
Flower: white, trumpet-shaped, 3-7 cm across, scentless; sepals 5, enclosed by 2 slightly longer bracts.
Flower arrangement: solitary, on long stalks.
Flowering time: July-September.
Leaf: arrow-shaped, up to 15 cm long, stalked, shortly hairy or not.
Fruit: capsule, enclosed by bracts.

SEA BINDWEED
Calystegia soldanella
The stems of this small plant creep along the sand or pebbles of the beach. It grows 10-60 cm long and is hairless.
Flower: pink or mauve, trumpet-shaped, 5 paler stripes within, 2·5-4 cm across; sepals 5, almost enclosed by 2 large bracts.
Flower arrangement: solitary, on long, 4-angled stalks.
Flowering time: June-August.
Leaf: kidney-shaped, rather thick.
Fruit: capsule, enclosed by bracts.

BOGBEAN FAMILY
Menyanthaceae

This is a small family of water plants in which the 5 white, pink or yellow flower petals are often hairy.

BOGBEAN
Menyanthes trifoliata
The leaves and beautiful fringed, pink and white flowers of this hairless water plant are borne above the surface of shallow water, the stems creeping through the mud. It is found in marshes, lake-edges and upland pools.
Flower: pink, paler within, about 1·5 cm across; petals 5, covered in long, white hairs, joined at base; anthers reddish.
Flower arrangement: clustered, on long stalk.
Flowering time: May-July.
Leaf: of 3 rounded leaflets, 3·5-7 cm, alternate, on stalk with sheathing base.
Fruit: capsule, spherical, with persistent style.
Uses: the underground stem contains a bitter substance called menyanthin, which was used as a tonic and to bring down fever.

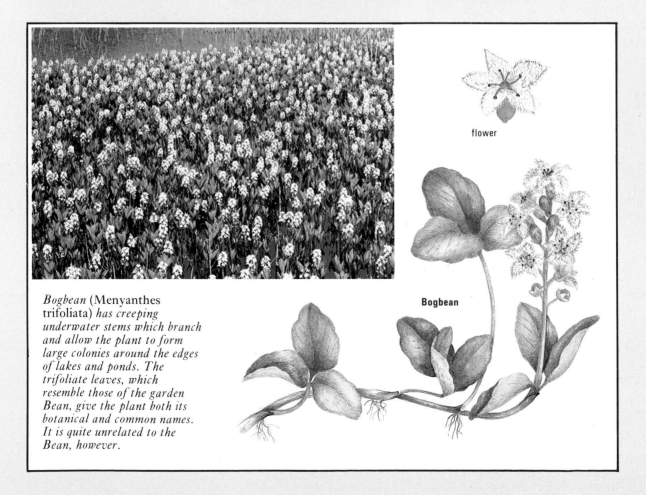

flower

Bogbean

Bogbean (Menyanthes trifoliata) *has creeping underwater stems which branch and allow the plant to form large colonies around the edges of lakes and ponds. The trifoliate leaves, which resemble those of the garden Bean, give the plant both its botanical and common names. It is quite unrelated to the Bean, however.*

POTATO FAMILY
Solanaceae

The very important economic crop plants, tomato, potato and tobacco all come from this family, as well as chillies and green and red peppers. Two of the more poisonous species are Mandrake and Henbane. The flowers in the family often have a central cone of yellow anthers and the fruits are usually berries.

THORN-APPLE
Datura stramonium
Thorn-apple is another very poisonous plant of the potato family, with large, spiny fruits. Originally from America it is more or less naturalized on rubbish tips and waste ground in southern parts of N. Europe. It is branched, hairless and grows 50-200 cm high.
Flower: white, sometimes purple, 5-10 cm, trumpet-shaped, erect; calyx 5-angled.
Flower arrangement: solitary, short-stalked.
Flowering time: July-October.
Leaf: ovate, irregularly toothed, tip pointed, up to 20 cm long.

Fruit: capsule, spiny, 4-7 cm.
Uses: an extract of the leaves known as stramonium is still used medicinally by asthma sufferers.

DEADLY NIGHTSHADE
Atropa bella-donna
This uncommon, highly poisonous, narcotic plant grows in dry places on chalk or limestone. It is stout, branched and grows up to 150 cm high. It is missing from the greater part of Scandinavia.
Flower: lurid violet or greenish, 2·5-3 cm, nodding, bell-shaped, lobes pointed; sepals pointed.
Flower arrangement: solitary.
Flowering time: June-August.
Leaf: alternate, ovate, up to 20 cm.
Fruit: berry, 1·5-2 cm across, shiny, black, surrounded by persistent calyx.
Uses: the poisonous and medicinal properties of this plant have long been known. An infusion of plant juice was formerly dropped in womens' eyes causing dilation of the pupils to produce a 'wide-eyed' look, hence the name *bella-donna* (beautiful lady).

BITTERSWEET
Solanum dulcamara
The small, purple flowers, each with a cone of yellow anthers, are unmistakeable. The plant is mildly poisonous and climbs 30-200 cm

high in hedges, woods or waste places. The common name refers to the taste of the leaves – bitter at first but with a sweet aftertaste.
Flower: purple, with central cone of yellow anthers, 1-1·5 cm across; petals 5, pointed; calyx of 5 rounded lobes.
Flower arrangement: cyme.
Flowering time: June-September.
Leaf: ovate, pointed, stalked, with or without 1-4 lobes at base.
Fruit: berry, poisonous, shiny, ovoid, green when unripe, becoming yellow, then red.
Uses: collars of Bittersweet were worn by people and their animals to avert witchcraft.

BLACK NIGHTSHADE
Solanum nigrum
This species, like many others of the same family, is poisonous. The plant is hairless or with short hairs and grows up to 60 cm high on waste and cultivated land.
Flower: white, with central cone of yellow anthers, about 5 mm across; petals 5, pointed; calyx of 5 rounded lobes.
Flower arrangement: cyme.
Flowering time: July-September.
Leaf: ovate or diamond-shaped, pointed, stalked, toothed or not.
Fruit: berry, poisonous, black.

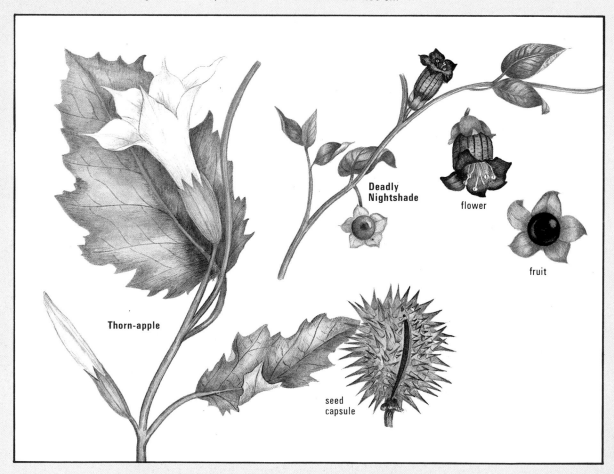

Thorn-apple

Deadly Nightshade

flower

fruit

seed capsule

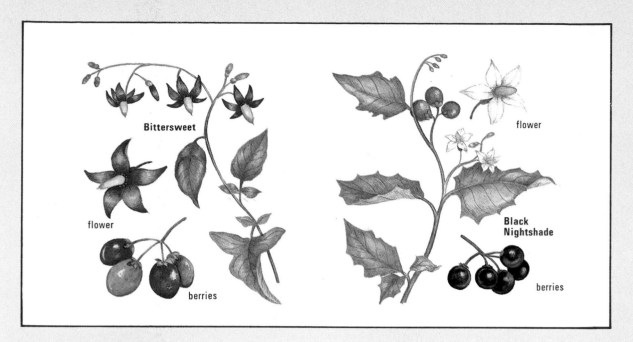

Bittersweet

flower

berries

flower

Black Nightshade

berries

FOXGLOVE FAMILY
Scrophulariaceae

Members of this large family come mainly from northern temperate regions. Some species are semi-parasitic, largely on Grasses. The flowers are usually tubular, with 2 lips, and attract specialized insect pollinators. The Mint family has similar flowers, but 4-angled stems. Many species, such as Snapdragons, are grown in gardens.

FOXGLOVE
Digitalis purpurea
The upright, softly hairy Foxglove plants with their spikes of purple bells are easy to recognize. They prefer acid soils and grow in open woodland, heaths and field borders. Children poke their fingers in the flowers to make a wish.
Flower: pinkish purple, sometimes white, 4-5 cm long, bell-shaped, shallowly 5-lobed, spotted and whiskery within; sepals 5.
Flower arrangement: long spike.
Flowering time: June-September.
Leaf: ovate, blunt-toothed, softly hairy above, woolly beneath; narrow border on each side of leaf-stalk.
Fruit: capsule, ovoid, with long, persistent style.
Uses: Foxgloves are still cultivated for the heart drug containing digitalin.

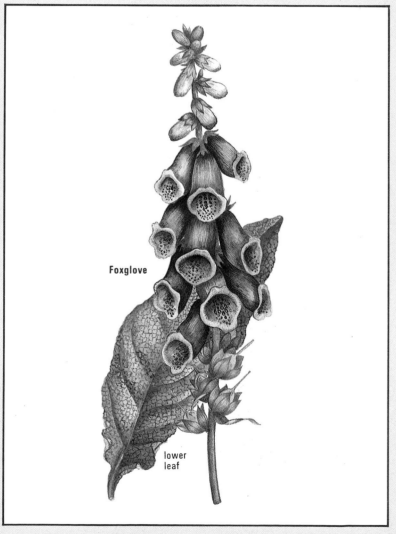

Foxglove

lower leaf

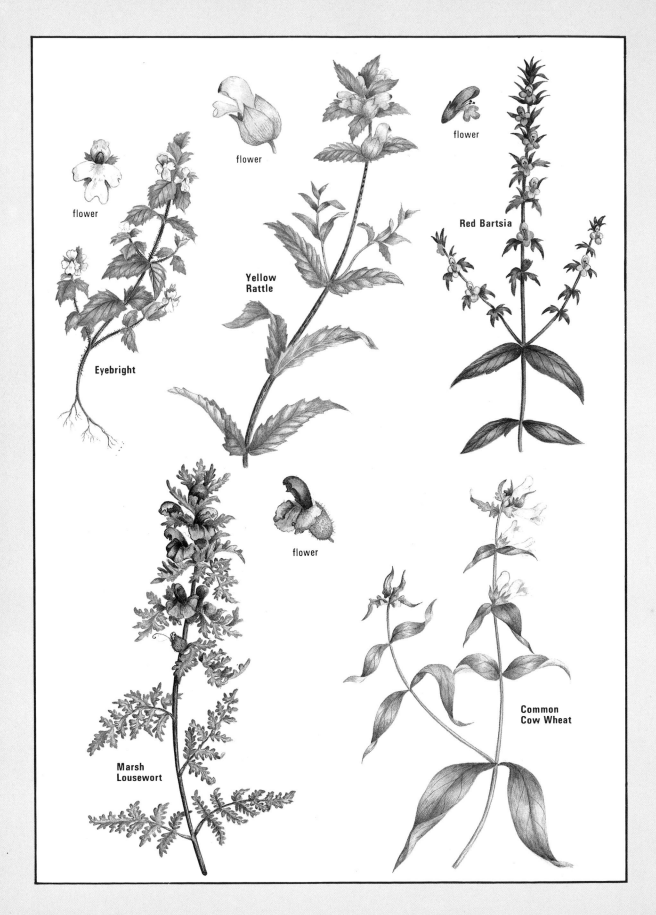

flower

Eyebright

flower

Yellow
Rattle

flower

Red Bartsia

Marsh
Lousewort

flower

Common
Cow Wheat

EYEBRIGHT
Euphrasia officinalis
The Eyebrights are extremely difficult to tell apart. The following description covers a group of species. All are semi-parasites on grasses and grow 1-40 cm high in grassy places. The stems are hairy and branched.
Flower: white or mauve, with yellow and purple marks; 2-lipped, lower lip of 3 notched lobes; calyx 4-toothed; bracts leaf-like.
Flower arrangement: in leaf-axils.
Flowering time: May-September.
Leaf: circular or oval, deeply toothed.
Fruit: capsule, fringed with hairs.
Uses: this little plant was used in the past to treat eye disorders.

YELLOW RATTLE
Rhinanthus minor
Yellow Rattle is semi-parasitic on grasses, amongst which it grows. The stem may be branched, 10-50 cm high and marked with black.
Flower: yellow, 1-1·5 cm long, tubular, 2-lipped, teeth of upper lip purple; calyx 4-toothed, inflated; bracts leaf-like.
Flower arrangement: crowded with bracts at top of stems.
Flowering time: May-August.
Leaf: oblong to lanceolate, toothed, opposite, stalkless, rough to touch.
Fruit: formed from enlarged calyx in which ripe seeds rattle.

RED BARTSIA
Odontites verna
Red Bartsia is very often tinged maroon, much branched and shortly hairy. It grows up to 50 cm high in grassland and waste ground, but is absent from much of Norway and N. Sweden. Curiously, there appears to be no old common name for this plant.
Flower: purple-pink, about 1 cm, tubular; 2-lipped, lower lip 3-lobed; calyx of 4 teeth; bracts leaf-like.
Flower arrangement: in spikes, flowers pointing one way.
Flowering time: June-August.
Leaf: lanceolate, toothed, opposite, stalkless.
Fruit: capsule, seeds ridged.

MARSH LOUSEWORT
Pedicularis palustris
This is a small, pretty plant with fern-like leaves and bright mauve-pink flowers. It is found only in damp grass or heathland. The common similar species of Lousewort (*P. sylvatica*) differs in having 3 teeth instead of 5 on the upper lip of the flower.
Flower: mauve-pink, 1·5-2·5 cm long, tubular; 2-lipped, upper lip with 5 small teeth; calyx hairy, blunt-toothed.
Flower arrangement: leafy spikes.
Flowering time: May-September.
Leaf: oblong, finely dissected, 2-4 cm.
Fruit: capsule, curved, calyx becoming inflated.

flower

Great Mullein

Common Toadflax

lower leaf

COMMON COW WHEAT
Melampyrum pratense
This small, slender plant is semi-parasitic on grasses. It grows 8-60 cm high in shady places and grassland and is branched in the upper part.
Flower: pale yellow, 1-1·5 cm long, tubular; 2-lipped, lower lip orange, calyx of 4 narrow teeth, about half as long as flower tube; upper bracts toothed.
Flower arrangement: in pairs in leaf-axils, each pair facing same way.
Flowering time: May-October.
Leaf: lanceolate or ovate, tapering to point, opposite, stalkless.
Fruit: capsule; seeds 4.

COMMON TOADFLAX
Linaria vulgaris
The flowers look like miniature yellow garden Snapdragons, to which Toadflax is related. Nectar is stored in the long spur behind the flower, accessible only to long-tongued bees. The plant is almost hairless, 30-80 cm high and grows along hedges and in grassy places.
Flower: yellow, top part of lower lip orange; 1·5-2·5 cm long; 2-lipped; spur almost straight; sepals 5, pointed.

Flower arrangement: dense raceme.
Flowering time: June-October.
Leaf: narrow, strap-shaped, pointed, alternate, 3-8 cm long, grey-green beneath.
Fruit: capsule, ovoid; seeds winged.
Uses: the plant is said to make a good fly poison if boiled in milk, the milk serving as an attractant.

GREAT MULLEIN
Verbascum thapsus
The leaves and stem of this tall plant are thickly covered in white wool. It grows in dry, waste places and chalk grassland.
Flower: yellow, 1·5-3 cm across; petals 5, rounded, joined at base; sepals 5, pointed; 3 stamens covered with pale hairs, 2 hairless.
Flower arrangement: tall, dense spike.
Flowering time: June-August.
Leaf: oblong, pointed or rounded at tip; base running down stem as narrow border; basal leaves in rosette.
Fruit: capsule, enclosed by sepals; seeds tiny.

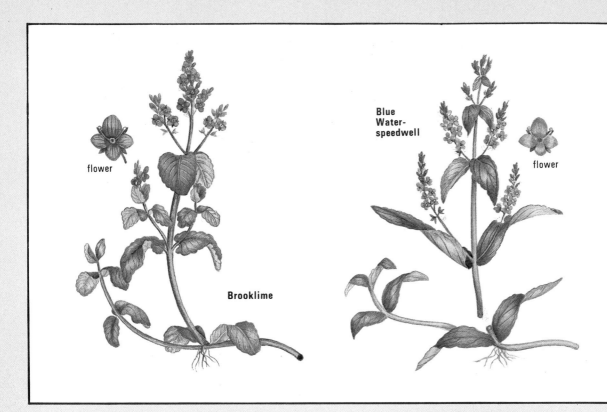

Blue Water-speedwell

flower

flower

Brooklime

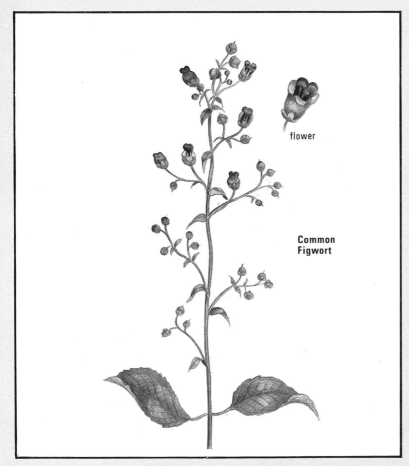

flower

Common Figwort

COMMON FIGWORT
Scrophularia nodosa
This is a rather tall, hairless plant growing in wet woods and ditches. The stem is 4-angled. The dull maroon flowers smelling of decay attract wasps by mimicking carrion.
Flower: upper part maroon, lower green, 1 cm long; 5-lobed, upper 2 slightly longer; sepals 5, rounded.
Flower arrangement: branched clusters.
Flowering time: June-September.
Leaf: ovate, pointed, toothed, opposite, 6-13 cm long.
Fruit: capsule, ovoid, pointed.
Uses: the knobs on the roots were taken as signs that this plant cured both piles and goitre.

BROOKLIME
Veronica beccabunga
Both stem and leaves of this water-loving plant are hairless and rather fleshy. The bases of the hollow stems creep and root in wet mud or shallow fresh water.
Flower: blue, 5-8 mm across; petals 4, upper petal larger than lower 3; sepals 4; stamens 2.
Flower arrangement: racemes in leaf-axils.
Flowering time: May-September.
Leaf: circular to oval, opposite, slightly fleshy, shiny, blunt-toothed, short-stalked.
Fruit: capsule, spherical, slightly notched.
Uses: the sharp-tasting leaves have been eaten as a substitute for Water-cress.

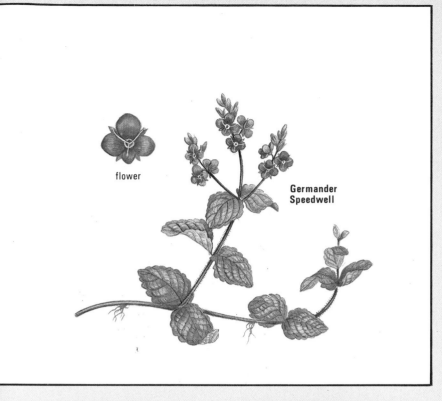

flower

Germander
Speedwell

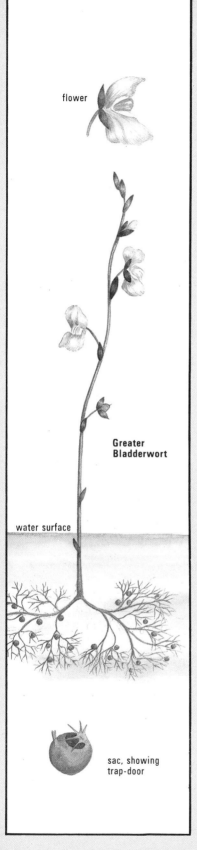

flower

Greater
Bladderwort

water surface

sac, showing
trap-door

BLUE WATER-SPEEDWELL
Veronica anagallis-aquatica
This is one of the larger Speedwells
and grows in or near fresh water.
The rather thick, branching stems
are green and hairless. growing
20-30 cm high.
Flower: pale blue, 5-6 mm across;
petals 4; sepals 4; stamens 2.
Flower arrangement: racemes in
upper leaf-axils.
Flowering time: June-August.
Leaf: lanceolate, pointed, blunt-
toothed, opposite, stalkless.
Fruit: capsule, slightly notched,
stalk curving up, not at right-angle
to stem.

GERMANDER SPEEDWELL
Veronica chamaedrys
Common in grassy places, hedges and
woods, this small Speedwell grows
7-25 cm high. The stem, with its 2
lines of hairs, lies along the ground,
rooting at intervals and turning up at
the tip. Speedwell flowers characteristically drop from the calyx at the
lightest touch.
Flower: bright blue, white circle
at centre, 1 cm across; petals 4,
upper largest; sepals 4; bracts
shorter than or equalling individual
flower stalks; stamens 2.
Flower arrangement: raceme
springing from leaf-axil.
Flowering time: March-July.
Leaf: oval, blunt-toothed, hairy,
shortly stalked or stalkless.
Fruit: capsule, heart-shaped, hairy,
shorter than sepals.

BLADDERWORT FAMILY
Lentibulariaceae

Plants in this small family are
insectivorous and live in wet or
damp places. They trap and
digest insects by rolling up sticky
leaves (Butterworts) or by means
of small, underwater sacs or
bladders (Bladderworts).

GREATER BLADDERWORT
Utricularia vulgaris
This strange, underwater plant has
no roots and grows suspended in
still water. Small sacs on the finely
divided leaves trap mainly water fleas,
which are digested by the plant. If
touched by a passing flea, sensitive
hairs at the mouth of the sac trigger
the opening of a trap-door. Water,
together with the flea, are sucked
into the previously air-filled sac.
Flower: bright yellow, 12-18 mm
across; 2-lipped, short spur behind.
Flower arrangement: 2-10 flowers
on long stalk, above water surface.
Flowering time: July-August.
Leaf: finely divided, each thread-like
segment minutely toothed, with
bristles; all leaves green (other
species with some colourless leaves),
bearing small sacs.
Fruit: capsule, spherical.

MINT FAMILY
Labiatae

Plants in this large family are often aromatic and include many kitchen herbs, such as Sage and Marjoram. Plant stems are square in cross-section, and the flowers are 2-lipped, often in whorls. Chemicals called *terpenes* are found in the family, and can act as growth inhibitors on surrounding plants. A Californian species exudes terpenes as 'weedkiller' to prevent growth of competing grasses.

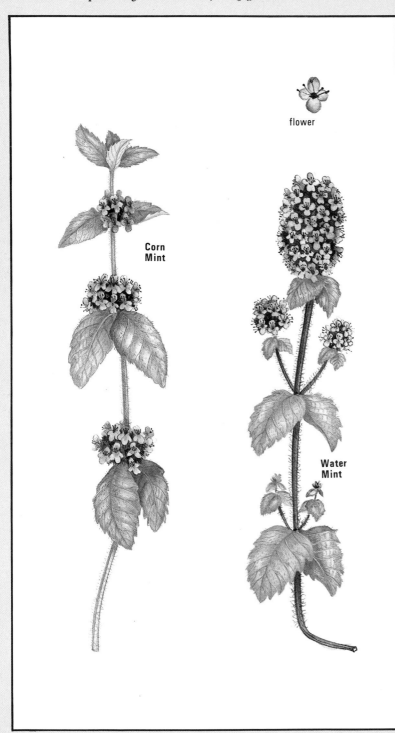

flower

Corn Mint

Water Mint

WATER MINT
Mentha aquatica
The often reddish stems of Water Mint are erect, rising from a creeping underground stem, and 15-90 cm tall. Water Mint grows in wet places. It breeds with escaped garden Spear Mint (*M. spicata*) to give the hybrid Peppermint (*M. piperita*).
Flower: mauve; petals 4; calyx 5-toothed, hairy; stamens long with red anthers.
Flower arrangement: shoots ending in dense, rounded heads of 1-3 whorls.
Flowering time: July-October.
Leaf: ovate, teeth blunt or pointed, opposite, more or less hairy, stalked; if growing in water, the submerged leaves are rounded, toothless.
Fruit: 4 nutlets, smooth.
Uses: as with many other Mints, Water Mint has been used as a stomach medicine and as a herb for strewing on floors of houses.

CORN MINT
Mentha arvensis
Corn Mint grows up to 60 cm high in damp rather than wet places. It is not one of the useful Mints owing to its rather unpleasant smell. The stem is 4-angled and hairy.
Flower: mauve, 4-lobed; calyx with 5 short teeth, hairy; stamens 4, protruding.
Flower arrangement: in dense whorls, shoots not ending in flowers.
Flowering time: May-October.
Leaf: shape variable, usually elliptic and rounded at tip; toothed, stalked, opposite, more or less hairy.
Fruit: 4 nutlets, each ovoid.

GIPSYWORT
Lycopus europaeus
Gipsywort is tall (20-120 cm) and unbranched, growing in wet places. Unlike many other Labiates this one has no smell when crushed.
Flower: white with purple marks, 3-4 mm; 4-lobed; stamens 2; calyx with spiny teeth.
Flower arrangement: in dense whorls.
Flowering time: June-September.
Leaf: ovate to lanceolate; tip pointed; deeply lobed and toothed, opposite, short-stalked.
Fruit: 4 nutlets, each 5-sided.
Uses: gipsies stained their skin with a black dye from this plant. Another name for the plant is Egyptian's Herb because gipsies, on arrival in Europe were first called Egyptians. It is thought they came from Egypt, though probably before that from India.

MARJORAM
Origanum vulgare
This is a plant of dry places on chalk or limestone, smelling aromatic when crushed, due to tiny translucent oil-filled glands on the leaves, seen if held

flower

Gipsywort

Marjoram

Ground Ivy

flower

flower

Selfheal

to the light. The 4-angled stems, 30-80 cm long, are erect and branched in the upper parts.
Flower: mauve, 6-8 mm across; 4-lobed; calyx 5-toothed; stamens 4; bracts often purple.
Flower arrangement: in flat-topped or rounded clusters at top of stems.
Flowering time: July-September.
Leaf: ovate, opposite, slightly toothed or not, short-stalked.
Fruit: 4 nutlets, each ovoid.
Uses: this native species is more pungent than the cultivated, frost-tender species from the Mediterranean used in cooking. Tea can be made from the dried leaves.

GROUND IVY
Glechoma hederacea
Many species in the Mint family have purplish, 2-lipped flowers, all looking rather similar. Ground Ivy is distinguished by having only 2-5 flowers in each whorl and the top petal-lobe being flat, not hooded. Creeping and rooting, it grows in woods and waste places.
Flower: pale violet, 1·5-2 cm long; 2-lipped, upper lip flat, not hooded, lower purple-spotted; calyx 5-toothed.
Flower arrangement: in loose whorls, directed to one side.
Flowering time: March-May.
Leaf: kidney-shaped to almost circular, blunt-toothed, often tinged purple, opposite, long-stalked.
Fruit: 4 nutlets, smooth.

SELFHEAL
Prunella vulgaris
Selfheal is a low-growing, slightly hairy plant of grassland, often tinged purple. The stem is 4-angled, creeping in the lower part and ending in an oblong head of flowers. The plant has no smell when crushed.
Flower: violet, 1-1·5 cm long; 2-lipped, upper lip hooded, lower 3-lobed; calyx of 5 teeth in 2 lips; bract beneath each flower almost circular.
Flower arrangement: in oblong or squat head at top of stem, pair of leaves immediately beneath.
Flowering time: June-September.
Leaf: ovate, tip pointed, 2-5 cm long, shallowly toothed or not, opposite, stalked.
Fruit: 4 nutlets, each oblong.

RED DEAD-NETTLE
Lamium purpureum
Red Dead-nettle is a softly hairy weed of cultivated ground. It has a 4-angled stem and grows 10-45 cm high. Dead-nettles, as the name implies, have no stinging hairs.
Flower: mauve-purple, 1-1·5 cm long; 2-lipped, upper hooded, lower spotted; ring of hairs near flower base; calyx 5-toothed.
Flower arrangement: in whorls in leaf-axils.
Flowering time: March-October.
Leaf: ovate to almost circular, blunt-toothed, often tinged purple, surface puckered, opposite, stalked.
Fruit: 4 nutlets, 3-angled.

WHITE DEAD-NETTLE
Lamium album
Although a very common plant of waste places and roadsides, the tight whorls of plump-looking, pure white flowers make this an attractive plant. The 4-angled stem is un-branched, hairy and 20-80 cm high. This Dead-nettle is not related to the Common Nettle and does not sting, although the leaves are similar.
Flower: white, 2-2·5 cm long; 2-lipped, upper lip pronouncedly hood-ed, hairy, lower lip with 2 or 3 short teeth each side; calyx with 5 narrow, pointed teeth.
Flower arrangement: in compact whorls.
Flowering time: May-December.
Leaf: ovate, tapering to point, coarsely toothed, opposite, stalked.
Fruit: 4 nutlets, 3-angled.
Uses: country children have made whistles out of the hollow stems.

COMMON HEMP-NETTLE
Galeopsis tetrahit
The branched, roughly hairy stem has red or yellow glandular hairs and is swollen where the leaf stalks join. The swellings contain special cells to enable the plant to make slight movements. This plant is 10-100 cm tall and found on cultivated land, less often in damp places.
Flower: mauve with darker mark-ings, occasionally white or pale yellow, 1·5-2 cm long; 2-lipped, upper lip hooded, lower 3-lobed, middle lobe notched or not; calyx with 5 narrow teeth.
Flower arrangement: in whorls.
Flowering time: July-September.
Leaf: ovate, tapering to point, blunt-toothed, stalked, blue-green.
Fruit: 4 nutlets, 3-angled.

HEDGE WOUNDWORT
Stachys sylvatica
The tough stems of this rather tall plant are roughly hairy and 4-angled. The plant grows 30-120 cm high in the shadier parts of hedgerows. If crushed the whole plant, in par-ticular the creeping, underground stem, gives off a foul smell.
Flower: light maroon with white marks, 1-1·5 cm; 2-lipped; calyx

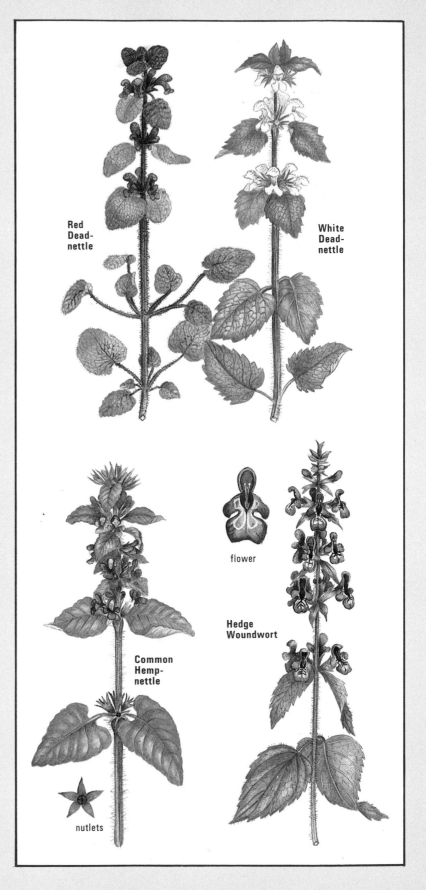

Red Dead-nettle

White Dead-nettle

flower

Hedge Woundwort

Common Hemp-nettle

nutlets

with 5, narrow teeth and glandular hairs.
Flower arrangement: spike of whorls.
Flowering time: July-August.
Leaf: ovate, tip pointed, toothed, stalked, opposite, sparsely hairy.
Fruit: 4 nutlets.
Uses: the common name refers to the old use of this plant in staunching bleeding wounds. The plant also contains antiseptic properties.

SKULL-CAP
Scutellaria galericulata
This is a slender plant of 7-50 cm, found in damp, grassy places, often by streams. The stem is 4-angled.
Flower: blue-violet, whitish toward base, 1-2 cm long; 2-lipped; tube long, slightly curved; calyx 2-lipped.
Flower arrangement: in pairs in leaf-axils.
Flowering time: June-September.
Leaf: lanceolate, tips rounded or bluntly pointed, blunt teeth widely spaced; short-stalked.
Fruit: 4 nutlets, rounded.

PLANTAIN FAMILY
Plantaginaceae

This is a family of temperate areas and tropical mountains. The small flowers, clustered into tight spikes, are mainly wind-pollinated, producing large amounts of powdery pollen.

RIBWORT PLANTAIN
Plantago lanceolata
The ribbed leaves of this Plantain are long and narrow, forming rosettes. The plant grows in grassy places.
Flower: browny-black, tiny; anthers cream, protruding, wind-pollinated.
Flower arrangement: in dense, short spike of 1-2 cm, on grooved, tough stalk, much longer than leaves.
Flowering time: April-August.
Leaf: lanceolate, in rosette; 10-15 cm long, usually without teeth, strongly ribbed.

Fruit: capsule, about 5 mm.
Uses: the seeds become slimy-coated when wet. In France the coating was used as a fabric stiffener, especially of muslin.

GREATER PLANTAIN
Plantago major
The rosettes of tough, ribbed leaves, often flattened by, but very resistant to trampling, are seen at the sides of almost every path and piece of trodden ground.
Flower: greenish yellow, tiny; anthers mauve, becoming yellow, protruding, wind-pollinated.
Flower arrangement: in long, dense, stalked spike, 10-15 cm, encircled by whorl of anthers.
Flowering time: May-September.
Leaf: broadly elliptic, in rosette; 10-15 cm long, usually without teeth, strongly ribbed, abruptly narrowed into broad stalk.
Fruit: capsule, 2-5 mm.
Uses: when in seed the flower spikes may be hung up for cage-birds to feed on.

stem section   flower

Skull-cap

Greater Plantain

Ribwort Plantain

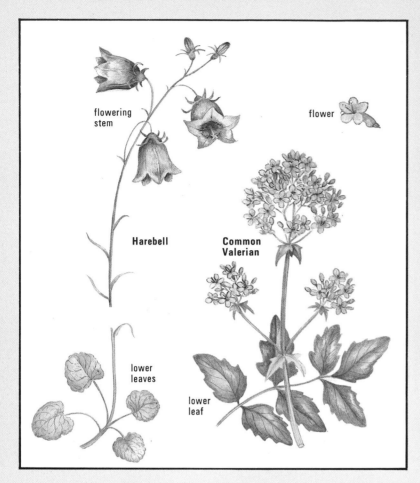

flowering
stem

flower

Harebell

Common
Valerian

lower
leaves

lower
leaf

BEDSTRAW FAMILY
Rubiaceae

As well as the Bedstraws, plants yielding coffee and the drug quinine are included in this very large family. Bedstraw seeds taste of coffee if roasted.

LADY'S BEDSTRAW
Galium verum
The stems of this yellow-flowered Bedstraw are more or less erect, 15-100 cm high, with 4 raised lines and without the minute, hooked bristles used by other Bedstraw species for climbing. The plant becomes black when dried and grows in dry grassland.
Flower: golden yellow, 2-4 mm across; petals 4.
Flower arrangement: in many-flowered clusters at ends of branches.
Flowering time: July-August.
Leaf: in whorls of 8-12, grass-like, 6-25 mm long, bristle-tipped; margins rolled under; dark green and shiny above, paler beneath.
Fruit: of 2 joined lobes, 1·5 mm, hairless, black when ripe.
Uses: this Bedstraw in particular was used to turn and colour the milk in cheese-making.

COMMON MARSH-BEDSTRAW
Galium palustre
Wet places are the habitat of this Bedstraw. The leaf tips are blunt and have no bristle – an important characteristic. The 4-angled stem straggles over other vegetation by means of minute, hooked bristles. It is up to 120 cm long and slightly rough to the touch.
Flower: white, 3-4·5 mm across; petals 4.
Flower arrangement: in clusters, on long stalks, with whorl of leaf-like bracts.
Flowering time: June-July.
Leaf: in whorls of 4-6, narrow, tip blunt, single-veined.
Fruit: of 2 joined lobes, 1 mm, without bristles, black when ripe.

CLEAVERS
Galium aparine
This scrambling plant of 15-180 cm clings to other vegetation, often in dense masses, with minute hooked bristles, rough and tacky to the touch. A characteristic to look for is the bristle at the leaf tip. The stem is 4-angled and branched. The plant grows in hedges and woods and is a weed of cultivation.
Flower: white, 2 mm across; petals 4.
Flower arrangement: in clusters of 2-5, on long stalks, with whorl of leaf-like bracts.
Flowering time: June-August.
Leaf: in whorls of 6-9, narrow, tip ending in bristle, single-veined.
Fruit: of 2 joined lobes, 3-6 mm, covered with tiny, white, hooked bristles; purplish when ripe.

BELLFLOWER FAMILY
Campanulaceae

Many of the flowers in this family are blue and bell-shaped and are grown as garden ornamentals. A sugar (*inulin*) occurs in the sap that is identical to that found in plants of the Daisy family. The two families are thought to be closely related.

HAREBELL
Campanula rotundifolia
Called Bluebell in Scotland, the Harebell is unrelated to the English Bluebell of woods. It is a very slender, hairless plant of dry, grassy places and grows 15-40 cm.
Flower: pale blue, 1-2 cm, bell-shaped with 5 pointed lobes, nodding; calyx with 5 narrow, pointed teeth; stigmas 3.
Flower arrangement: solitary or in loose cluster, on thread-like stalk.
Flowering time: July-September.
Leaf: very narrow, pointed, un-stalked on stem; basal leaves ovate or circular, blunt-toothed, stalked.
Fruit: capsule, papery, 3-5 mm.

VALERIAN
FAMILY Valerianaceae

Plants in this family give off an unpleasant smell. Cats are often drawn to the smell, and appear to become intoxicated. The small, clustered flowers each have a tiny pouch near the base. In many species there is a plume of hairs on the fruit for wind dispersal.

COMMON VALERIAN
Valeriana officinalis
Often tall and erect, Valerian is usually hairless and not much branched. It differs from other Valerian species in having all the leaves divided into leaflets. The plant has a sickly smell when crushed. It is mostly found in damp places.
Flower: pale pink, about 5 mm across, 5-lobed, tubular at base; pouch at base of tube; stamens 3.
Flower arrangement: clustered.
Flowering time: June-August.
Leaf: divided into pairs of broad or narrow leaflets, toothed or not, lower leaves stalked.
Fruit: 2-5 mm with plume of hairs.
Uses: the roots contain medicinal properties used as a sedative.

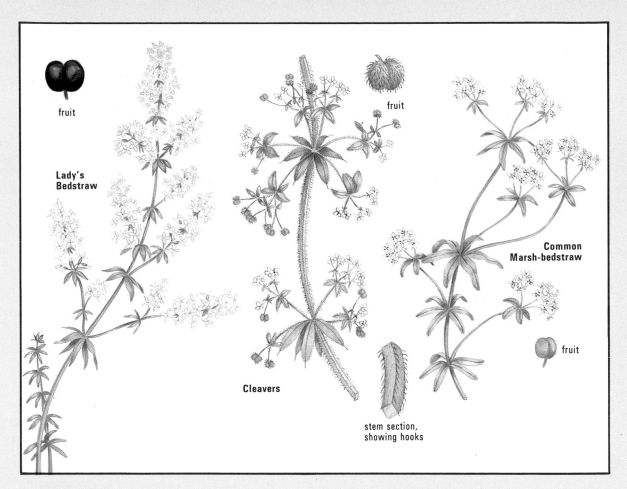

fruit

Lady's
Bedstraw

Cleavers

fruit

Common
Marsh-bedstraw

fruit

stem section,
showing hooks

HONEYSUCKLE FAMILY
Caprifoliaceae

Most of the species in this family are shrubs, some of them climbing. The flowers are often tubular, and the fruits are usually berries. There are many garden ornamentals, including Honeysuckles, Snowberries and Viburnums.

HONEYSUCKLE
Lonicera periclymenum
A climbing shrub of up to 6 m, Honeysuckle may also be found sprawling over the ground. It grows in hedges and woods and is planted in gardens for the scented flowers.
Flower: cream, tinged with pinky red; trumpet-shaped with 4 upper lobes, 1 lower; 4-5 cm long, stamens and style protruding.
Flower arrangement: in head, flowers directed outwards.
Flowering time: June-October.
Leaf: elliptic or oblong, tip usually pointed, opposite, no teeth, stalkless, 3-9 cm long, dark green above, paler beneath.
Fruit: tight head of red berries.

Honeysuckle

berries

Honeysuckle (Lonicera periclymenum) *climbing on a Douglas Fir* (Pseudotsuga menziesii) *in a plantation. The flowers produce abundant nectar and attract moths in the early evening.*

TEASEL FAMILY
Dipsacaceae

This is a small family which includes Teasels and Scabious. The tight heads of tiny flowers look like those of the Daisy family, except for the stamens which stand out from each flower.

FIELD SCABIOUS
Knautia arvensis
The beautiful mauve flower-heads, made up of many tiny flowers, are often larger than the other Scabious species. The erect plants grow 25-100 cm high on dry banks and fields, and the stem has rough bristles, at least at the base.
Flower: mauve, 4-lobed; outer flowers larger than inner; stamens protruding.
Flower arrangement: in flattish head, 3-4 cm across, on long stalk; bracts directly below head ovate, in 2 overlapping layers, not reaching edge of head.
Flowering time: July-September.
Leaf: variable, deeply lobed, opposite, hairy; basal leaves often forming rosette, some unlobed.
Fruit: 5-6 mm, crowned by 8 bristles; dispersed by ants, which find them attractive.

DEVIL'S BIT SCABIOUS
Succisa pratensis
This Scabious has undivided leaves and an erect, slightly hairy stem 15-100 cm high. It grows in damp places, including woods. The curious root gives the plant its name. After the first year's growth the tip of the thick root falls away leaving an abrupt end, as if bitten off.
Flower: mauve, 4-lobed; outer flowers not much larger than inner; stamens protruding.
Flower arrangement: in domed head, 1·5-2·5 cm across, on long stalk; sepal-like bracts lanceolate, in 2 overlapping layers, reaching edge of head.
Flowering time: June-October.
Leaf: elliptic, tip pointed or rounded, opposite, untoothed or with a few teeth; basal leaves stalked, forming rosette.
Fruit: 5 mm, crowned by 5 bristles.

DAISY FAMILY
Compositae

This is one of the largest flowering-plant families, with more than 25,000 species occurring throughout the world. Most European members are herbs, but in the tropics there are also shrubs, trees and climbers. The family is characterized by tiny flowers (*florets*) grouped

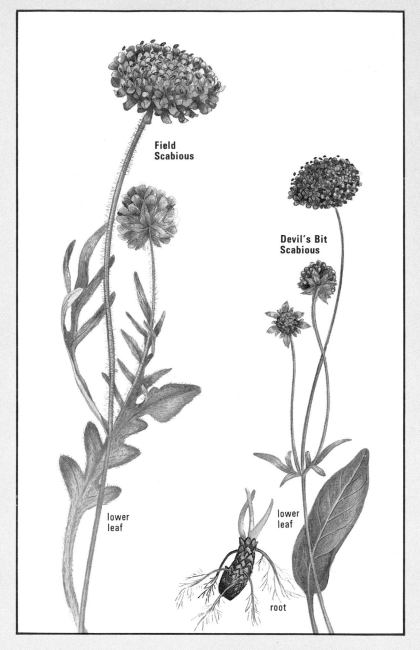

Field Scabious

Devil's Bit Scabious

lower leaf

lower leaf

root

together in a head, or *capitulum*. These heads often look like a single large flower, and the bracts surrounding the head resemble petals. The florets are of two kinds: a simple tube made up of 5 fused petals known as a *disc floret*, and a tube elongated on one side into a strap shape and called a *ray floret*. The heads may consist entirely of disc florets, as in the Thistles, or all ray florets, as in the Dandelion, or both together, as in the Daisy. In a few species, such as the

Groundsel, ray florets may or may not be present in some heads. Members of the family cultivated for food include the Lettuce, Chicory, Artichoke and Sunflower. Many are also grown as ornamental plants, including Chrysanthemums, Marigolds, Dahlias and Everlasting Flowers. A number of species are serious weeds capable of rapidly colonizing bare or disturbed ground and producing vast quantities of wind-dispersed seeds.

Ox-eye Daisy

flower bud

lower leaf

Daisy

Sea Mayweed

DAISY
Bellis perennis
Familiar in the short grass of meadow, lawn and verge, the Daisy is known to all who have ever made a daisy chain. The flower stalks rise straight from a rosette of leaves and the flowers close at night and in wet weather.
Flower: ray florets white, tinged pink beneath, many; disc florets yellow; head 1·5-3 cm across.
Flower arrangement: head solitary, on long stalk.
Flowering time: March-October.
Leaf: spoon-shaped, with or without a few teeth.
Fruit: achene, 1·5-2 mm, downy.

OX-EYE DAISY
Leucanthemum vulgare
The Ox-eye Daisy has large, Daisy-like flower-heads, smaller in exposed places. The almost hairless stems grow 20-70 cm tall in grassy places.
Flower: ray florets white; disc florets yellow; head 2·5-5 cm across; sepal-like bracts with purplish borders.
Flower arrangement: heads solitary, on long stalks.
Flowering time: June-August.
Leaf: Often forming non-flowering rosettes, dark green, toothed; lower stem leaves rounded or spoon-shaped, long-stalked; upper leaves oblong, stalkless.
Fruit: achene, pale grey, ribbed.

SEA MAYWEED
Matricaria maritima
This Mayweed has Daisy-like flower-heads and ferny leaves. It has no smell when crushed. The branched stem is 10-30 cm high, usually prostrate. The whole plant is hairless, and is found near the sea.
Flower: ray florets white; disc florets yellow; heads 1·5-5 cm across; sepal-like bracts with narrow, papery margins.
Flower arrangement: heads solitary, on long stalks.
Flowering time: July-September.
Leaf: ferny, very finely dissected; segments sometimes fleshy.
Fruit: achene, with 2 dark dots near top.

flower without ray florets

Sea Aster

Pineappleweed

Blue Fleabane

lower leaf

PINEAPPLEWEED
Chamomilla suaveolens
Familiar by the warm, aromatic smell when walked on (supposed to resemble a pineapple smell), Pineappleweed is low-growing on trampled ground. It is a weed introduced to Europe, probably from N. America, and has ferny leaves and little greeny-yellow, petal-less flower-heads.
Flower: yellow-green, disc florets only; heads domed, 5-8 mm across; sepal-like bracts rounded, pale-bordered.
Flower arrangement: heads on branched stalks.
Flowering time: June-July.
Leaf: finely dissected, fern-like.
Fruit: achene.

SEA ASTER
Aster tripolium
Closely related to the Michaelmas Daisy of gardens and with similar flowers, Sea Aster has fleshy leaves and grows 15-100 cm high in salt marsh and on sea cliffs.
Flower: ray florets mauve or whitish, many or none; disc florets yellow; head 8-20 mm across; sepal-like bracts rounded at tip.
Flower arrangement: in clusters, often flat-topped.
Flowering time: July-October.
Leaf: fleshy, hairless; upper leaves narrow, pointed, stalkless; lower leaves rounded at tip, stalked.
Fruit: achene, with brownish pappus.

BLUE FLEABANE
Erigeron acer
The flower-heads are of similar colour to those of the Sea Aster but the mauve ray florets are erect, not spread out. The slender, roughly hairy stems are 8-60 cm high, often reddish and branched in the upper part. This Fleabane grows in dry places, especially on chalk.
Flower: ray florets pale mauve, erect, in 2 or more rows; disc florets yellow; head 12-18 mm across; sepal-like bracts narrow, pointed, red-tinged.
Flower arrangement: in long-stalked cluster, less often solitary.
Flowering time: July-August.
Leaf: lanceolate, untoothed, stalkless, leaf base clasping stem; basal leaves stalked.
Fruit: achene, with pinkish pappus.

TRIFID BUR-MARIGOLD
Bidens tripartita
The branched stem of this rather dull-looking plant is 10-60 cm high. The plants grow near fresh water, and the fruits are dispersed by catching on the fur of passing animals or on clothing.
Flower: brownish-yellow; disc florets only; head 1-2.5 cm across; inner sepal-like bracts brownish-green; outer collar of 5-8 leaf-like bracts spreading beyond head.
Flower arrangement: solitary, nodding slightly.
Flowering time: July-September.
Leaf: of 3 toothed segments or undivided, stalked, opposite.
Fruit: achene, each barbed with 2-4 bristles.

GROUNDSEL
Senecio vulgaris
Groundsel grows on waste and cultivated ground. The branched stem is 8-45 cm high. The common name is very old, coming from an Anglo-Saxon word meaning 'ground swallower', from the way this weed spreads.
Flower: yellow; disc florets only, occasionally rayed; heads about 4 mm across; sepal-like bracts dark-tipped, outer short.
Flower arrangement: heads in loose clusters.
Flowering time: all year.
Leaf: lobed, the lobes irregularly toothed; upper leaf bases clasping stem; hairless or slightly hairy.
Fruit: achene, with pappus forming clocks.

COMMON RAGWORT
Senecio jacobaea
Neglected fields are often overgrown with this species of Ragwort. It is also found on waste ground. The grooved stem branches above the middle and grows 30-150 cm high.
Flower: ray florets yellow, 12-15; disc florets orange; heads 1.5-2.5 cm across; sepal-like bracts black-tipped.
Flower arrangement: heads in flat-topped clusters.
Flowering time: June-October.
Leaf: deeply lobed, lobes blunt-toothed, end lobe rounded; dark green, hairless or with sparse hairs beneath.
Fruit: achene, ribbed, with pappus.

Trifid Bur-marigold

flower without ray florets

flower with ray florets

Groundsel

Common Ragwort

lower leaf

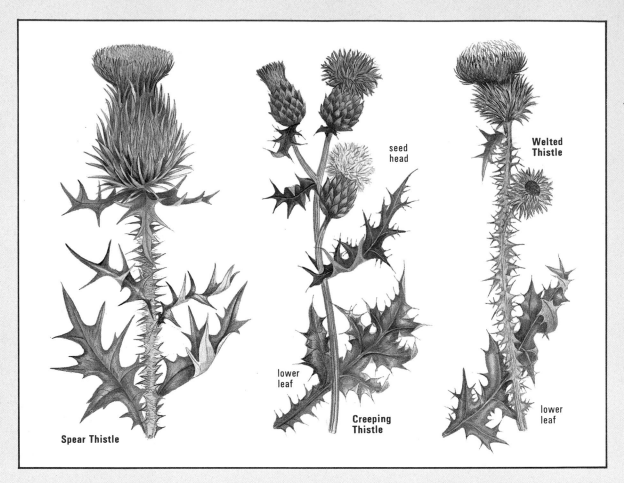

Welted Thistle

seed head

Creeping Thistle

lower leaf

lower leaf

Spear Thistle

SPEAR THISTLE
Cirsium vulgare
Thin, spiny ridges run down the stems of this common thistle. The stems have white, woolly hairs and grow 30-150 cm tall in fields and waste places, and by roadsides.
Flower: mauve; disc florets only; head 3-5 cm across; sepal-like bracts spiny, hairy.
Flower arrangement: solitary, or cluster of 2-3.
Flowering time: July-October.
Leaf: lanceolate, margins wavy, very spiny; end segment sword-shaped; white-hairy or rough beneath.
Fruit: achene, yellow with black streaks; pappus long, white.

CREEPING THISTLE
Cirsium arvense
Creeping Thistle is a stubborn weed on cultivated and waste land. The creeping roots send up new plants. The grooved stem is not contin-uously spiny-ridged, as in the com-mon Spear Thistle, and grows 30-120 cm high.
Flower: mauve; disc florets only; head 1·5-2·5 cm across; sepal-like bracts sharply pointed but not spiny, purple-tinged.
Flower arrangement: solitary, or in clusters.
Flowering time: July-September.
Leaf: lanceolate, margin undulating,

very spiny, hairless above, white-hairy or not beneath.
Fruit: achene; pappus long, fawn.

WELTED THISTLE
Carduus acanthoides
The common name refers to the matted white hairs on the stem and undersides of the leaves, though the degree of hairiness varies. Thin, spiny ridges run up the stem, ending short of the flower head. The plant grows 30-150 cm tall in hedges, verges and stream-sides.
Flower: reddish purple; disc florets only; head 2-2·5 cm across; sepal-like bracts many, sharply pointed.
Flower arrangement: in clusters of 3-5.
Flowering time: June-August.
Leaf: margins spiny, wavy, white hairs beneath; upper leaves narrow, lower deeply lobed.
Fruit: achene, with long pappus.

COMMON KNAPWEED
Centaurea nigra
The Thistle-like flower-heads of this Knapweed may be shaped either like a shaving brush or with the outer florets enlarged and dissected. The unspined plants grow 15-100 cm tall in grassland and along roadsides.
Flower: reddish purple; disc florets only or outer florets enlarged, dis-sected; head 2-4 cm across; sepal-

like bracts browny-black, each edged by dark fringe.
Flower arrangement: solitary.
Flowering time: June-September.
Leaf: lanceolate, with or without a few teeth, hairy; lower leaves stalked.
Fruit: achene, fawn; pappus short.

LESSER BURDOCK
Arctium minus
Stout, sometimes bushy, Lesser Burdock grows 50-150 cm high in waste places and on roadsides. After flowering the hooked bracts of the seed-heads attach themselves as burs to clothing and animal fur, so transporting the seeds.
Flower: red-purple; disc florets only, in thistle-like, ovoid heads, 1·5-4 cm; bracts hooked.
Flower arrangement: in leaf-axils below; upper heads clustered.
Flowering time: July-September.
Leaf: ovate, tip pointed, toothed, up to 30 cm long; hairless above, sparse hairs beneath; stalk hollow.
Fruit: achene, with short pappus; whole seed-head forming bur.

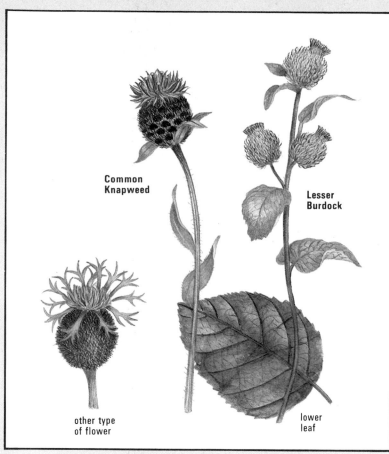

Common Knapweed

Lesser Burdock

other type of flower

lower leaf

DANDELION
Taraxacum officinale

There are many species of Dandelion, all very variable and difficult to identify. This description covers a group of species. Dandelions grow in grassy and waste places. The pappus forms the familiar 'clocks' of children's games.

Flower: yellow; ray florets only, outer brown or mauve beneath; heads 3-7·5 cm across; outer sepal-like bracts turned down or spread out.

Flower arrangement: heads solitary, stalk unbranched, stout, hollow, exuding milky sap if broken.

Flowering time: March-October.

Leaf: in basal rosette, lobes deep, toothed, pointing down, hairless.

Fruit: achene, with stalked pappus.

CAT'S EAR
Hypochoeris radicata

Important features are the rosette of rough, lobed leaves and tiny bracts on the upper parts of the branched, hairless stem. The stem bears Dandelion-like flower-heads and exudes milky sap if broken. The plant grows 20-60 cm high in grassy places.

Flower: yellow; ray florets only, outer green or grey beneath; heads 2·5-4 cm across.

Flower arrangement: heads on hairless, few-branched stalks with tiny bracts.

Flowering time: June-September.

Leaf: in basal rosette, roughly hairy, lobed, end lobe rounded.

Fruit: achene, pappus fawn, stalked.

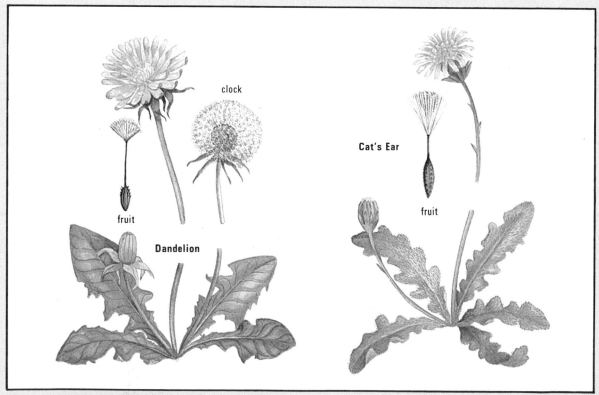

clock

fruit

Dandelion

Cat's Ear

fruit

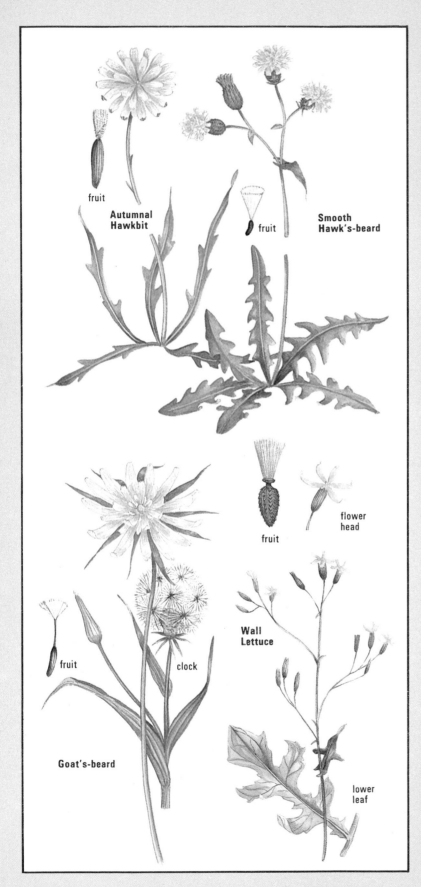

fruit

Autumnal Hawkbit

fruit

Smooth Hawk's-beard

fruit

flower head

fruit

clock

Wall Lettuce

Goat's-beard

lower leaf

AUTUMNAL HAWKBIT
Leontodon autumnalis
The outer petals of the Dandelion-like flower-heads are often striped red beneath. The stems are branched, usually hairless, with tiny bracts towards the top. If broken, the stem exudes milky sap. The plants grow 5-60 cm high in grassy places.
Flower: yellow; ray florets only, striped red beneath; heads 1-3·5 cm across; buds erect; sepal-like bracts hairless (with dark hairs on mountain plants).
Flower arrangement: heads on branched, usually hairless stalks.
Flowering time: June-October.
Leaf: in rosette, lobed or with widely spaced teeth, tip pointed, hairless or slightly hairy.
Fruit: achene, with pappus.

SMOOTH HAWK'S-BEARD
Crepis capillaris
The branched stems of this rather slender, Dandelion-like plant are 20-100 cm high. It grows in grassland and waste places.
Flower: bright yellow; ray florets only, outer often reddish beneath; heads 1-2·5 cm across; sepal-like bracts lanceolate, with black bristles or not, in 2 layers, outer bracts pressed close to inner.
Flower arrangement: loose clusters.
Flowering time: June-September.
Leaf: variable; lower leaves with many narrow lobes or toothed; upper leaves narrow, stalkless, with base having 2 pointed lobes which clasp stem.
Fruit: achene, fawn, 10-ribbed; pappus white.

GOAT'S-BEARD
Tragopogon pratensis
The Dandelion-like flower-head of this curious-looking plant is over-topped by long bracts and closes around noon. The stem bears grass-like leaves and grows 30-70 cm high in grass- and waste land.
Flower: yellow; ray florets only; heads broad; sepal-like bracts longer than head, narrow.
Flower arrangement: head solitary.
Flowering time: June-July.
Leaf: grass-like, often clasping stem at base, white-veined, hairless.
Fruit: achene, with stalked pappus, forming large clock.

WALL LETTUCE
Mycelis muralis
The flower-heads, on branched stalks, each have only 5 pale yellow florets. The stem bears leaves, often purple-tinged, with red veins. Wall Lettuce is hairless and grows 20-100 cm high on walls, and in rocky places and woods.
Flower: pale yellow; 5 ray florets only; heads about 1 cm across; sepal-like bracts in cylinder shape.
Flower arrangement: heads on branched stalks.
Flowering time: July-September.
Leaf: alternate, deeply lobed,

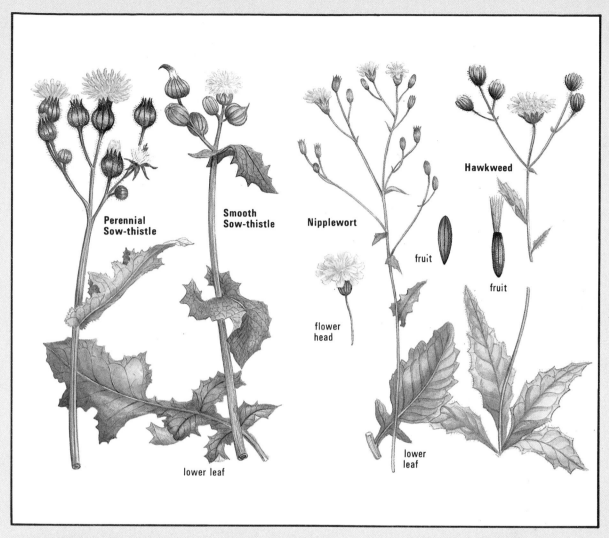

Perennial Sow-thistle

Smooth Sow-thistle

Nipplewort

flower head

Hawkweed

fruit

fruit

lower leaf

lower leaf

coarsely toothed; basal lobes of upper leaves clasping stem; often purple-tinged, red-veined.
Fruit: achene, with pappus.

PERENNIAL SOW-THISTLE
Sonchus arvensis
The plant has Dandelion-like flower-heads, and leaves with rounded basal lobes. The hollow stem is 30-150 cm tall with sticky hairs on the upper parts. If cut, the stem oozes milky sap. The plant grows in waste places, by streams and on the coast.
Flower: golden yellow; ray florets only; heads 4-5 cm across; sepal-like bracts with yellow-tipped, sticky hairs.
Flower arrangement: heads in loose, flat-topped clusters.
Flowering time: July-October.
Leaf: oblong, lobed, margins weakly spiny; leaf bases clasping stem with 2 rounded lobes.
Fruit: achene, with white pappus.

SMOOTH SOW-THISTLE
Sonchus oleraceus
This plant has Dandelion-like flower-heads and pointed basal lobes to the

leaves. The stem is hollow, 20-150 cm high and usually lacks sticky hairs. If cut, it oozes milky sap. The plants grow in waste places and as a weed of cultivation.
Flower: pale yellow; ray florets only; heads 2-2·5 cm across; sepal-like bracts usually without sticky hairs.
Flower arrangement: heads clustered.
Flowering time: June-August.
Leaf: variable in shape, often deeply lobed, margins weakly spiny; leaf bases clasping stem with 2 pointed lobes; blue-green.
Fruit: achene, with white pappus.

NIPPLEWORT
Lapsana communis
The flower-heads are like small Dandelions on branched stalks, and the leaves grow up the stem. The plant can grow up to 90 cm high in shady, waste places. The common name is said to come from the shape of the flower buds.
Flower: yellow; ray florets only; heads 1·5-2 cm across; sepal-like bracts narrow, tips rounded, dark-

striped down centre.
Flower arrangement: heads on branched stalks.
Flowering time: July-September.
Leaf: alternate, toothed; lower leaves with toothed lobes; all often slightly hairy.
Fruit: achene, ribbed, no pappus.

HAWKWEED
Hieracium Sect. Vulgata
Hawkweed species are extremely numerous and difficult to identify. A section containing some of the most common species is described here. The branched, hairy stem grows 15-80 cm tall and exudes milky sap if broken. Hawkweeds are found in shady or rocky places.
Flower: yellow; ray florets only, Dandelion-like; sepal-like bracts dark green, glandular, hairy.
Flower arrangement: heads on branched, glandular hairy stalks.
Flowering time: June-September.
Leaf: elliptic to lanceolate, variably toothed, not lobed, both ends narrowed, hairy in parts; basal leaves in rosette.
Fruit: achene; pappus brownish.

COLTSFOOT
Tussilago farfara
Coltsfoot is found on waste and arable land, especially on clay soil. The flowering stems appear before the leaves in early spring, rising from a creeping, underground stem, as do the leaves later on.
Flower: yellow; disc florets surrounded by many narrow ray florets; head 1·5-3·5 cm across, drooping after flowering.
Flower arrangement: head solitary; stalk thick, scaled, 5-15 cm high.
Flowering time: February-April.
Leaf: appearing after flowers, 10-30 cm across, in clumps, heart-shaped, irregularly toothed, stalked, white-woolly beneath.
Fruit: achene, pappus forming clock.

BUTTERBUR
Petasites hybridus
The rather short, large-leaved plants of Butterbur are found in damp places, often growing in masses. Flowering stems with broad bracts appear before the leaves.
Flower: pink or mauve; disc florets only; heads 3-12 mm; sepal-like bracts narrow, purplish.
Flower arrangement: heads in dense racemes.
Flowering time: March-May.
Leaf: 10-90 cm across, kidney-shaped, toothed, grey beneath, stalked.
Fruit: achene, with pappus.
Uses: the large leaves were used to wrap butter, hence the common name.

YARROW
Achillea millefolium
The stem is erect and 8-60 cm high, with soft hairs. Yarrow grows in grass- and waste land and the narrow, ferny leaves may be found creeping through lawns. The plant looks Umbellifer-like, except that the flower stalks do not all join at one point. If crushed, the plant smells aromatic.
Flower: ray florets white or pink, 5; disc cream; head 4-6 mm across.
Flower arrangement: in flat-topped clusters.
Flowering time: June-August.
Leaf: very finely dissected, fern-like, alternate, 5-15 cm long, narrow; lower leaves stalked.
Fruit: achene, 2 mm, greyish.

MUGWORT
Artemisia vulgaris
The backs of the finely cut leaves are strikingly white, and the plant is faintly aromatic. The stem is 60-120 cm tall, erect and often red. It grows on roadsides and in waste places.
Flower: brownish-yellow; disc florets only in bell-shaped heads, 3-4 mm long; sepal-like bracts hairy.
Flower arrangement: branched raceme.
Flowering time: July-September.
Leaf: deeply dissected, segments toothed, main vein translucent, almost hairless above, densely white-hairy beneath.
Fruit: achene, about 1 mm.

TANSY
Tanacetum vulgare
The flower-heads are like little yellow buttons clustered at the ends of stems 30-100 cm high. The plant is highly aromatic and grows in hedgerows and waste places. It is often found as an escape from gardens, where it has been grown for ornament and medicine.
Flower: orange-yellow; disc florets only; heads 7-12 mm across.
Flower arrangement: heads in flat-topped clusters.
Flowering time: July-September.
Leaf: ferny, divided into narrow, toothed segments, alternate, dark green, hairless, gland-dotted, 15-25 cm long.
Fruit: achene, 5-ribbed.

GOLDENROD
Solidago virgaurea
Goldenrod grows in woods, on heaths and in grassy places. The height of this erect plant varies widely, up to 100 cm in lowland areas and 5-20 cm in mountain forms. The garden Goldenrod (*S. canadensis*), which often escapes, has leaves with 3 main veins.
Flower: yellow; ray florets 6-12 surrounding disc florets; heads 6-10 mm across; sepal-like bracts with pale margins.
Flower arrangement: heads in branched clusters.
Flowering time: July-September.
Leaf: ovate or lanceolate, short-stalked, toothed, with 1 main vein.
Fruit: achene; pappus whitish.

Coltsfoot
clock
leaf

Coltsfoot is often found on waste ground such as railway banks.

flower head
leaf
Butterbur

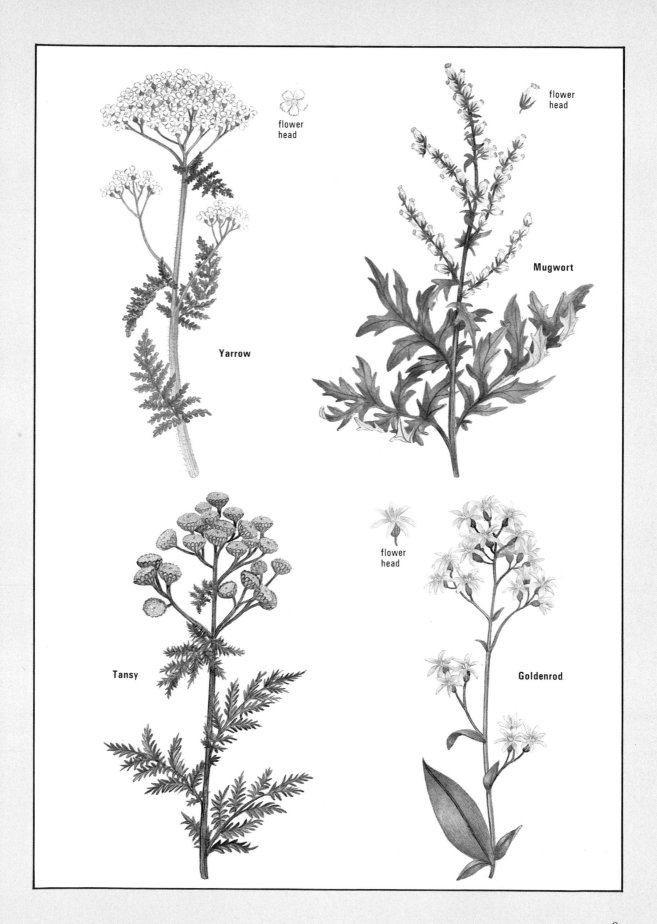

flower
head

Yarrow

flower
head

Mugwort

Tansy

flower
head

Goldenrod

HEMP AGRIMONY
Eupatorium cannabinum
The tall plants grow 30-170 cm high in masses in damp places. The tiny pink flower-heads are gathered in fairly loose clusters.
Flower: pinkish; disc florets only; styles protruding; head of 5-6 florets, 2-5 mm across; sepal-like bracts purple-tipped.
Flower arrangement: heads in rather loose, domed clusters.
Flowering time: July-September.
Leaf: divided to base into 3-5 toothed segments, almost stalkless, opposite; upper leaves undivided.
Fruit: achene, black, with pappus.
Uses: tea made from the leaves was taken at the onset of influenza; also used as a purge.

MARSH CUDWEED
Gnaphalium uliginosum
The leaves and branched stems of this small plant are covered in white wool. It grows 4-20 cm high in damp places.
Flower: yellow; disc florets only; heads 3-4 mm across; sepal-like bracts brown, papery, pointed.
Flower arrangement: in dense, rounded clusters at the branch-tips, shorter than surrounding leaves.
Flowering time: July-August.
Leaf: white-woolly, narrow, tip rounded or pointed.
Fruit: achene, usually hairless, with pappus.
Uses: Cudweed boiled in water makes a gargle for sore throats.

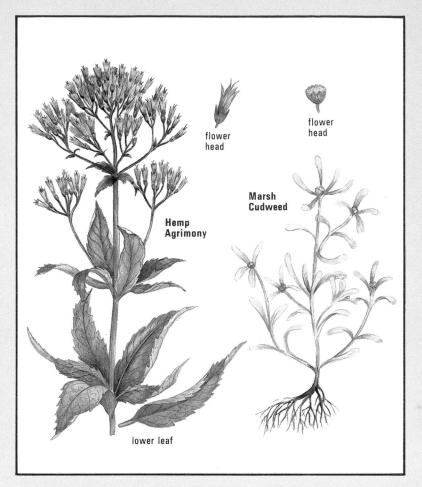

flower head

flower head

Marsh Cudweed

Hemp Agrimony

lower leaf

MONOCOTYLEDONS

The following families are all *monocotyledons* – that is, they differ from the preceding dicotyledon families in their usually narrow leaves with parallel veins. The flower-parts are usually in threes, and there is a single *cotyledon*, or seed leaf, rather than two. Monocotyledons are mostly soft-stemmed, or *herbaceous*, plants, although some, such as the Palms, are tree-like and produce a soft-wooded trunk. The flowers vary from the simple construction found in the Lily family (Liliaceae) to the most elaborate of all flowers, those of the vast Orchid family (Orchidaceae), which includes at least 18,000 species. The flowers of the Grass family (Graminae), another large group, have flowers specialized for wind pollination. This family includes the most important crop plants: cereals.

ARROW-GRASS FAMILY
Juncaginaceae

The small Arrow-grass family is made up of marsh plants. They are not Grasses, but look Grass-like, and grow in cold and temperate, often coastal, areas. The flowers are inconspicuous and wind-pollinated.

MARSH ARROW-GRASS
Triglochin palustris
This plant is not a Grass despite the common name and Grass-like leaves. It grows 15-50 cm high in marshes, often hidden among tall Grasses. Marsh Arrow-grass is most common in Scandinavia, Scotland and N. England. A similar species of Arrow-grass (*T. maritima*) grows in salt-marsh at the coast.
Flower: green, edged with purple, tiny.
Flower arrangement: on long spike.
Flowering time: June-August.
Leaf: long, narrow, grass-like, fleshy, channelled towards base.
Fruit: narrow, opening from below by 3 valves.

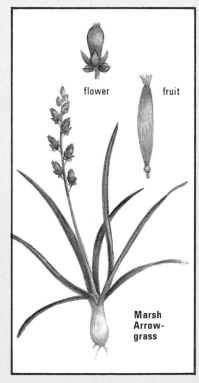

flower

fruit

Marsh Arrow-grass

WATER-PLANTAIN FAMILY
Alismataceae

All the plants in this small family grow near or standing in fresh water. The flowers have 3 white or pink petals rarely lasting more than a day.

WATER-PLANTAIN
Alisma plantago-aquatica
This is a pretty plant which grows in the wet mud or shallow water of ditches, ponds and slow rivers. The flowers are 3-petalled and the whole plant is hairless and 20-100 cm high. This Water-plantain differs from other, more narrow-leaved species by its ovate leaves with abrupt, not tapering bases.
Flower: very pale pink to white, up to 1 cm across; petals 3, rounded; sepals 3; open 1-7 pm.
Flower arrangement: in branched whorls.
Flowering time: June-August.
Leaf: broadly ovate, tip pointed; base joining long stalk abruptly, not tapering.
Fruit: flat seeds in a ring.
Uses: the leaves and root have been used medicinally for many ailments, such as epilepsy and cystitis.

ARROWHEAD
Sagittaria sagittifolia
The arrow-shaped leaves and 3-petalled flowers on stout, 3-sided stems poke up out of shallow water. From root to tip the plant is 30-90 cm tall and hairless.
Flower: white, purple blotch at centre, 2 cm across; petals 3, rounded; sepals 3.
Flower arrangement: in short-stalked whorls of 3-5 on long stems.
Flowering time: July-August.
Leaf: arrow-shaped, long-stalked, held above water; floating leaves ovate with smaller basal lobes; submerged leaves ribbon-like.
Fruit: in tight, rounded head.
Uses: the Chinese and Japanese cultivate it for the starchy edible tubers.

FROGBIT FAMILY
Hydrocharitaceae

Some members of this family grow partly or wholly submerged in fresh water, and some grow in the sea (rare in flowering plants). There are several unusual methods of pollination in the family. In the Tape-grasses (*Vallisneria*) the male flowers break off the submerged plant and float about on the water-surface until they meet and pollinate the long-stalked female flowers.

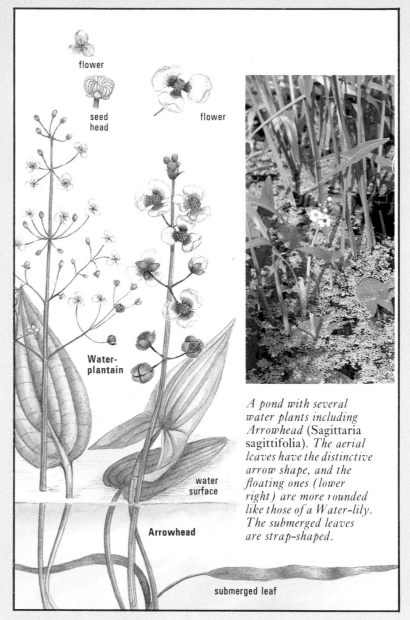

flower

seed head

flower

Water-plantain

water surface

Arrowhead

submerged leaf

A pond with several water plants including Arrowhead (Sagittaria sagittifolia). The aerial leaves have the distinctive arrow shape, and the floating ones (lower right) are more rounded like those of a Water-lily. The submerged leaves are strap-shaped.

CANADIAN PONDWEED
Elodea canadensis
This waterweed has many little dark green leaves closely spaced up the long stems. It grows submerged in slow-moving fresh water. Male and female flowers are on separate plants, females flowering occasionally, males very rarely.
Flower: white, tinged pink, 5 mm across; petals 5.
Flower arrangement: solitary, floating, on long stalk.
Flowering time: May-October.
Leaf: dark green, translucent, lanceolate, tip pointed or rounded, in overlapping whorls of 3.
Uses: this plant is widely grown in aquaria for the large amounts of oxygen it produces and for the shelter it provides.

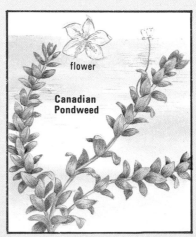

flower

Canadian Pondweed

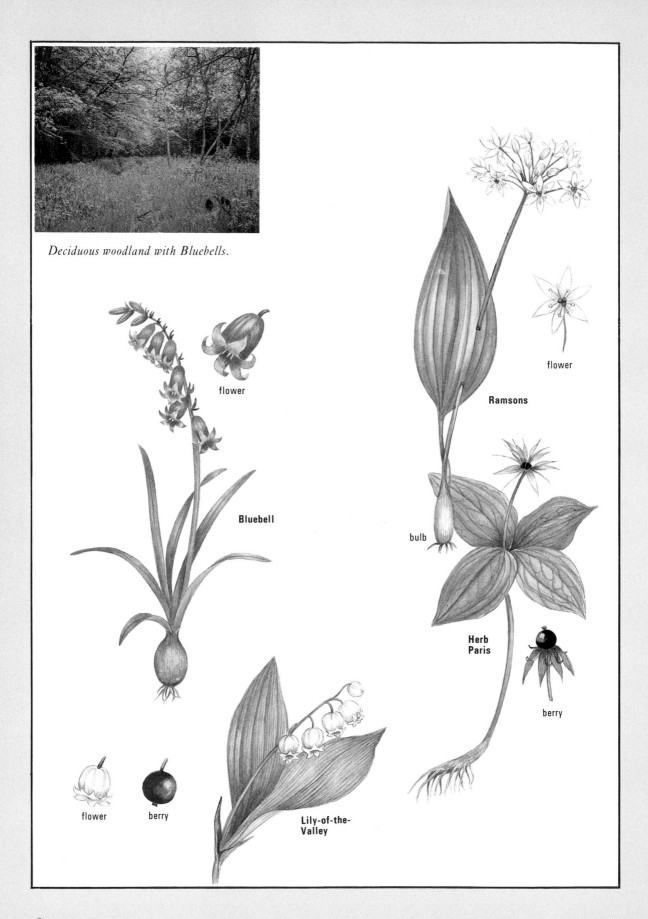

Deciduous woodland with Bluebells.

flower

Bluebell

flower   berry

Lily-of-the-Valley

Ramsons

flower

bulb

Herb Paris

berry

LILY FAMILY
Liliaceae

This is one of the largest of the flowering plant families. Many members have bulbs as storage organs. Included in the family are onions, leeks and very many garden plants such as the many hybrid Tulips, and the Lilies. The flowers appear 6-petalled, having 3 true petals and 3 petal-like sepals.

LILY-OF-THE-VALLEY
Convallaria majalis
This little plant may sometimes be found escaped from gardens, where it is commonly grown. It is also native to Europe in woods, mostly on chalk or limestome. There is a pair of broad leaves at the base of the flowering stem.
Flower: white, sweet-scented, bell-shaped, nodding, 8 mm.
Flower arrangement: in raceme of 6-12 flowers, all directed one way.
Flowering time: May-June.
Leaf: broad, elliptic, stalked, hairless, in a pair; scales sheathing base of leaf-stalks and flowering stem.
Fruit: red berries.

Uses: the plant contains a heart drug close to that found in Foxgloves. It was used to revive gassed soldiers in World War I.

RAMSONS
Allium ursinum
Walkers through woods may notice the strong garlic smell before the plants themselves. Ramsons also grow in hedges. There is a small, narrow bulb at the base of the 3-angled stem. The leaves are broad and spring from the bulb.
Flower: white; petals 6, pointed; stamens 6.
Flower arrangement: 6-20 flowers in rounded umbel on unbranched, 3-angled stem 10-45 cm high.
Flowering time: April-June.
Leaf: broad-elliptic, tip pointed, stalked, hairless.
Fruit: 3-lobed, containing black seeds.

HERB PARIS
Paris quadrifolia
This strange-looking little plant can hardly be mistaken for any other, with its ring of 4 leaves near the top of the stem, just below the greeny-yellow flower. It grows 15-40 cm high in damp woods on chalk or limestone. *Paris* is a Latin word meaning equality and refers to the balance between the number of leaves and flower parts.
Flower: green-yellow; sepals petal-like, 4-6; petals thread-like, 4-6; stamens 8.
Flower arrangement: solitary, stalked.
Flowering time: May-August.
Leaf: in whorl of 4 or more, broadly ovate, tip pointed, short-stalked, hairless.
Fruit: black berry.

BLUEBELL
Hyacinthoides non-scripta
This species of Bluebell is native to the western, Atlantic part of Europe. It was not known to the ancient Greek recorders of plants, hence the species name of *non-scripta,* meaning 'not written upon'. The plant grows 20-50 cm high, often carpeting woods.
Flower: purplish blue, 1·5-2 cm long, bell-shaped; rim with 6 curled-back teeth; anthers cream; bracts paired, bluish.
Flower arrangement: raceme, drooping at tip; buds erect; open flowers nodding, all directed to one side of long stem.
Flowering time: April-June.
Leaf: long, narrow, all rising directly from bulb, keeled, shiny.
Fruit: about 15 mm.
Uses: a slimy glue can be obtained by scraping the bulbs.

PONDWEED FAMILY
Potamogetonaceae

Most plants included in this world-wide family grow in fresh, some in brackish, water. Some species have broad, floating leaves while others are narrow-leaved and submerged.

BROAD-LEAVED PONDWEED
Potamogeton natans
Rooting in the mud of ponds and rivers, the stems of this Pondweed are up to 100 cm long and bear both broad, floating leaves and narrow, submerged ones. Although many of the Pondweed species are difficult to identify this one can be recognized by the bend, often with 2 tiny flaps, which occurs between the floating leaf-blade and its stalk.
Flower: green, inconspicuous, wind-pollinated.
Flower arrangement: in dense spike above water surface.
Flowering time: May-September.
Leaf: alternate; floating leaves elliptic, tip more or less pointed, stalked, slightly leathery; base of young leaves inrolled; submerged leaves narrow; stipules long.
Fruit: dark green, slightly flattened, dispersed by floating on water surface and eventually sinking.

Broad-leaved Pondweed (Potamogeton natans), *showing the broad, floating leaves which give the plant its common name. The flower spikes produce small green fruits which contain air spaces. These cause the fruits to float so that they are widely distributed by water currents until they become waterlogged and sink.*

Broad-leaved Pondweed

water surface

DAFFODIL FAMILY
Amaryllidaceae

This is an important family for garden plants, in particular the Narcissus and Daffodil, many of which are hybrids. The species are mainly from warm-temperate and tropical regions of the world, with relatively few from northern Europe.

WILD DAFFODIL
Narcissus pseudonarcissus
The Wild Daffodil is native in woods and grassland in N. Europe and naturalized in Scandinavia, Scotland and Ireland. The flower stem and leaves end in a bulb of 2-3 cm. The bulbs are poisonous and have been eaten in mistake for onions.
Flower: trumpet golden yellow, as long as or slightly shorter than surrounding 6 paler yellow petals, 3·5-6 cm long; flower-sheath brown, papery.
Flower arrangement: solitary, drooping, on flattened stalk 20-35 cm high.
Flowering time: February-April.
Leaf: linear, 12-35 cm long, grey-green.
Fruit: capsule.

SNOWDROP
Galanthus nivalis
Snowdrops are native to Central and S. Europe. In N. Europe they are commonly planted in gardens and widely naturalized in damp woods and hedges. There is a small bulb at the base of the plant, from which spring the leaves and flower stem.
Flower: white and green, bell-shaped, 14-17 mm long; outer petals 3, white; inner petals 3, shorter than outer, deeply notched, green-tipped and striped, forming tube; flower-sheath green.
Flower arrangement: solitary, nodding, on long stem.
Flowering time: January-March.
Leaf: linear, grey-green, keeled.
Fruit: capsule.

IRIS FAMILY
Iridaceae

Many of the plants in the Iris family are widely grown in gardens, such as Crocus, Gladiolus and Iris, of which there are many hybrids. The flowers appear 6-petalled, and the leaves often form a flattened fan-shape at the base. Storage organs mostly take the form of swollen underground stems.

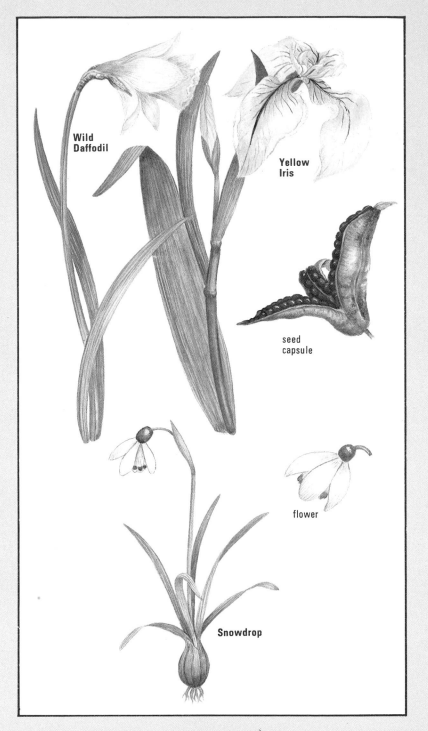

Wild Daffodil

Yellow Iris

seed capsule

flower

Snowdrop

YELLOW IRIS
Iris pseudacorus
The leaves and flower-stem are tall and stiff, growing 40-150 cm high in river or ditch margins, marshes or marshy woods. The thick rhizomes often arch up above the soil surface.
Flower: yellow, 8-10 cm across; outer petals 3, broad, drooping, often dark-veined; inner petals 3, erect; stigmas 3, petal-like, forked at tip.
Flower arrangement: 2-3 on long, flattened stem.
Flowering time: May-July.
Leaf: very long, narrow, blue-green, 1·5-2·5 cm across, midrib raised; together, leaves form a flattened fan-shape at base.
Fruit: capsule; seeds brown.
Uses: the rhizomes give a black dye and black ink.

ORCHID FAMILY
Orchidaceae

The beautiful flowers of this large family are cultivated commercially. They have 6 petal-like segments, the lowest, called the *lip*, often projecting as a nectar-filled spur behind. Pollen is often amassed into stalked pellets (*pollinia*) which stick to the insect visitor's body for transference to the next flower. The tiny seeds have no food store and need a fungus partner to start growth, the fungus often continuing to live in the root of the mature plant. Orchids, in particular, are not for picking, often being rare or sporadic.

flower

Early
Purple
Orchid

tubers

EARLY PURPLE ORCHID
Orchis mascula
These spring-flowering Orchids are found growing 15-60 cm high in woods and grassland. They often grow among Bluebells and Dog's Mercury. The lovely purple or mauve flowers have the unlovely smell of tom cats.
Flower: purple or mauve; lip pale with dark spots at top-centre, broad, 3-lobed; spur thick, blunt; bracts purple.
Flower arrangement: spike.
Flowering time: April-June.
Leaf: usually dark-spotted, alternate, slightly fleshy, oblong, tip shortly pointed or rounded; bases sheathing stem.
Fruit: capsule.
Uses: because of the twin tubers, looking like testicles, this orchid was used as an aphrodisiac. The name Orchid comes from the Greek for testicle.

COMMON SPOTTED ORCHID
Dactylorhiza fuchsii
This conspicuous Orchid is also one of the more common, and grows 15-50 cm high in damp or dry grassy places and open woods. Like many other Orchids, this one hybridizes readily with other species.
Flower: pale pink or whitish with dark red marks; segments each side of hood pointing up; lip broad, 3-lobed; middle lobe pointed, slightly longer than broader side lobes; spur 5·5-8·5 mm long; bracts equalling or longer than flowers.
Flower arrangement: dense spike.
Flowering time: June-August.
Leaf: usually dark-blotched, alternate, slightly fleshy, bases sheathing stem; lower leaves broad-elliptic, tip rounded; upper leaves narrower.
Fruit: capsule.

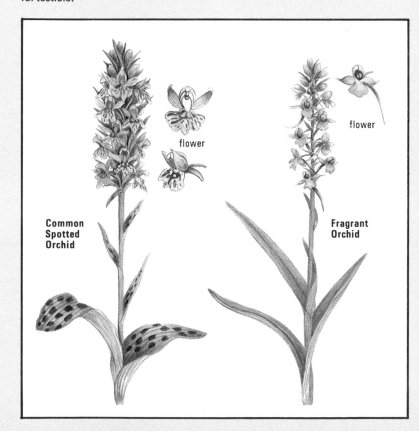

flower

Common
Spotted
Orchid

flower

Fragrant
Orchid

FRAGRANT ORCHID
Gymnadenia conopsea
The scent of this Orchid is strongest in the evening, when it attracts pollinating moths. The spurs on the flowers are very narrow and long, as are the leaves. The stems grow 15-40 cm high in grassland and marshy ground, particularly on chalk or limestone.
Flower: pink-lilac; lip of 3 rounded lobes; spur 11-13 mm long, slender; bracts equalling flowers.
Flower arrangement: dense spike.
Flowering time: June-August.
Leaf: long, narrow, folded down midrib, tip more or less rounded, slightly fleshy; bases sheathing stem.
Fruit: capsule.

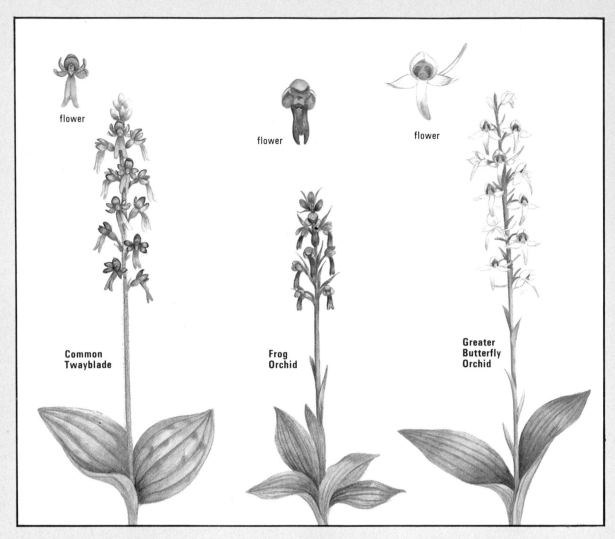

flower

flower

flower

Common Twayblade

Frog Orchid

Greater Butterfly Orchid

COMMON TWAYBLADE
Listera ovata
The common name refers to the 2 broad leaf-blades just below the middle of the stem. The stem is 20-60 cm high and hairy above the leaves. The plant grows in damp woods and grassland, particularly on limestone or chalk. A smaller species of Twayblade (*L. cordata*) can be found in pine woods and moorland.
Flower: yellow-green; lip oblong, furrowed down centre, forked at tip; no spur; bracts tiny.
Flower arrangement: long spike.
Flowering time: June-July.
Leaf: pair of very broad, ovate leaves, slightly fleshy; bases sheathing stem.
Fruit: capsule.

FROG ORCHID
Coeloglossum viride
This unassuming little green-flowered Orchid is often hard to spot in the grass of high land, where it usually grows. The stem is 6-25 cm high and often reddish above.
Flower: yellow-green, tinged with red-brown; upper segments in round hood; lip oblong, 3-toothed at tip; spur 2 mm long; bracts long.
Flower arrangement: spike.
Flowering time: June-August.
Leaf: alternate, slightly fleshy; bases sheathing stem; lower leaves broad, tip rounded; upper leaves narrow, tip pointed.
Fruit: capsule.

GREATER BUTTERFLY ORCHID
Platanthera chlorantha
The pale, rather widely spaced flowers of this Orchid attract moths as pollinators by their clove-like evening scent. The plant grows 20-40 cm high in grassy and wooded areas, particularly on chalk. The less common Lesser Butterfly Orchid (*P. bifolia*) has smaller flowers.
Flowers: greeny white, 18-23 mm across; side segments long, narrow, spread out; lip long, narrow; unlobed; spur long, narrow, curved; bracts almost equalling flower stalks.
Flower arrangement: loose spike.
Flowering time: May-July.
Leaf: pair of elliptic leaves at stem-base; upper leaves much smaller, narrower, alternate, tips short-pointed, bases sheathing stem, slightly fleshy.
Fruit: capsule.

BROAD-LEAVED HELLEBORINE
Epipactis helleborine
There are up to 3, often tall stems, short-hairy at the top, to this Helleborine. They rise from a short length of underground stem and grow up to 80 cm high in hedge-banks and woods. This Orchid is rare in Scotland and N. Scandinavia. The cup-shaped lip of the flower holds nectar for visiting bees and wasps.
Flower: green to dull purplish, scentless; lip cup-shaped with narrow, turned-back tip; no spur; bracts almost equalling flowers.
Flower arrangement: loose spike of drooping flowers turned to one side.
Flowering time: July-October.
Leaf: alternate, broadly ovate, tip pointed, middle leaves longest, margins rough.
Fruit: capsule.

ARUM FAMILY
Araceae

Members of this large, mainly tropical family include Arum Lilies of florists' shops (not Lilies at all) and the Swiss Cheese Plant (*Monstera deliciosa*), a common house-plant. The poker-like flower-spike is surrounded by a large sheath; many exude unpleasant smells to attract pollinating flies.

LORDS-AND-LADIES
Arum maculatum

The tiny flowers are hidden at the base of a purple, poker-shaped stalk, half-enclosed by a yellow-green hood. Midges are trapped in the base of the hood and pollinate the flowers. They later escape and effect cross-pollination by becoming trapped in other flower-hoods. The plants grow in shady hedges and woods.

Flower: tiny.
Flower arrangement: inside hood.
Flowering time: April-May.
Leaf: arrow-shaped, usually dark-blotched, shiny; stalks rising directly from roots.
Fruit: spike of orange berries.
Uses: the roots were a source of laundry starch, especially for ruffs in the 16-17th centuries. They were also thought to be aphrodisiac.

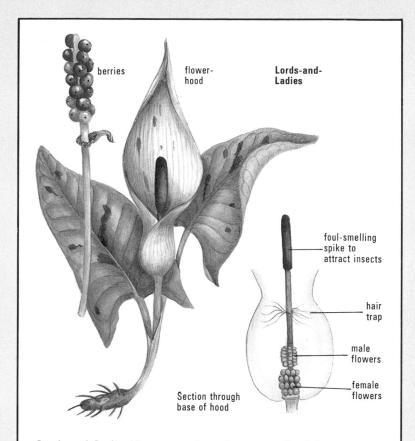

berries   flower-hood   **Lords-and-Ladies**

foul-smelling spike to attract insects

hair trap

male flowers

female flowers

Section through base of hood

Lords-and-Ladies (Arum maculatum) *on a woodland floor.*

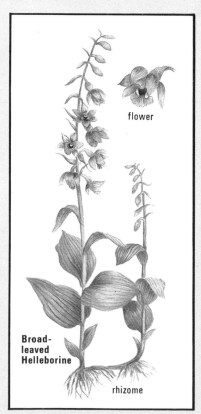

flower

Broad-leaved Helleborine

rhizome

BUR-REED FAMILY
Sparganiaceae

Some plants in this small family float in fresh water, while others grow erect at the water-side. The tiny flowers are gathered into round heads on the same stem, male separate from female. Most species are found in temperate regions.

BRANCHED BUR-REED
Sparganium erectum
This is a stout, erect, hairless plant of 50-150 cm, growing at the edge of still or slow-moving fresh water. The long, stiff leaves look like Iris leaves except for the 3-angled bases. The less common Unbranched Bur-reed (*S. emersum*) has a single stem of flower-heads.
Flower: tiny, greenish, black-edged.
Flower arrangement: males and females in separate, round heads on branched, leafy stem (male above female).
Flowering time: June-August.
Leaf: long, narrow, 3-angled and sheathing stem at base.
Fruit: in bur-like head, each bearing spike.
Uses: stands of Bur-reed shelter wild-fowl, and the fruits provide food for them in winter.

Branched Bur-reed (Sparganium erectum) *in flower and fruit.*

Branched
Bur-reed

stem
section

Duckweed

water surface

Duckweed (Lemna minor) *grows vegetatively until vast numbers of plants are produced and the surface of the water is covered by them. Often, as seen here, the plants accumulate on one side of the pond because they are blown together by the wind.*

DUCKWEED FAMILY
Lemnaceae

The plants in this family are very small and made up of simple, leaf-like lobes which float on fresh water, especially in ponds. They are found in suitable freshwater habitats throughout the world. Included in the family are species of *Wolffia*, the smallest known flowering plants. The minute flowers are borne in pouches on the leaf surface.

DUCKWEED
Lemna minor
The tiny, round, leaf-like lobes of this plant spread on the surface of still water, often covering large areas. A single thread-like root hangs in the water from each plant. The plants normally reproduce by the budding of new lobes, and over-winter in the mud of pond- or ditch-bottoms.
Flower: minute (flowers fairly uncommon).
Flower arrangement: in pouch on lobe-surface.
Flowering time: June-July.
Leaf: leaf-like, rounded lobe, 1·5-4 mm across, almost flat, not swollen below.
Uses: eaten by water-fowl.

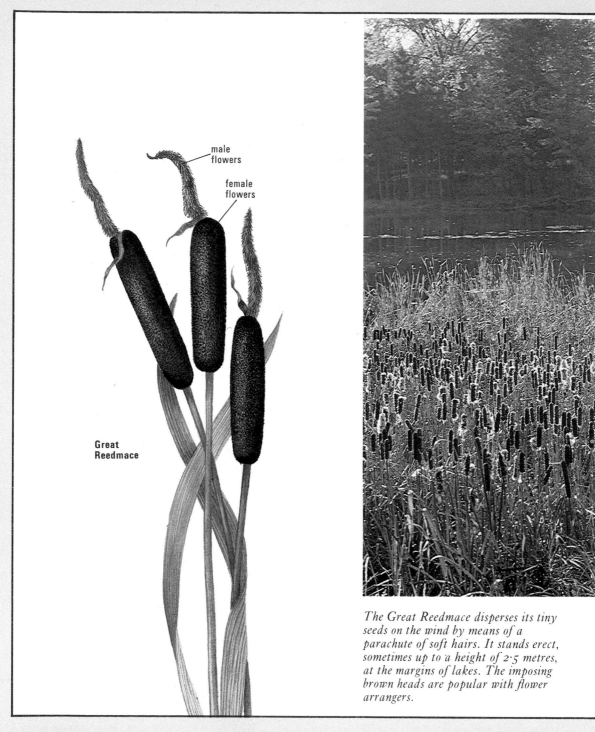

male flowers

female flowers

Great Reedmace

The Great Reedmace disperses its tiny seeds on the wind by means of a parachute of soft hairs. It stands erect, sometimes up to a height of 2·5 metres, at the margins of lakes. The imposing brown heads are popular with flower arrangers.

REEDMACE FAMILY
Typhaceae

Most species in this small family are very tall and grow in shallow, fresh water. The tiny flowers form a long, dense club-shape. The plants are commonly known as 'Bulrushes'.

GREAT REEDMACE ('BULRUSH')
Typha latifolia

Great Reedmace is very tall (1·5-2·5 m), and grows in large stands in the shallows of still or slow-moving fresh water. It is often found growing with Reed (*Phragmites communis*), a tall water-side grass.
Flower: tiny, dark brown.
Flower arrangement: females in large, dense club-shape, continuous with thinner, paler male spike above (Lesser Reedmace, *T. angustifolia*, has a gap between).
Flowering time: June-July.
Leaf: very long, narrow, 10-18 mm wide, grey-green, rather leathery.
Fruit: wind-borne.
Uses: the leaves can be used for weaving and basketry.

Glossary

Achene: Small, dry one-seeded fruit, not splitting when ripe.

Adventitious roots: Roots which arise from aerial parts of the stem.

Aggregate: Group of very closely related species.

Alternate: Not arranged in opposite pairs, describing leaves.

Angiosperms: The group of seed-producing plants which possess flowers instead of cones.

Annual: A plant which completes its entire life cycle in a single year.

Anther: Top part of a stamen, containing pollen.

Axil: The upper angle formed where the leaf meets the stem.

Berry: A fleshy fruit which has no stony layer and usually contains many seeds.

Biennial: A plant which completes its life cycle in two years, usually growing during the first year and flowering in the second.

Bract: A small leaf-like structure on, or at the base of, a flower stalk.

Bracteole: A minute bract.

Bulb: An underground storage organ consisting of swollen leaf bases around a short stem; it may also act as a means of vegetative reproduction.

Calyx: The collective name for all the sepals of a flower.

Capitulum: A kind of inflorescence in which there are many crowded florets, typically found in the Daisy family (Compositae).

Capsule: A dry fruit, splitting open to shed seeds.

Carpel: A single female organ of a flower, which contains one or more ovules.

Compound leaves: Leaves made up of several leaflets.

Compound umbel: An umbel, itself made up of several umbels.

Corm: An underground storage organ consisting of a swollen stem base with adventitious roots.

Corolla: The collective name for all the petals of a flower.

Cotyledon: An embryonic leaf contained within a seed which may act as a food reserve or may grow and photosynthesize.

Cyme: A flower cluster in which each growing point ends in a flower, the oldest flowers being at the top, or centre, of the cluster.

Deciduous: Having leaves which are all shed during a particular season.

Dentate: With a toothed margin, as in some leaves.

Dicotyledons: One of the two groups of seed-producing plants, characterized by the presence of two cotyledons in each seed.

Dioecious: With male and female flowers borne on separate plants.

Disc floret: A floret without a strap-shaped petal; the lobes of the petals are equal in size and shape.

Drupe: A fleshy fruit in which the seed is encased within a hard stony layer.

Elliptic: Oval with narrowed ends.

Entire: Untoothed (leaf margin).

Environment: The surroundings and prevailing conditions which influence the life of a plant.

Epidermis: The thin outer layer of cells which covers many parts of a plant, such as the leaves.

Evergreen: A perennial or biennial plant which does not shed all its leaves during any season.

Fertilization: The joining of male and female sex cells, resulting in seed formation.

Fibres: Elongated cells with thickened walls which add strength to stems and other parts of plants.

Filament: The stalk of a stamen, attached to the anther.

Follicle: A fruit which develops from a single ovary, dries out on ripening and splits along one side only to release the seeds.

Fruit: The structure which contains the ripe seeds.

Genus: A group containing a number of species which are shown to be closely related by their possession of one or more distinctive features.

Germination: The start of growth at the end of a resting, or *dormant*, stage, as for example in pollen grains or seeds.

Glands: Tiny, disc-shaped structures on a plant containing oil or resin; they may be stalked and called *glandular hairs*.

Glaucous: With pale bloom, as on grapes, due to a waxy surface.

Habit: The characteristic growth form or overall appearance of a plant.

Habitat: The surroundings in which a plant grows.

Head: Another name for a *capitulum* (q.v.) or other closely grouped structure.

Herb: Any flowering plant without a woody stem.

Honey guides: Patterns or markings on petals which lead visiting insects to the nectar.

Hybrid: A plant produced when one species interbreeds with another.

Inflorescence: The arrangement of more than one flower on a plant.

Insectivorous: Describes a plant which traps and digests insects.

Keel: A boat-shaped fold in a leaf, petal or the lowest pair of petals in a flower of the Pea family.

Lanceolate: Narrowly ovate.

Latex: A milky white or yellow juice produced by stems and roots of some plants, such as the Dandelion.

Linear: Strap-shaped.

Lip: A group of petals divided from the rest and more-or-less joined.

Lobed: Describes leaves or other plant parts that are deeply indented.

Mealy: Pale-powdery.

Midrib: The central and largest vein of a leaf.

Monocotyledon: One of the two groups of Angiosperms (q.v.), characterized by the single cotyledon in each seed.

Monoecious: Having separate unisexual male or female flowers on the same plant.

Naturalized: Describes a foreign plant that has been introduced and become established.

Nectary: A gland in a flower which produces sugary fluid (nectar) to attract insect visitors.

Nut: A woody, one-seeded fruit, not opening when ripe; a *nutlet* is a tiny nut.

Ochrea: A papery sheath surrounding the stem and the base of a leaf stalk.

Opposite: Occurring in pairs on either side of the stem, describing leaves.

Osmosis: The process by which water passes through the membranes between cells from a weaker solution, such as soil water, to a stronger one, such as the cell sap.

Ovary: The female part of a flower which contains the ovules.

Ovate: Egg-shaped in outline.

Ovoid: Egg-shaped in three dimensions.

Ovule: The structure inside an ovary which contains a female egg cell.

Palmate: Describes a leaf made up of lobes radiating from a central point.

Panicle: An inflorescence made up of branching racemes (q.v.).

Pappus: A tuft of hairs on fruits of the Daisy family.

Parasite: A plant which obtains its food from the living tissues of a plant of a different kind.

Perennial: A plant which completes its life cycle over a period longer than two years.

Petal: Part of a flower which is leaf-like in shape but usually brightly coloured to attract insects.

Petiole: The stalk of a leaf.

Phloem: The plant tissue which transports food substances from one part to another.

Photosynthesis: The process by which green plants manufacture sugars from water and carbon dioxide, using energy from sunlight trapped by the green pigment (chlorophyll).

Pinnate: Describes a leaf made up of leaflets in two rows along a common stalk; *double pinnate*, etc., describes leaflets that are themselves pinnate.

Pistil: The female reproductive organs of a flower, consisting of carpels, each with stigma, style and ovary.

Pod: A dry fruit which contains several seeds and splits along both sides.

Pollen: Dust-like bodies produced in the anthers which contain the male sex cells.

Pollination: A process by which pollen is transferred from the male to the female part of a flower. In self-pollination the pollen is transferred to the stigma of the plant from which it originates; in cross-pollination it is transferred to another plant.

Prostrate: Lying along the ground.

Pseudocopulation: A type of pollination effected by male insects attempting to mate with part of a flower which resembles the female insect.

Raceme: A cylindrical head of stalked flowers.

Ray: A spoke-like stalk in an umbel.

Ray floret: A floret in which the petals are elongated into a strap shape on one side.

Receptacle: The end part of a stem to which the petals, sepals, stamens and ovaries are attached.

Reproduction: The process, normally involving fertilization, by which new individuals are produced.

Rhizome: A horizontal underground stem which may act as an organ of vegetative reproduction.

Rosette: A ring of leaves at the stem base.

Runner: A long, creeping stem which roots and forms new plants.

Saprophyte: A plant which obtains its food from decomposing plant remains rather than from photosynthesis.

Seed: The product of fertilization of an embryo which can develop into a new individual.

Semi-parasite: A plant which obtains part of its food by parasitism but is also photosynthetic.

Sepal: A usually green, leaf-like part of a flower, arranged in a ring beneath the petals and enclosing the flower when it is in bud.

Shrub: A woody plant which is perennial and has several stems arising at ground level. Unlike a tree, it has no main trunk and is smaller.

Simple: Undivided.

Species: A subdivision of a genus, the members of which can usually breed with each other but not with members of other species.

Spike: A cylindrical head of unstalked flowers.

Spur: A hollow, usually cone-shaped, projection at the base of a petal.

Stamen: The male part of a flower, made up of a pollen-producing anther on a stalk.

Stigma: The tip of the female part of the flower which receives pollen.

Stipule: A small, scale-like structure at the base of the leaf-stalk.

Stomata: The microscopic pores in the epidermis, mainly of leaves, through which gases and water pass in or out of the plant.

Style: The stalk between stigma and ovary.

Succulent: Juicy or fleshy, describing those parts of a plant which contain stored water.

Tendril: A spiral, thread-like structure on a stem or leaf for climbing.

Transpiration: The process by which water is lost by evaporation through the stomata.

Trifoliate: A pinnate leaf with three leaflets.

Tubular: A flower with fused petals forming a tube.

Tuber: Part of a stem or root used for food storage, lasting one year.

Umbel: An umbrella-shaped inflorescence in which flower stalks of equal length arise from the same point on the stem.

Umbellifer: A plant of the Carrot family.

Valve: One of the pieces a capsule breaks into on ripening.

Vegetative reproduction: Reproduction not involving fertilization, for example, the branching of a rhizome to produce new plants.

Venation: The pattern of veins of a plant organ.

Whorl: Leaves or flowers arranged in a ring around a stem.

Xylem: The water-conducting tissues of a plant made up of dead cells which in large numbers make up wood.

Bibliography

Clapham A. R., Tutin T. G. & Warburg E. F. *Excursion Flora of the British Isles*. Cambridge University Press 1959

Fitter R., Fitter A. & Blamey M. *The Wild Flowers of Britain and Northern Europe*. Collins 1980

Grey-Wilson C. *The Alpine Flowers of Britain and Europe*. Collins 1979

Grieve M. *A Modern Herbal*. Penguin Books 1978

Hunt P. F. *Discovering Botany*. Longmans 1979

Hyde M. *Hedgerow Plants*. Shire Publications 1976

Keeble-Martin W. *The Concise British Flora in Colour*. Ebury Press 1965

Mabey R. *Food for Free*. Collins 1972

McClintock R. & Fitter R. *Collins Pocket Guide to Wild Flowers*. Collins 1956

Press J. R., Sutton D. A. & Tebbs B. M. *Field Guide to the Flowers of Britain*. Reader's Digest 1981

Index

Page numbers in *italics* refer to illustrations.

Acknowledgements

The author and publishers wish to thank the following for their help in supplying photographs for this book on the pages indicated:

A-Z Collection 53 (Jacques Remazeilles), 117, 121, 148, 153; Heather Angel 8–9, 10–11, 15, 25, 29, 34 top, 39, 46 top, 48, 49, 51, 52, 54, 55, 56 top and bottom, 60–1, 65 bottom, 70, 71, 73, 74 top and bottom, 75, 82, 83, 84 top and bottom, 85, 89, 92 bottom, 93, 95, 98, 99 bottom, 105, 106, 109 top, 112–13, 116, 123, 129, 131 left and right, 134, 135, 137, 149, 152, 155, 171, 183, 185, 189, 190 top and bottom, 191; G. E. Barrett 79; British Museum (Natural History) 47, 65 top; M. Chinery 31 bottom, 40 bottom, 94 bottom; Brian Hawkes 16 top and bottom, 22, 23, 27, 31 top, 32, 41, 46 bottom, 66, 67, 78, 86, 88 top and bottom, 90, 91, 92 top, 94 top, 99 top, 100, 101 bottom, 103, 108 top and bottom; Mansell Collection 97, 101 top; P. Morris 26, 35 bottom, 64, 142; Nature Photographers Ltd/Brinsley Burbidge 34 bottom, 35 top, 37, 38, 40 top, 80 bottom, 81, 96, 102, 104, 109 bottom, 133;/A. A. Butcher 80 top;/N. A. Callow 19, 50;/Andrew Cleave 42 top, 72 top and bottom;/D. M. T. Ettlinger 42 bottom;/C. K. Mylne 76;/Owen Newman 77, 87;/W. S. Paton 159; N.H.P.A./R. G. Argent 110;/G. M. Bain 115;/Stephen Dalton 45;/E. A. Janes 12–13, 136, 180;/Hugh Newman 184 ZEFA/Paul Freytag 6–7

Front cover: N.H.P.A. Back cover: ZEFA

Picture Research: Penny J. Warn

Artwork: Wendy Bramall; line drawings: Shirley Willis; maps: Tudor Art